Proudhon and His Age

Proudhon and His Age

John Ehrenberg

HUMANITIES PRESS
NEW JERSEY

First published 1996 by Humanities Press International, Inc.
165 First Avenue, Atlantic Highlands, New Jersey 07716

© John Ehrenberg, 1996

Library of Congress Cataloging–in–Publication Data

Ehrenberg, John, 1944–
    Proudhon and his age / John Ehrenberg.
        p. cm.
    Includes bibliographical references (p.) and index.
    ISBN 0–391–03891–5 (cloth)
    1. Proudhon, P.-J. (Pierre-Joseph), 1809–1865. 2. Anarchists–
–France—Biography.   I. Title.
HX893.7.P78E47 1995
335.2—dc20
[B]   95–19461
                                                                                              CIP

A catalog record for this book is available from the British Library.

Printed in the United States of America

To Charles Drekmeier and Nannerl Keohane,
who were there in the beginning
To Stephen Bronner, who was there at the end
To Kathleen, who was there all the time

Contents

Acknowledgments

Longer ago than I care to remember, Stanford University's Political Science Department made it possible for my wife and me to travel to France for two years of research at the Bibliothèque Nationale. Sally Holt, Jenny Jones, Piotr Kowalski, and Paul Volsik were the best friends we could have had there. Since then, Alfred DiMaio, Bertell Ollman, and many other colleagues and friends have shared ideas and offered important encouragement. The support of the Long Island University Research Time Awards Committee and of the Library staff was vital. Keith Ashfield was a pleasure to work with from beginning to end. Cassie and David, who were "just air" at the beginning of this project, are very much flesh and blood now. In many ways this book is for them. All translations are mine.

Introduction

Any individual life carries with it a permanent but incomplete record of the historical period and social order in which it is lived. General history is revealed in the isolated data of specific experience, and the present partially preserves the past even as it breaks with it. But individuals also retain considerable autonomy, for contemporary affairs carry more than the undiluted reflection of prior experience and an individual life is richer than any mirror. If broad qualities of a social order can be discerned in what appear to be unique matters of biography, contextual investigation can yield truths which run deeper than what is immediately obvious. These broad considerations shape the boundaries of the "social biography" which follows.

The life and work of Pierre-Joseph Proudhon (1809–1865), one of the nineteenth century's most prominent social theorists, was shaped by France's transition to a modern capitalist economy organized around coal and iron. General patterns of bourgeois development were conditioned by the particularities of French nineteenth-century history, and the sweep and depth of her Great Revolution interacted with some distinctive features of her social structure to produce an exceptionally rich ideological environment. Proudhon was one of an impressive group of nineteenth-century intellectuals and activists who were trying to understand the new world that was taking shape, and it is no accident that the vast majority of them were French.

If French economic and political history provides a remarkably clear object-lesson in the development of modern capitalism, it illustrates the power of the "dual revolution" in politics and economics which began in northwest Europe and went on to transform the world. The impact of the market is still very much with us, and the crisis of what remains of the socialism of the Third International suggests that we will be coping with its effects for some time to come. As constrained as it was by its own conditions, time and place, Proudhon's life may illustrate more about our past, present and future than we expect. This may be as true of his limitations as it is of his strengths, of his blind spots as well as of his insights.

Proudhon was not an isolated individual trying to understand what was happening in France. From the very beginning of his career his self-defined project was to defend the interests of France's large, powerful, and vulnerable *petite bourgeoisie*—that immense stratum of small proprietors which has proven so important to modern history and whose political and ideological motion have always been problematic for the left. The market crushes this grouping as remorselessly as it recreates it, and Proudhon's effort to understand and defend its interests provides a clear example of how social class conditions ideology. His work was driven by a strong desire to protect the combination of work and ownership which he judged the condition of equality, the foundation of justice and the key to France's well-being. The petty bourgeoisie's democracy was shaped by its objective social position as surely as were the bourgeoisie's liberalism and the proletariat's socialism. At the same time, capitalism's small proprietors continue to be a large and important force in contemporary social life, and their political perspectives are formed by the same forces which shaped Proudhon's orientation. In studying him we can learn a great deal about our present and future, and if we look at him in historical and social context we can learn even more.

Like many of his colleagues on the left, Proudhon was trying to understand the development of capitalism in France in order to consciously control its enormous productive capacity and direct it toward the ancient goal of the full satisfaction of human needs. The possibilities he glimpsed and the obstacles he encountered sound very contemporary, yet the past lived in him as surely as it does in all of us. He was trying to understand the new with theoretical tools partly inherited from an earlier period, and his career demonstrates the unformed character of human understanding as surely as it reflects the transitional nature of the period in which it was shaped. His very real limitations notwithstanding, Proudhon was better able than many of his contemporaries to grasp the uniquely contradictory character of French life even if his reluctance to break with the past sharply limited the impact of his intellectual strength and political insight.

The first two chapters present a broad sketch of the environment which shaped Proudhon's development and conditioned his thought. The extensive damage, deep contradictions, and undeniable achievements which would mark France's later history were evolving in a rudimentary form during his lifetime. She had emerged from her Great Revolution with a classical bourgeois political order but a distorted bourgeois economic environment. A high level of class struggle was shaped by a capitalist transformation of the economy accompanied—and increasingly constrained—by a narrow and rigid political regime. A concentrated industrial proletariat began to take shape as France's ancient peasantry disintegrated, and its unending conflict with its bourgeois antagonist conditioned the unremitting pressure to which her large stratum of small proprietors was subjected throughout the century.

Molded by the *petite bourgeoisie*'s real concerns, an exceptionally productive generation of French social theorists dominated European social thought during the 1830s and 1840s. The spread of market relations illustrated both the achievements and limits of the Great Revolution, and as they turned their attention to "the social question" theorists and activists alike tried to understand how political freedom could coexist with economic inequality. As the bourgeoisie's liberalism confronted the workers' socialism and the petty bourgeoisie's "pure democracy," the growing importance of industry illuminated the role of social forces in the evolution of political ideology. Social reform had become the chief priority of the left by the time Proudhon reached maturity as the scientific organization of productive life replaced the traditional Jacobin reliance on the seizure of political power. The generation of French social theorists which followed the pioneering work of Saint-Simon and Fourier—a generation whose outstanding representative was Proudhon—was shaped by the problems to which their predecessors had addressed themselves, the questions they had asked and the answers they had provided.

Chapter 3 traces the classical petty-bourgeois egalitarianism which rested at the heart of Proudhon's early theoretical development. It drove his brilliant critique of bourgeois social relations, summarized only partially in *Qu'est-ce que la Propriété?*'s famous assertion that "property is theft." The first systematic socialist criticism of bourgeois property, the book called it the "right" to appropriate the fruit of someone else's labor and a rigorous analysis revealed Proudhon's core position that only the fusion of ownership with work could make possible a just, rational and egalitarian social order. If he recognized that the appropriation of collectively-produced surplus rested at the heart of modern inequality and that French society was built on a deep antagonism between those who produce and those who own, his petty-bourgeois viewpoint led him to assert that only the universalization of "possession" could eliminate unproductive ownership and enable the direct producer to appropriate the full measure of value he provided. Proudhon's conviction that economic liberalism was "illogical" and that the unsupervised market could not provide justice lay at the center of his lifelong effort to protect the independence of France's many small autonomous producers. It would bring him into direct contact with the newly aroused proletariat during the Revolution of 1848, and his reactions to an intensifying class struggle revealed as much about his own attitudes as about those of the *petite bourgeoisie* for which he became the acknowledged spokesman during a period of acute crisis and rapid change.

Chapter 4 traces the distinctively modern set of problems which the Revolution of 1848 presented and follows their characteristically pure French resolution. As liberalism, democracy, and socialism began to separate out from the "general democratic" movements of an earlier period, social issues became central to the poor and thus began to drive the political activity of every class. The "right to work" became the basic demand of the left during the spring, and the contradiction between a "liberal republic," a "democratic republic" and a "social republic" testified to the different perspectives of the classes whose interaction propelled the Revolution forward and eventually framed its limits. Proudhon was an influential journalist and parliamentary representative throughout this period, and if he understood the need for a widespread social transformation he also wanted to preserve the sort of property which was associated with productive labor. Like other leaders of the left, he tried to fashion a political and ideological alliance between the proletariat and the petty bourgeoisie—but he wanted it on his terms. The organization of credit and exchange came to replace the organization of work, and attempts to create equal exchange of "constituted" value expressed his notion of a republic of small producers. Caught between the increasingly incompatible perspectives of propertyless workers and small proprietors, Proudhon's twists and turns provide a perfect illustration of the pressures to which intermediate strata of the population were subject as they tried to develop an independent position while it was becoming increasingly difficult to do so. Early hopes for a peaceful and gradual social reorganization died as political antagonisms intensified, and Proudhon's increasing suspicion of political activity led him to celebrate the spontaneous effervescence of society and try to organize a pluralist exchange between equal contracting centers whose voluntary agreement would replace politics and the state.

Louis-Napoleon's Second Empire provided the political framework for the post-1848 industrialization of France, and Proudhon's late commitment to mutualism and federalism took shape within the regime's rigidly-defined boundaries. Chapter 5 traces his attempts to reconcile the requirements of egalitarian "justice" with those of market society, an effort which culminated in his attempt to preserve existing social units in a mutualist economy whose stable "reciprocity" would protect the individual from the liberal market's amoral indifference. Equilibrium and balance would maintain social peace and guarantee independence by protecting the integrity of free transactions in a stateless "mutualist" society. If Proudhon is "the father of anarchism" and urged the trade-union movement to abstain from all political activity, federalism expressed his sense of mutualist justice and summarized his discomfort with the workers' collectivism. He remained convinced to his dying day that only free networks of mutual exchange could protect liberty, and the federal republic of his late writings was organized around autonomous centers of production and exchange. In the long run his was a socialism of exchange rather than of production, and his influential hostility to politics ranks as one of the most problematic of his many influences on the French left in the years before and after the Paris Commune.

The relationship between the socialist proletariat and the democratic petty bourgeoisie continued to dominate the French left after Proudhon's death, and the problems to which he addressed his considerable energy continue to haunt socialists and democrats today. His desire to protect independent economic activity and the small property on which it is based rested at the center of his life's work and provide eloquent testimony to the pressures which were inexorably forcing the petty bourgeoisie to act and simultaneously compressing its sphere of activity. The development of a distinct proletarian current whose antipathy toward property and orientation toward the use of state power in the name of social revolution weakened his appeal, but the contemporary disarray of the left and a momentarily triumphant neo-liberalism are forcing a reexamination of basic assumptions. No matter what the outcome, such a development would have pleased him.

1

Politics and Society

PAST AND FUTURE

The singular path of French nineteenth-century economic and social development shaped the context within which Proudhon's life and work can be understood. Contrary to what one might expect given the classical bourgeois form of the Great Revolution, France's economic development stood in surprising contrast to her military strength, population, level of culture, and diplomatic importance. French economic progress was relatively delayed, her industrialization progressing rather unevenly throughout the period. The early establishment of a powerful export-oriented British industry against which she was unable to compete contributed to her relative backwardness, but the paradoxical legacy of the Revolution's class settlement was the most important factor shaping her economic, social, and political development.

Whatever its other virtues, the Revolution's land settlement made impossible an English "solution" to the agrarian problem. In distributing land to the peasants, guaranteeing a rural economy of small production and anchoring the peasantry to the soil, the Republic won the decisive struggle for the rural population's political allegiance and was able to defend itself against European reaction, but it paid a great economic price in the long run. The growth of an internal market was slowed, the transfer of resources from agriculture to industry was retarded, and the development of a modern class structure was distorted. The continuing weight of agriculture and resulting political importance of the peasantry acted as a powerful brake on industrialization and colored the development of a modern national polity throughout the century. As late as 1861, 88 percent of the French people lived in the *département* of their birth and by the end of the century fully 70 percent of the population still lived on the land.[1] Purchasing power and income were significantly handicapped as a result, and this tended to limit the development of an internal market and to discourage investment in industry. The result was that French capitalism was marked by a relatively

6

important "moneyed bourgeoisie" and a correspondingly important role of finance compared to that of England. Landed property and capital that could be lent to the state played disproportionately greater roles in French economic life than elsewhere and, since a large internal market for cheap mass-produced commodities did not exist for most of the century, French producers tended to emphasize the production of high-quality goods and catered to their wealthier customers at home and abroad. The economy was dominated by partnerships and family firms throughout the period.[2] Industrial production was generally small-scale and tended to resist concentration, each firm producing for a relatively small local market. Manufacturing methods were dominated by habits inherited from the past and a "peddlar" approach dominated merchandising techniques.[3] Strongly shaped by the influence of small capitalists, the industrialization of the French economy was slow and halting. This was true even in such industries as iron and steel and it continued to influence French history until fairly recently:

> The ironmaster's ignorance, provincialism, love of routine, and individualism are characteristic of the industry in France in 1815, and are of vital importance to an understanding of its condition and lack of progress. To describe inadequate means of transportation, remoteness of coal, and scarcity of capital is not an adequate explanation of the prevalent backwardness. Small-scale production in France was not due to these important economic, geographical, and geological factors: it was due also to profound love of individualism combined with devotion to thrift and to tradition, and it has remained typical of French industry and agriculture right down to our age of mass production at ever increasing speed.[4]

Industrialization was so slow in France that even by 1870 she could not rival the more advanced European economies.[5] Despite the growth of factories, the gradual increase in the number of people living in large cities, and the appearance of a modern proletariat, the country remained profoundly stamped by the influence of small proprietors—so much so that "France, compared with her neighbors to the north and east, appears to be the country of the uncompleted revolution."[6] One important and paradoxical consequence of the French Revolution, then, is that this most classically bourgeois of political upheavals created near-perfect legal and institutional conditions for the full flowering of capitalist social relations but simultaneously left intact important social barriers to their realization in economic affairs.

The pattern of French industrialization thus presented two faces. On the one hand, its slowness and incompleteness meant that the country's class structure and the Revolution's political legacy would continue to affect each other in complicated ways for some time. A strong and entrenched sector of the population whose roots lay in small property and small production imposed serious limits on the extent to which modern social relations could penetrate industry and agriculture. On the other hand, it is important to remember that, as limited and distorted as it was, French industrialization *did* move forward. The gradual extension of the country's railroad system during the 1840s stimulated a more general economic expansion; if only 1,800 kilometers of railroads were in use at the outbreak of the Revolution of 1848, it is no less true that the powerful industrialization of the second half of the century was driven by coal and iron.[7] Much of the social, political, and ideological history of nineteenth-century France was shaped by the relations between her politics and her economics. There is nothing surprising about this of course, but the purity of her class struggle and the intensity of her politics gave her history the sharp edge which continues to make it singularly useful for understanding the *ensemble* of capitalist social relations.

If the favorable legal foundations which the Revolution established for the development of bourgeois social relations preceded the social and economic conditions for industrialization, this tended to give a momentary advantage to the small-scale forms of capitalism associated with petty production. Under these circumstances it is particularly important to understand the social roots, economic problems and ideological perspectives of the French *petite bourgeoisie*, for this large and powerful section of the population exercised a great deal of influence in all areas of French public life through the nineteenth century and retains considerable importance in contemporary affairs as well.

In general terms, the *petite bourgeoisie* is best understood as the poorest and most vulnerable section of the property-owning bourgeoisie itself. It is such a diverse grouping that it cannot be called a social class in its own right, consisting as it does of small and middle peasants, artisans, farmers, handicraftsmen, small merchants, independent businessmen of all sorts, and the lower levels of the intelligentsia and the professions. It occupies an ambiguous social position and is thus able to attain a measure of economic independence, its ownership of some property partially freeing it from the necessity of working for someone else. On the other hand, it does not own enough property to attain complete independence, and it is thus partially dependent on—and partially exploited by—the upper levels of the bourgeoisie. While able to reach a level of economic independence through its ownership of property, it must partly work for others to support itself.

The dual character of the *petite bourgeoisie* stems from the fact that it partly owns and partly does not own, is partly independent and partly dependent, partly idle and partly working. It has characteristics of both the bourgeoisie and proletariat, between which it occupies an unstable, sensitive, and threatened position. The most basic conditions of its existence are marked by continual difficulties, for its behavior is more likely to be a reaction to the pressures operating on it—and over which it seldom exercises full control—than the result of a clear understanding of its needs.

The contradictions which tear modern societies apart and move them forward play themselves out with particularly devastating effect among the petty bourgeoisie. Its frequent fractures bear witness to the difficulty of generalizing about it with great precision, yet it often exhibits enough coherence to permit an analysis of the conditions in which it exists and the actions it is likely to take. In spite of the pressures under which it is forced to live, its ownership of small property enables it to hold on and regenerate itself. It is both actor and battleground, agent and subject. Its large size and strategic location make it an important, often pivotal, group. Nowhere in nineteenth-century Europe was this more true than in France.

The French petty bourgeoisie was well-established long before 1789, and in many ways the Revolution could do little more than register its importance. It played a major role in defining the limits beyond which the Revolution could not go. It succeeded to some extent in safeguarding small property from real and imagined threats during the Revolution and was strong enough to limit the spread and extent of capitalist industrialization in France after the political transformations of the Revolution were over. Even the Jacobins, at the height of their power in 1793, had been forced to compromise with it. This is why

they established that impregnable citadel of small and middle peasant proprietors, small craftsmen and shopkeepers, economically retrogressive but passionately devoted to Revolution and Republic, which has dominated the country's life ever since. The capitalist transformation of agriculture and small enterprise, the essential condition for rapid economic development, was slowed to a crawl, and with it the spread of urbanization, the expansion of the home market, the multiplication of the working class and, incidentally, the ulterior spread of proletarian revolution. Both big business and the labor movement were long doomed to remain minority phenomena in France, islands surrounded by a sea of corner grocers, peasant small-holders, and cafe proprietors.[8]

The *petite bourgeoisie* continued to be a powerful force after the Revolution. Unwilling to give up the important political and economic gains it had won in the struggle against feudalism,[9] it exercised such political influence in France that at least one perceptive observer called it "the living and progressive part of the nation" in these years before the appearance of a modern proletariat.[10]

The continuous destruction of small property by big property tended to make the big bourgeoisie an enemy of the small bourgeoisie, and the latter functioned best in a decentralized economy dominated by small firms engaging in limited production for a local market. Resistance to the concentration of wealth continued throughout the century and would color much of the *petite bourgeoisie*'s economic, social, and ideological orientation. Domestic industry generally held its own with the factories throughout the century, although the latter became more important after 1815. Important limits to industrialization and concentration in the towns and the capitalist penetration of agriculture were largely set by the powerful and entrenched French petty bourgeoisie.

Although its relative slowness and incompleteness were important aspects of the development of French capitalism, it should not be forgotten that industry was growing. While the factory system appeared relatively timid and hesitant during the first half of the century, it did constitute a serious threat to the old artisan classes and small manufacturers.[11] Not only were small businesses increasingly unable to compete with the factories, but it was also clear that industrialization would eventually destroy many traditional skills of the *petite bourgeoisie* if allowed to develop unchecked.[12]

The small property, fragmented labor, and special skills of the petty bourgeoisie were continually threatened by socialized production. Such production was the key to developing a modern form of capitalism, and the small proprietors who had been strengthened by the Revolution's economic and political settlement were always under threat from the social forces set in motion by it. They could not compete for very long with an enterprise manned by a disciplined, organized, interdependent, and divided labor force. Threatened by the spread of industry, the petty bourgeoisie was most successful when it exercised its considerable influence to slow and retard the growth of factories. It was much less fortunate in its attempt to compete with industry on the latter's terms, for it was hampered not only by the disadvantages that came with smaller size but also by past habits whose effects were exacerbated by its deeply-rooted individualism.[13]

The social pressures at work on the large and powerful mass of small proprietors were important in shaping French history throughout the period, although it took some time for them to precipitate major social upheavals. Such pressures were important because they eroded the petty bourgeoisie's ability to maintain its position. Where the threat of big masses of capital and property appeared as "industrial feudalism," the threat of more efficient social production appeared as the slowly developing proletariat. The *petite bourgeoisie* was threatened by both because its small property was jeopardized by both. Constantly faced with the loss of its modest degree of economic security in a struggle with either, its survival depended on preserving both so it could eke out a measure of independence from the struggle which simultaneously threatened to chew it up. Its social position tended to drive it toward policies of conciliation and compromise. But the continued struggle between both classes, a struggle which accelerated and intensified as the century developed, meant that the space between the antagonists tended to shrink over time. This was particularly true when periods of acute class struggle undermined the tendency of the petty bourgeoisie and its spokesmen to try to preserve capitalism while ending its unavoidable class conflicts. This was the basic thrust and the most profound problem facing all petty-bourgeois ideologies during this period, and it formed an important theme of Proudhon's work as well.

Yet small proprietors were also threatened by the "normal" operations of capitalism, and so they were always pulled by deeply contradictory forces. Their ownership of property tied them to the bourgeoisie. Their need to work tied them to the proletariat. Thus they tended to waver and vacillate between the two great classes of modern capitalism. To the extent that the petty bourgeoisie was able to articulate a distinctive ideology, it gravitated toward a crude and simplistic sort of egalitarianism which would culminate in a republic of small producers. Faced with continuing pressure from the social forces accompanying largescale capitalism, it was predisposed to demand protection from the state in the name of substantial equality of conditions. Yet guaranteeing a minimum standard of living to all citizens often required interfering with property relations and exercising a measure of social supervision of the "free" market, and vague plans for the redistribution of wealth often characterized petty bourgeois schemes for social reform. This did not necessarily conflict with its equally fervent demand that the state protect the small property which rested at the foundation of its deeply cherished independence. Its desire to establish and protect its personal independence and economic liberty made it deeply antifeudal, and the Revolution had succeeded in winning it to the Republic. Visibly productive and obviously hard-working, it based its understanding of property on individual labor and dreamed of a society of independent small owners protected by a democratic state from the new centers of "industrial and financial feudalism." Its egalitarianism was designed to protect it from both the bourgeoisie and the proletariat but, threatened by and fearful of both, it was faced with a series of choices which could not be avoided in periods of crisis. It was continually breaking up and reforming, and its ideological perspectives faithfully reflected the material conditions of its existence.

Just as it looked to a democratic state to protect it from its enemies, the petty bourgeoisie was forced to confront the centralizing tendency of nineteenth-century French politics. The French system has long subordinated local and regional authority to central control, and Paris so dominates the country that *everywhere* else is called "the provinces." The hyper-politics of the French Revolution and the residual Jacobinism of the nineteenth century democratic and socialist left reflected both the historical legacy of French centralization and the fact that the irreversible political tendency of the century was for the state to became centralized in lockstep with the economy. The French petty bourgeoisie would come to develop a uniquely articulated political sensibility as a result of the interplay between its social position and the particularities of its country's history.

POLITICS AND STATE

The victors of Waterloo attempted to end the French Revolution by imposing the Bourbons on the nation in 1815, but the Restoration bourgeoisie now dominated the country and was willing to tolerate the aristocracy, nobility, and Church only if they accepted the Revolution's fundamental political settlement.[14] The Restoration laid the foundations for the further expansion of both industry and credit,[15] and this not inconsiderable accomplishment occurred within the context of a greatly restricted franchise, counter-revolutionary policies at home, and a peaceful foreign policy.[16] But despite the common desire of all parties concerned to consolidate the gains already won, the class alliance which provided the foundation of the Restoration could last only as long as the aristocracy, Church, and king were willing to live in a society which was slowly industrializing under the leadership and for the benefit of the upper levels of the bourgeoisie.[17] The alliance fell apart because the old feudal classes and institutions could not live with capitalism and—more important—because the classes that now mattered could no longer live with them.[18]

The accession of Polignac, an *ultra* of the *ultras*, to head the government in August 1829 brought the Restoration's permanent political crisis to a head. It coincided with the overt clerical counter-revolutionism of Charles X and signaled an intensification of the reactionaries' attempts to undo some of the most fundamental results of the Revolution itself. Virtually the entire French middle class had expressed its opposition to the reaction by becoming liberals during the 1820s, and when the king responded to widespread popular dissatisfaction with Polignac by suspending freedom of the press, annulling elections, and modifying the electoral law to the benefit of the great landowners, the royal *coup* did not go unchallenged.[19] The July Revolution featured the appearance of the dreaded barricades and was led by the liberal bourgeoisie at the head of the people.[20]

The Revolution of 1830 was a watershed in French history because it completed the dismantling of domestic feudalism through a mass revolution which abolished the remaining political and economic privileges of the ancient nobility and began to establish bourgeois political supremacy in its characteristic French purity. Louis-Philippe, the head of the younger branch of the Bourbon family and a large property-owner in his own right, was installed as a constitutionally limited monarch.[21] Placed on the throne by a handful of bourgeois politicians and journalists in the tumultuous days following the "Trois Glorieuses," he ruled the kingdom as the "citizen-king" for eighteen years.[22] Alexis de Tocqueville described the extent to which the bourgeoisie monopolized state power after 1830 with his customary clarity:

> Our history from 1789 to 1830, viewed from a distance and as a whole, affords as it were the picture of a struggle to the death between the Ancien Regime, its traditions, memories, hopes, and men, as represented by the aristocracy, and the New France led by the Middle Class. The year 1830 closed the first period of our revolutions, . . . In 1830 the triumph of the middle class had been definite and so thorough that all political power, every franchise, every prerogative, and the whole government was confined and, as it were, heaped up within the narrow limits of this one class, to the statutory exclusion of all beneath them and the actual exclusion of all above. Not only did it thus rule society, but it may be said to have formed it. It entrenched itself in every vacant place, prodigiously augmented the number of places and accustomed itself to live almost as much upon the Treasury as upon its own industry.[23]

Faced with potentially explosive threats to its power from both right and left, the new government set about protecting the upper bourgeoisie from both aristocracy and people. While it was anticlerical, tolerated some religious dissent, and refused to restore any of the aristocracy's feudal privileges, it was simultaneously determined to rule through an extremely restricted franchise, was violently anti-republican, and sided with the employers in almost every labor dispute.[24] The only class allowed to vote ("le pays légal"), the upper bourgeoisie was not prepared to make any compromises with the peasantry, nascent proletariat, or middle and lower bourgeoisie. It ruled through a "government of resistance," and the familiar cycle of French politics reappeared as the July Monarchy matured: a rigid, unyielding, narrow government representing the interests of a small minority of the population made revolution inevitable because compromise and reform would have equally exposed it to ruin.

The unity of the different fractions of the bourgeoisie had melted away almost as soon as Louis-Philippe assumed the throne. In general they were able to unite and express their common class interests only when the old aristocracy or the new proletariat threatened it.[25] The *grande bourgeoisie financière* was able to impose its will on its former allies because it was better organized and possessed a more complete understanding of how to attain its ends than did the others. The proletariat remained within the bounds of bourgeois politics because French capitalism had not developed far enough for it to assume an independent political position,[26] the petty bourgeoisie followed the upper bourgeoisie because of its hostility to the aristocracy and was unable to offer a viable alternative to Louis-Philippe for the moment, and the section of the bourgeoisie which was tied to manufacturing wanted nothing more than a share of power. In contrast, the *grande bourgeoisie* moved quickly to establish a "government of interest" whose sole purpose was to enable it to enrich itself.[27] While the petty bourgeoisie, the urban poor, and the small proletariat had provided the popular force which delivered the death-blow to the Restoration, the upper bourgeoisie emerged in full control of the country; "the 'king of the barricades' quickly became the king of the boutique and was soon to become the king of the Stock Exchange."[28] The Revolution thus appeared to have been little more than an insignificant change in regime,[29] and Casimir Perier—an important banker and one of the early leading figures of the July Monarchy—acknowledged this when he told one of his associates that "there hasn't been a revolution; there's been only a simple change in the person of chief of state."[30]

It could hardly have been different, for neither the small proletariat nor the more numerous petty bourgeoisie was in a position to mount a serious challenge for power. The French labor movement would take a series of dramatic steps forward during the 1830s, but it would not begin to play an important part in national politics until the following decade. Strikes and occasional local riots did testify to the increasing militancy and political orientation of the workers' movement, however, and the insurrections in Lyon and Paris early in the 1830s served as harbingers of the future. Hobbled by the relatively slow pace of industrialization and by the stubborn survival of artisanal production, the French proletariat could do little but follow in the wake of the same bourgeoisie whose consolidation of power it had made possible and which was becoming its remorseless antagonist.

Thus the circumstances of the July Monarchy's birth expressed the basic paradox common to all of French politics from 1789 through the end of the nineteenth century. It owed its existence to the active participation of "the people" in July, yet its social base was so narrow and its politics were so unyielding that it soon became clear that it rested on a betrayal. The possibility of revolution haunted the upper bourgeoisie through the July Monarchy.[31] Fearful of democracy and republicanism, anxious to limit the revolutionary implications of 1830 yet dependent on the popular movement which had brought it to power in the first place, it tried to maintain itself on a very narrow social base for eighteen years, the "financial aristocracy" steadfastly refusing to do anything to broaden the base of the regime.[32]

The *petite bourgeoisie* was in deep trouble throughout the July Monarchy, for it was subject to the pressure of steady industrialization and it became progressively less able to defend itself without assistance. Yet when it appealed to the state for help it often found that the government and bureaucracy were as hostile to it as they were to the working and nonworking poor.[33] In many ways, the class in whose interest the government ruled was itself the greatest threat to the petty bourgeoisie.[34] Trapped between the concentrated masses of landed property and big capital, France's small proprietors tried desperately to maneuver between them throughout the eighteen years of the July Monarchy. They got no help from the state and it soon became clear that their attempts to defend themselves were limited by their political weakness.[35] The rapid growth of petty-bourgeois democracy and socialism during the early 1840s resulted from their beleaguered economic position and their attendant political isolation.

Unable to obtain credit, unable to compete against bigger industry and agriculture, and unable to get satisfaction from a government monopolized by its enemies, the *petite bourgeoisie* first became disenchanted and then went into active opposition. It was soon joined by the growing proletariat, and a formidable threat to the July Monarchy began to mature as working people and small proprietors began organizing to defend themselves against wage cuts, unemployment, and bankruptcy.[36] It was in conditions of nearly universal alienation and constant struggle that a political alliance between the French *petite bourgeoisie* and the proletariat, led for the moment by the former, began to take shape in the late 1830s. A characteristically modern popular movement fused political and social concerns, for it became obvious that both the proletariat's struggle for a living wage and full employment and that of the petty bourgeoisie for protection and equality necessitated a struggle against the state which supported big property as a matter of policy.[37] Ths struggle tended to be defensive at first, but as the century progressed it developed more amplitude, became more generally political in orientation, and slowly became more self-assertive and aggressive in tone:

> The decision to keep political power in the hands of the upper middle class gave the Government far too narrow a base. As industry developed, the number of voters increased, but there arose another class of 'new men,' the smaller factory owners and shopkeepers, who greatly resented their lack of the vote. Such men are slow to combine and to agitate, but their numbers were such that when they felt they had real cause for dissatisfaction with the policy of the State they had the means to publicize their demands.[38]

Economic and political concerns thus began to come together for both the *petite bourgeoisie* and the proletariat during this period. A dynamic economy which was creating and shaping large new blocs of small owner-workers and modern laborers was in conflict with a narrow political system which could neither serve nor absorb them.[39] The result was a long-term crisis which had a great influence on nineteenth-century political affairs, helped to form the ideological perspectives of the modern left, and contains important implications for contemporary politics.

Proudhon was coming to maturity during the July Monarchy, and it is important to understand the deeply contradictory position of the *petite bourgeoisie* if one wants to understand what he was trying to do. It is also important to note that the same forces that were shaping his outlook were at work among a whole generation of petty-bourgeois and proletarian radicals. While post-1830 liberalism made property the pivot of political life, the social forces unleashed by the development of market society interacted with the political legacy of the Revolution to produce an unprecedented contestation of property and bourgeois supremacy. For all the triumph of bourgeois society which the July Monarchy seemed to register, it was in France that modern socialism and democracy developed in a particularly clear and intense fashion. Under these circumstances many thinkers and actors were trying to understand and change political and economic forces, and their efforts were as reflective of the society in which they lived as they were instrumental in changing it.

NOTES

1. E. J. Hobsbawm, *The Age of Capital* (New York: New American Library, 1975), 227 and F. F. Ridley, *Revolutionary Syndicalism in France* (Cambridge: Cambridge University Press, 1978), 15.
2. Louis Dunham, *The Industrial Revolution in France 1815–1848* (New York: Exposition Press, 1955), 423.
3. *Ibid.*, 184.
4. *Ibid.*, 119–20.
5. Louis Girard, "Problèmes Francais," in Max Beloff et al eds., *L'Europe du XIXe et du XXe Siècle* (Milan: Marzorati, 1959), 519.
6. *Ibid.*, 521.
7. Tom Kemp, *Industrialization in Nineteenth-Century Europe* (London: Longmans, 1969), 65.
8. E. H. Hobsbawm, *The Age of Revolution 1789–1848* (New York: New American Library, 1961), 93.
9. Albert Léon Guérard, *French Civilization in the Nineteenth Century* (New York: Century, 1914), 189.
10. Eugène Fournière, "Le Règne de Louis-Philippe" in Jean Jaurès ed., *Histoire Socialiste* (Paris: Jules Rouff, 1907), 8:51.
11. Pierre Léon, "L'évolution démographique, économique et sociale" in Beloff et al, 344.
12. Louis Girard, "Problèmes Français," 520.
13. Dunham, 185.
14. Rene Viviani, "La Restauration" in Jaurès ed., vii:92.
15. Dunham, 224.
16. Guerard, 95. One had to pay 300 francs per year in order to vote and 1,000 francs to be eligible for election to the Chamber. Hence 90,000 people could vote in 1815, and 15,000 could be elected out of a total population of 38,000,000. Viviani, 91.
17. For an interesting description of the relations between classes in Restoration France, see Frederick B, Artz, *Reaction and Revolution 1814–1832* (New York: Harper, 1934), ch. 2.
18. Paul Lewis, *Histoire du Socialisme en France 1789–1945* (Paris: Rivière, 1946), 40–43.
19. See M. D. R. Leys, *Between Two Empires: A Study of French Politicians and People Between 1814 and 1848* (London: Longmans, Green, 1955), 157–75.

20. Guerard, 100. See also Fournière, 48.
21. Among other things, the Orleans family owned two of the most important French canals in 1830. "This singular opportunity for personal profit by the sovereign at the expense of the nation was utilized fully." Dunham, 29.
22. Leys, 176–87.
23. Alexis de Tocqueville, *Recollections*, trans. Alexander Teixeria de Mattos and J. P. Mayer (New York: Columbia University Press, 1949), 2–3.
24. From 90,000 during the Restoration the number of eligible voters rose to about 200,000 in 1830 and by the end of the monarchy to 250,000. With universal manhood suffrage it would have been between seven and eight million. Less than one percent of the population could vote. Georges Lefebvre, *La Monarchie de Juillet* (Paris: Centre de Documentation Universitaire, 1936), 93.
25. Fournière, 49.
26. Vivianni, 255–57.
27. Jean Lhomme, *La Grande Bourgeoisie au Pouvoir 1830–1880* (Paris: Presses Universitaires Françaises, 1960), 49–50.
28. Celestin Bouglé, *Chez les Prophètes Socialistes* (Paris: Alcan, 1918), 134.
29. Guerard, 89. This characterized the situation: "From 1814 to 1848 the government of France was a constitutional monarchy, closely modeled on that of England. . . . As the richest taxpayers alone had the right to vote, only one class, a limited aristocracy of wealth, the upper bourgeoisie, was directly represented. No radical change took place in the financial and foreign policies of France under three kings and two flags: it was a time of recuperation, economy, and peace. . . . In many respects, therefore, these thirty-four years of constitutional monarchy form a well-characterized unit."
30. This famous assessment was reported by Odilon Barrot in his memoirs and is quoted in Fournière, 116.
31. Leys, 188–201.
32. Guérard, 102.
33. See, for example, Fournière's description of Casimir Périer, 115.
34. *Ibid.*, 48.
35. *Ibid.*, 380.
36. Guérard, 193.
37. Dunham, 201.
38. Leys, 191.
39. Hobsbawm 1961, 360.

2

Class, Ideology,
and Social Theory

BOURGEOIS LIBERALISM AND
PETTY-BOURGEOIS DEMOCRACY

The Revolution's Jacobin legacy and the July Monarchy's narrowness forced
spokesmen for the petty bourgeoisie to think in political terms in the early
years of the regime. Their initial tendency was to demand that the political
system be widened in the expectation that a measure of influence would be
enough to enable small proprietors to defend themselves against threats from
above and below. Republican and democratic ideologies flowered during the
early 1830s and although they attracted adherents from the growing proletariat they tended to express the viewpoint of the beleaguered petty bourgeoisie.

The fact that working-class and petty-bourgeois ideologies were forced to
develop outside the "official" political system explains why they reflected
the opposition of these two classes so clearly. Political and economic developments deeply affected every class in French society, and this interacted
with Louis Philippe's isolation and stubbornness to produce an extraordi-
narily rich group of writings. The resulting ferment deeply affected the *petite bourgeoisie* and the proletariat, and as 1848 approached both the inability
of the government to hold back social change and its isolation from the
majority of the population were becoming increasingly clear. Tocqueville
described the situation:

> The country was at that time divided into two unequal parts, or rather zones: in
> the upper, which alone was intended to contain the whole of the nation's politi-
> cal life, there reigned nothing but languor, impotence, stagnation, and boredom;
> in the lower, on the contrary, political life began to make itself manifest by
> means of feverish and irregular signs, of which the attentive observer was easily
> able to seize the meaning.[1]

The Revolution of 1830 had shown the power of the "little" people and
their desire to end feudalism once and for all, yet as the government in-

18

creasingly showed itself to be ruling for the benefit of a small clique it became clear that one oligarchy had been substituted for another while the "free" operations of the economy exposed more and more people to ruin. As the 1830s developed and a genuine proletarian movement began to take shape it became increasingly apparent that the "liberty" which the July Monarchy defended was little more than a mask for privilege.

The "haute bourgeoisie" expressed its ideological opposition to both the *ancien régime* and democracy with liberalism and took the early moderate years of the Great Revolution as its model. Deeply committed to property and admiring the English bourgeoisie's "Glorious Revolution," French liberalism tended toward an abstract legalism and relied on laws and institutions, was bitterly antidemocratic, and opposed any extension of the franchise. It became the chief ideological weapon of a small financial aristocracy against the political and social claims of the laboring majority, and the narrowness of the class whose interests it represented gradually turned it into a straightforward antidemocratic defense of the status quo.

Whatever democratic possibilities liberalism embodied were undermined by the market's tendency to create a concentration of wealth at one pole of society and a concentration of poverty at the other.[2] If Benjamin Constant and François Guizot emphasized freedom at the expense of equality and sought to buttress political rights at the expense of social welfare, neither man was able to look beyond a limited set of parliamentary institutions and an understanding of liberty as the right to accumulate property. Both were unreservedly hostile to any proposals to widen the franchise, Constant invoking individual freedom and Guizot declaring that democracy constituted the greatest single danger to peaceful and orderly progress.[3] As liberalism became an apology for class dictatorship and economic inequality, it did not take Guizot long to justify his use of the same methods to suppress opposition that he himself had combatted when they had been used by the Bourbons against the financial bourgeoisie. His acknowledgement that the specific purpose of the July Monarchy was to defend the new aristocracy against democracy only confirmed what had long been suspected.[4] Tocqueville traced the origins of the July Monarchy's decay right back to the upper bourgeoisie's capture of the state in 1830:

> No sooner had the Revolution of 1830 become an accomplished fact, than there ensued a great lull in political passion, a sort of general subsidence, accompanied by a rapid increase in public wealth. The particular spirit of the middle class became the general spirit of the government; it ruled the latter's foreign policy as well as affairs at home: an active, industrious spirit, often dishonorable, generally orderly, occasionally reckless through vanity or egoism, but timid by temperament, moderate in all things except in its love of ease and comfort, and last but not least mediocre.... Master of everything in a manner that no aristocracy has ever been or may ever hope to be, the middle class, when called

upon to assume the government, took it up as an industrial enterprise; it entrenched itself behind its power, and before long, in their egoism, each of its members thought much more of his private business than of public affairs; of his personal enjoyment than of the greatness of the nation.[5]

Since the *haute bourgeoisie* used liberalism to justify its privileges under the July Monarchy, the political struggle against Louis-Philippe's regime inevitably required a simultaneous ideological struggle against liberalism. As the *petite bourgeoisie* and the proletariat, the two most important classes in opposition during the July Monarchy, continued to clarify their respective positions, liberals proved increasingly unable to offer credible explanations of why things had to be the way they were.[6] The fate of modern French liberalism was tied to that of the class which elaborated and used it to justify its rule. It was compromised by its close identification with a restricted, authoritarian and unpopular regime,[7] it lost its hold as the attack on the July Monarchy developed, and it failed utterly as the French left began to address the connections between political liberty and economic inequality in the context of a developing market economy.[8]

The petty bourgeoisie's opposition took a political form at first and was shaped by the narrowness of the political system; democracy and republicanism, virtually synonymous during this period, arose as the progressive petty bourgeoisie began to lead the struggles of the lower classes for a measure of political influence.[9] The failure of the bourgeoisie's liberalism was mirrored by the increasing power of the petty bourgeoisie's democracy. Heavily influenced by Rousseau, favorable to the Great Revolution in general and to the Jacobin constitution of 1793 in particular, trusting the people's innate sense of justice and deeply anticlerical, "pure" democracy developed in great depth during the July Monarchy. In a clear break with liberalism, it talked of extending the Revolution's political equality to everyone; appealing to "the people"—which it defined as all who worked for a living and were politically unrepresented—to take direct action and establish popular sovereignty and a democratic republic, it was a political movement from the very beginning. Many of the traditions of the revolutionary and republican past were revived and deeply-held petty-bourgeois aspirations were tapped; the movement's orientation was expressed by its claim that broad political democracy would help small property-owners defend themselves against both big capital and the mob.[10] A heavily egalitarian petty-bourgeois democracy gave direction to the opposition through the 1830s before the national economy developed to the point where a politically independent proletariat could appear and begin to challenge the institution of private property as such.[11] In the meantime, all the leading republican and democratic leaders of the period stressed the need to widen the franchise and establish true popular sovereignty. Arago and Ledru-Rollin of the *Réforme*,

Garnier-Pagès of the *National*, Marrast of the *Tribune*, and the democratic poet Lamartine demanded that the right to vote be extended to all classes and that a republic replace the July Monarchy. Jules Michelet and Edgar Quinet developed the democratic aspects of the opposition while appealing to the infallible "people," glorifying the Great Revolution's pre-Terror accomplishments, trying to unite all Frenchmen against unearned wealth and arbitrary privilege while preserving private property, and relentlessly attacking both the power of the Church and the aristocratic pretensions of the upper bourgeoisie.

Its position under the July Monarchy enabled the petty bourgeoisie to understand that the alliance between large-scale production, big landholdings, concentrated capital and an oppressive state worked against its interests— and those of other groups as well. To some extent it was prepared to ally itself with the proletariat and defend its interests, for it was also vulnerable to uncontrolled concentration and mechanization and could see the connection between its imminent ruin and that of the peasantry and the smaller proletariat.[12] Democrats tended to appeal to all classes, men like Michelet often recognizing the particular importance of the proletariat as the most oppressed but claiming that the workers' interests were identical to those of small proprietors and the peasantry.[13] Even if its demands were often limited to attempts to defend the working and nonworking poor from starvation, however, the petty bourgeoisie did begin to share some common positions with the developing working class. The alliance between the two continued to develop as the "social question" intruded itself into the national consciousness.

As the July Monarchy matured and factory capitalism continued to develop, it became increasingly clear that exclusion from political power was not the basic cause of the petty bourgeoisie's difficulties. Attention began to shift from political to social matters as the attempt to understand the economic conditions which made possible the political hegemony of the financial aristocracy became primary.[14] The increasing preoccupation with "the social question" marked the beginning of petty-bourgeois socialism as the more narrowly political approaches slowly died away.

SCIENCE, INDUSTRY, AND "THE SOCIAL QUESTION"

If the Great Revolution confirmed that nineteenth-century France was the home of the modern state and the hyper-politics which accompanied its consolidation, it is no less true that French socialism drew a good deal of its strength from and directed much of its attention toward an analysis of the social and economic questions raised by the industrialization of the country. Even in so "jacobin" and "political" a social order, the unfolding emphasis on economic matters was not entirely unfamiliar to French social theory.

Economic concerns run through Rousseau's writings, particularly the *Second Discourse*.[15] Holding that society is based on economics; linking inequality with private property; emphasizing solidarity, cooperation, and community; and deriving all rights from society, Rousseau was trying to elaborate a social order based not on the king, not on God, not on the isolated individual, but on society's objective interests. He thought private property lay at the root of both inequality and society.[16] A clear materialist current runs through the *Second Discourse*, early advances in social organization being linked to technical innovations in production.[17] Inequality was heightened in society because increased human appetites established an atmosphere in which work provided an opportunity for some men to enrich themselves at others' expense:

> the stronger did more work; the cleverer turned his mind to better advantage; the more ingenious found ways to shorten his labor; the farmer had greater need of iron or the blacksmith greater need of wheat; and working equally, the one earned a great deal while the other barely had enough to live. Thus does natural inequality imperceptibly manifest itself along with contrived inequality; and thus do the differences among men, developed by those of circumstances, become more perceptible, more permanent in their effects, and begin to have a proportionate influence over the fate of individuals.[18]

Rousseau's concern with economic matters is an important and often-neglected aspect of his work. His attempt to understand the connection between political affairs and social matters stands as a bridge between the *philosophes* of the eighteenth century and the men who helped elaborate the ideology of the Revolution, Restoration and July Monarchy—all of whom were talking about "la question sociale" in different ways.[19]

Sièyes is often considered one of the founders of a purely political Jacobinism, but a large part of his discussion of representation and participation was based on an economic analysis.[20] In opposing the Physiocrats he held that labor, rather than the ownership of property, held society together and defended the Third Estate, not because it was more numerous than the clergy or nobility, but because it produced the goods and performed the tasks which made a settled and stable society possible. Anticipating a later tendency to define "the people" as those who work rather than those who are outside the formal political system, he included manufacturers, speculators, and entrepreneurs with the working class in the group of socially useful citizens and claimed that their activity entitled them to direct state affairs. Although he did try to solve the misrepresentation of the *ancien régime* by focusing on the formal structures of power and authority,[21] his understanding of the historical importance of the way societies organize the production of what they need anticipated some of the themes which later social theorists would enlarge upon.

The Great Revolution had as great a social as a political content, and much of its political history was written in the contradictory relationship between the bourgeois understanding of liberty and the plebian conception of equality. If the defense of property underlay the bourgeoisie's politics through the course of the Revolution, the social and economic needs of the peasantry and the urban poor determined their activities just as surely.[22] The peasants' desire for food, land, and protection from aristocratic restoration drove their assault on the structures of feudalism during the summer of 1789 and married them to the republic after the Jacobins committed themselves to land reform. The enormous impact of hunger in country and town radicalized the *sans-culottes'* social egalitarianism, and their desire for restrictions on property rights in the interest of small proprietors lay behind the popular movement's conceptions of popular sovereignty, democratic accountability, the right of revolution, and the need for repression. The Jacobins' alliance with the popular movement made possible the Revolution's final victory over counter-revolution and intervention but Robespierre's break with the *sans-culottes'* desire to subordinate liberty to social welfare doomed the Revolution at its hour of victory and opened the path to Thermidor. In the long run the Jacobins proved more committed to defending property than following through on the social gains of the Terror, and the reluctance of even the most radical wing of the revolutionary bourgeoisie to countenance serious long-term restrictions on freedom of property in the interests of social equality stood as a start reminder of what lay in the future.

For their part, plebian leaders such as Babeuf and Marat were demanding equality and justice at the expense of property rights as early as 1795.[23] They saw property as the worst of all the evils afflicting the poor and were among the first major figures on the French left to move away from the petty-bourgeois desire to generalize property to something approaching a communist position of collective ownership and use. Babeuf was also favorable to industry and thought in terms of dispossessing the rich for the benefit of the poor.[24] His egalitarianism has often been singled out as his most important single legacy to French socialism,[25] and he stood at the beginning of the French left's tendency to pay more attention to equality and fraternity than to liberty. This tendency was a reflection of the immediate needs of the poor and the left's suspicion of the uses to which bourgeois notions of freedom had been put in the past.[26]

The 1820s and 1830s saw a heightened preoccupation with the economic roots of modern society's *malaise*. One of the reasons so many early socialist theoreticians were French was that the Great Revolution's thoroughness meant that the contemporary situation was relatively uncomplicated by any factors other than "the social question." The left's traditional focus on the state notwithstanding, it became apparent that political explanations alone could not account for what was happening in the country. Modern socialism's origins lay in the increasing emphasis it placed on the economic order, rather than on political affairs, as the central cause of the chaos and anarchy of modern life. The central contradiction of the French Revolution, a harbinger for all bourgeois revolutions of the future, was that a classically democratic political upheaval seemed to have set the conditions for the development of a wildly chaotic and increasingly unequal social order. If political democracy had been made more concrete and extended to wider sections of the population than ever before, the inequities of an individualistic and competitive economy stood in stark contrast to the expectation that equality before the law would translate formal equality of opportunity into substantive equality of condition. Economic liberalism clashed violently with social democracy, and whether the conflict appeared to be an unfortunate legacy of the past or inherent to the dynamics of a market economy it soon became clear that the left would have to base itself on the demand for social regulation of the market in the name of values different from, or in addition to, the classical bourgeois demand for freedom.

Even if they often analyzed modern society with a mode of thought which derived from a preindustrial egalitarianism, the early socialists sought to preserve the Enlightenment's prime accomplishment by trying to combine social supervision of the market with a commitment to personal liberty and a presumption that social harmony could arise spontaneously through the liberation of private initiative. The chief theoretical novelty of the new "socialist" movement, however vague and diffuse it proved to be, was that it began to differentiate itself from the far more widespread petty-bourgeois democratic radicalism of the period by stressing the virtue of cooperation, looking to public regulation, and slowly beginning to dispute the claims of private ownership. This would later mark one of the lines of demarcation which separated the "pure" democrats from the socialists and it indicated that the latter were prepared to move beyond deploring the condition of the poor to rejecting the central claims of liberalism as such. If egalitarian distribution of the social product marked an earlier phase in the theoretical development of the nineteenth-century left, social regulation of the market would point the way to a political movement which stood for something deeper than the elimination of poverty or the organization of social equality.

The theoretical sophistication of the early French socialists contrasted with the organizational backwardness of the workers' movement. From 1815 through the Revolution of 1848, the French left developed unevenly because the theoretical insights of two generations of social critics could not yet be matched by the practical accomplishments of a labor movement which remained relatively weak for some time.[27] As a theoretical trend, modern socialism was born in the half-century which separated the Great Revolution from the upheaval of 1848 but it could not influence or find support from an organized and active labor movement until the end of the 1850s. The slow pace of French industrialization and the survival of artisanal production hobbled both the practical development of the "real movement" and the theoretical maturation of socialism, each of which could grow only as it drew strength from and fostered the development of the other.

Building on the foundation laid by Sièyes, Rousseau, and Babeuf, then, modern socialism arose because liberalism, democracy and republicanism could provide neither convincing explanations of nor remedies for what was wrong with France. Yet it did not emerge ready-made, and its spokesmen often retained many attitudes and positions which were rooted in the very society they were trying to understand and change.[28]

Most members of this first generation of modern French social critics, whose outstanding representatives were Henri de Saint-Simon and Charles Fourier, were born before the Great Revolution. They had witnessed the end of feudalism, the Revolution's "gigantic broom," Napoleon's wars and the beginnings of the factory system with their own eyes. Their life-histories were themselves reflections of the tumultuous times in which they lived and served as a source of their wisdom and experience—and of their bewilderment, frustration, and anger, for they had seen momentous events and had all been personally affected by the great changes in French society. They were able to compare early industrialization with the *ancien régime* precisely because they had known both firsthand. All their analyses and panaceas bore the imprint of their experiences. They were able to be so penetrating about the society in which they lived because an important period of European history was written in their own lives. Saint-Simon, for example, fought in the American War of Independence, renounced his ancient family title during the French Revolution, made a fortune by speculating in Church lands and then lost it in the commercial chaos of Napoleon's early reign. He was deeply struck by the passing of feudalism, the bulk of his life's work being devoted to hastening the coming of the "Industrial Age." Fourier was shaped more by the difficulties of the petty bourgeoisie than by anything else, much of his desire to end the anarchy of economic life taking its direction from his desire to save small property and small production.[29] Although they differed in many important ways, both men were links between the eighteenth and nineteenth centuries. Not socialists themselves, they were nonetheless fathers of modern socialism; irritated and annoyed that the modern world had not done away with the arbitrariness and unfairness of the *ancien régime*, they retained a modified belief in the virtues of inequality and fiercely defended private property.

The members of the second generation of modern European socialists, whose outstanding French example was Proudhon, were molded by a very different set of experiences. For the most part they were born after Napoleon had been defeated. What direct knowledge they had of prerevolutionary France came from their parents' generation. They themselves were children of the industrial age, and their kind of socialism was radically different from that of their predecessors as a result.

They had the accumulated knowledge of the first generation to build on, and an understanding of what they were trying to do must begin with a discussion of what they had inherited. They were not nearly as shocked as their forefathers had been. They had fewer illusions about the world and tended to be far more angry, for they had a clearer sense that industry could enable modern society to finally satisfy human needs and were disappointed and embittered when they saw it being used to reinforce privilege and exploitation. They dealt with the problems they encountered in different ways because early capitalism was an overwhelming force to nearly everyone in France, and the depth and variety of their approaches is a testament to the magnitude of the transformations that were sweeping over the country. Peasants, rural laborers, landlords, factory workers, the petty bourgeoisie, large capitalists—nearly everyone in France was directly affected by the social changes set in motion by the development of industrial capitalism. The result was a body of theoretical work which has few rivals in the breadth, complexity, imagination, or originality of its diagnoses of social illness or its schemes for social renewal. It was "a period fertile in ideas so simple, so noble and so utopian that it seems difficult to take them seriously today, yet the seed-bed of nearly all political thought for the rest of the century."[30] Its representatives appealed to fraternity, brotherhood, and collective action, elaborating a powerful challenge to the individualistic concern with liberty which seemed to reflect and reinforce the market's scarcities to divide people on the basis of their shared needs instead of uniting them in the common production of abundance. They tried to understand how machines could fulfill human requirements, although there was wide disagreement about how the damage that industry was inflicting could be minimized. They often advocated some kind of central planning to overcome the anarchy of production which they thought resulted from the uncontrolled pursuit of private profit. Widespread distrust of politics ran throughout their writings, emphasis being placed on the discovery and application of universal and knowable scientific laws. They did more than focus on specific examples of unfairness but tried to understand the essential mechanisms of the productive system, for "they could show not merely that capitalism was unjust, but that it appeared to work badly and, in so far as it worked, to produce the opposite results to those predicted by its champions."[31]

The effort to understand how capitalism worked itself proceeded from a basic acceptance of the Industrial Revolution, although there was a residual temptation to blame society's mounting problems on industry as such. Reactionary attacks on science, reason, and capitalism persisted throughout the period,[32] but all attempts to restore the *ancien régime* were doomed after 1830.[33] The power of early French socialism derived from its ability to analyze existing conditions, and to get at the way the world seemed to be working, it was necessary—at the very least—that the analyst not want to turn the clock back.[34]

The "social question" became important to the largely middle-class intellectuals of the French left because it was becoming important to the working and nonworking poor toward whom socialism was beginning to turn. The workers' developing class-consciousness was initially expressed as a recognition that there was an intrinsic connection between their own poverty and the wealth of those who owned property. This development had immediate repercussions, for the realization that the poor were poor *because* the rich were rich encouraged socialists to think about radically transforming the basic structure of society.[35]

That the social question was posed at all was a consequence of the development of the French proletariat, even if a full half-century would pass before the theoretical socialism of the intelligentsia and the practical movement of the workers turned toward each other. Interested in questions of social reform and slightly hostile to purely political problems and solutions, the proletariat had an unmistakable effect on the direction of French socialism from the beginning of the July Monarchy. "From 1830 on, the question of the workers, which had been called the social question for so long, was posed."[36] If workers were interested in "the social question" from the very beginning, the impact on the purely political approaches of the past would intensify as the economy developed:

> The proletariat, as a distinct class with a distinct outlook of its own, was the most important historical product of this period, the period of the development of great industry in France. While the *bourgeoisie*, great and small alike, concerned itself with the question of monarchy and republic, the factory proletariat showed from the first a certain indifference to political claims, and demanded social reforms: the right to work and the duty of society to provide means of subsistence.[37]

Virtually all the early socialists were forced to reevaluate the results and lessons of the Great Revolution,[38] and in almost every case they came to the same conclusion: deep-going and profound as it had been, the Revolution had not gone far enough because it had been so narrowly political. It was clear that the Revolution had substantially broadened the political and civil rights of most Frenchmen and had contributed to the destruction of feudalism, but the continued existence of poverty and exploitation a full half-century after the Bastille's fall encouraged many thinkers to begin investigating the non-political roots of inequality and misery. This left them vulnerable to charges from democrats that they were ignoring the need for political democracy and a republic as the indispensable foundations for economic and social justice.[39] They responded that the sterility of democratic thought was due precisely to its infatuation with the form of the state while it ignored the truly important social questions.[40] Democrats' naive faith that the traditional forms of political action and discourse could provide satisfactory answers to France's most basic problems did not appeal to them, for they saw that, as far as it had gone, the Revolution had merely transferred power from one social class to another. Oppression and inequality had not been ended; they had merely changed location, and many social theorists went on to add that a system of formal political democracy in which all citizens were theoretically equal before the law but manifestly unequal in social and economic conditions could result in only an everincreasing degree of inequality and a heightened level of social conflict. The only substantial result of the Revolution, it seemed, was that a slightly larger minority than before now exercised political and social power. If anything, post-revolutionary France seemed more unstable and unjust than ever.

Nowhere did these theoretical developments yield more fruitful or important results than in the works of Saint-Simon, the most influential and farsighted social theorist of the early nineteenth century. His emphasis on the importance of unifying and organizing mens' understanding and the world on the basis of scientific principles was the cornerstone of his work. Aghast at the chaos and disorganization of his time, he articulated a "science of humanity" which would permit the rational reorganization of economic life and which stands at the center of everything for which modern socialism has come to stand:

> Hitherto, the method of the sciences of observation has not been introduced into political questions; every man has imported his point of view, method of reasoning and judging, and hence there is not yet any precision in the answers, or universality in the results. The time has come when this infancy of science should cease, and certainly it is desirable that it should cease, for the troubles of the social order arise from obscurities in political theory.[41]

The scientific era that the Industrial Revolution was opening up would enable mankind to use the methods and findings of the natural sciences in economic, social and political affairs[42] and this would require an ideological struggle against all "metaphysical" approaches to social problems.[43] Saint-Simon had great faith in industry's capacity to liberate mankind from the arbitrariness of nature, believed that the production of useful things is man's most important activity and looked forward to full employment, a planned economy, universal peace, and the end of suffering.[44] Convinced that the future lay in liberating and organizing the enormous productive forces which were only beginning to manifest themselves, he adopted the basic liberal premise of a split between the state and civil society and looked forward to a social order in which politics could guide economic development but would ultimately die away as society spontaneously organized itself.

Saint-Simon is extraordinary in the clarity of his recognition that industrial production was becoming the motive force in social development, and he wanted those who direct production—*les industriels*—to direct society as well. Violently hostile to the obsolete political power of the "parasites"—the nobility, clergy, military, and idle landowners—he was insistent in demanding that the "useful" bankers, manufacturers, artisans, scientists, engineers, and workers exercise political power and use it to rationally organize the economy. If society is being organized by industry, so should the state:

> The progress of civilization has been leading the population of France to become basically industrial; thus the industrial class should be primary and the other classes should be subordinate to it. The industrialists certainly need an army and the courts; property-owners do not need to be forced to invest their money in industry; but it is outrageous that it should be the military, the lawyers and the idle landlords who are the principal directors of the public welfare given the current state of civilization.[45]

Saint-Simon's assertion that those who direct production should also administer the state systematized the financial and industrial bourgeoisie's political claims under the Restoration. The proletariat was not yet counted as one of society's productive classes, although he did view its plight with genuine sympathy. He took its suffering to be the paramount sign of France's social corruption and held that the amelioration of the lot of "la classe la plus nombreuse et la plus pauvre" was one of the tasks of enlightened government.

Living as he did before the proletariat was sufficiently developed to constitute a social force in its own right, Saint-Simon leveled most of his attacks against both the parasitical feudal aristocracy and the modern men of property who lived off other mens' labor—those he contemptuously called *les oisifs*. His insistence that those who contribute to production rather than those who own property be rewarded seemed very radical indeed[46] and prefigured similar claims which both petty-bourgeois socialists and proletarian communists would direct against the bourgeoisie itself.[47] His famous "parable" of 1819 compared the hypothetical loss to France of her 3,000 best scientists, artists, and artisans to that of the Duc d'Angoulème, the Duc de Berry, the Great Officers of the Royal Household, all the cardinals and archbishops of the Holy Roman Church, and the country's 10,000 richest landlords. Not surprisingly, he concluded that society would be harmed in the first instance and helped in the second.[48]

A wide-ranging attack on the powerful French tendency to use politics to solve social questions was also characteristic of Saint-Simon's approach, even if he did look to a measure of state-directed planning. He was convinced that industrialization meant that economics would determine politics much more directly than before, and he consistently rejected political solutions to problems which resulted from the birth of modern industry.[49] If this antipolitical figure looked to the state it was because he thought it could be an impersonal organizer of production which would lead the transition "from the exploitation of man to the administration of things." Politics could be cured of its arbitrariness only if it were depersonalized; it could be depersonalized only if it became a "science of production," and this would entail the gradual dissolving of politics into economics:

> The human species is destined by its organization to live in society; it has been called to live under a *governmental* regime. It is destined to pass from a governmental or military regime to an *administrative* or industrial one after having made sufficient progress in the positive sciences and industry. Finally, it has had to endure a long and violent crisis during its passage from a militaristic system to a peaceful one.[50]

Saint-Simon stands at the beginning of the nineteenth century's tradition of an antipolitical socialism. No democrat, he was concerned only that "expertise" rule and was convinced that such a development would be good for everyone.[51] He wanted political power to become economic, but although less chaotic and irrational it would remain power for all that. Hierarchy and inequality would remain but would now be based on proven capacity rather than the accidents of birth. The poor would still be led—only they would be better led.

If Saint-Simon believed that people suffered because industry was not sufficiently dominant in France, Charles Fourier held that there was entirely too much industry. Convinced that disorder was the great defect of the economy and that it resulted from a combination of industry and a lack of understanding, Fourier was hostile to machines, large-scale production and centralism of any kind.[52] Deeply offended by widespread impoverishment in the midst of riches, the ostentatious wealth of a handful of idle speculators and merchants, oppression of the weak, increasing social polarization, and periodic economic crises, he denounced commerce all his life and insisted that civilization be reorganized around the needs of the individual.[53] The anarchy of competition lay at the root of France's problems and Fourier joined Saint-Simon in calling for a new social science, for

> had the philosophers sought to discover a method of true and equitable commerce and declared open war against the system of falsehood, extortion, and complication which, under the name of free competition, reigns in commercial relations, they would have secured the thanks and approval of all classes.[54]

Fourier tried to escape the undeniable horrors of what he saw by placing his trust in voluntary rural communes which would fuse ownership and labor—the *phalanstères*.[55] People would work in common, industry would play a minor role, labor would be an integrating and satisfying activity, and local autonomy and administrative decentralization would combine the virtues of the conscious regulation of economic affairs with a maximum of personal liberty. Deeply suspicious of modern civilization, Fourier thought that if people organized their affairs in accordance with the harmony which guides the universe they could attain the moral perfection which had escaped them for millennia.

Like Saint-Simon, Fourier thought that the Great Revolution had been aborted because it had fallen prey to France's centralizing impulse and had failed to provide the economic and social institutions which could satisfy man's most basic needs.[56] Politics could never be a tool of social reform; Fourier was acutely aware that liberty had an economic underpinning and bitterly attacked constitutionalism, Jacobinism, and related political ideologies for promising freedom without knowing how to deliver it. The conflict between the grasping, artificial, and suffocating state and the multifaceted, spontaneous and free *phalanstère* was central to his desire to order society from the bottom up by relying on man's desire for association. A mordant critic of the prevailing wisdom from a materialist standpoint,[57] he held that the needed changes in individual and social life could be liberating only if they occurred outside the realm of politics.[58] His ultimate conclusions were similar to those of Saint-Simon: the Great Revolution had not gone far enough because it had stopped at the bourgeois notion of equality before the law without dealing with the more basic source of oppression. The promises of the Revolution remained unfulfilled because "the social question" had not been resolved.

Fourier and Saint-Simon shared three perspectives which were important to the development of socialism and directly affected the social theorists who came after them. First, they regarded the "social question" as primary, holding that the duty of any well-ordered society is to provide happiness for its members and satisfy basic human needs. They were sure that this lofty aim could not be reached unless societies were organized scientifically. Second, both men emphasized human sociability and association to counteract the harshly divisive effects of an economic system based on the uncontrolled competition of self-serving atoms. Finally, they shared a healthy distrust for politics and a preference for a social order directed by the "producers."

Deeply affected by the crisis of 1817–18, Simonde de Sismondi was horrified by the increase of pauperism in England despite tremendous advances in production. He identified persistent underconsumption as the cause of the crisis and saw clearly that the workers got the worst of it. Moved by genuine concern at the plight of both the workers and small producers, he supported efforts to form unions, urged that the working day be limited, called for an

end to child labor, recommended that Sunday be a day of rest, and advocated public assistance in cases of unemployment or sickness.[59]

If the *National* was the newspaper of the "political" republicans, the *Réforme*
expressed the views of those elements of the traditional left which shared
the developing awareness of the "social problem." Ledru-Rollin and Arago
were leaders of this tendency[60] and both men recognized that the legal
emancipation of the workers was not the same thing as their economic or
social liberation. The *Réforme* was decidedly hostile to socialism and defended
property but argued that social reform had to accompany political change.
It pressed for changes which would help the workers in their fight against
the new "féodalité" which was arising on the basis of industry and finance
and tended to emphasize universal suffrage and free public education. Oriented
toward the "pure" democracy of the petty bourgeoisie yet aware of the need
for some measures of social reform, Arago and Ledru-Rollin decried increasing
class polarization and warned of the consequences of mass immiseration.
Their solution was to urge a series of measures which would enlist the state
in the struggle to preserve a measure of free competition against a financial
aristocracy which was intent on using its political and financial power to
deny credit to small producers. Arago himself posed the social question to
the Chamber in 1841 in a manner which illustrated the common interest
of both the petty bourgeoisie and the proletariat in seeing it resolved:

> Once again Arago raised a heartfelt cry from the podium . . . and, in a speech
> about electoral reform, posed the social question in the following terms: 'there
> exists in the country,' he said, 'a part of the population which is in the grip of
> cruel suffering; this part is especially the manufacturing population.'
> 'Now,' he added, 'this evil can only get worse as the new productive system
> develops. Small industrial capital will not be able to compete against big capital;
> mechanized industry will triumph over industry which relies on human power;
> manufacturing which uses powerful machinery will always prevail over that which
> uses small machines.[61]

If social theorists were struck by the disparities between what political
economists promised and what the economy really did, it was not clear what
the remedy was. The chaos and anarchy of the new productive system was
painfully obvious, and as the 1830s developed it became clear that a general
attempt to organize some sort of public supervision of the market was becoming
an axiom of most social criticism and most schemes for social renewal.

CLASS STRUGGLE, PROPERTY, AND THE ANARCHY OF PRODUCTION

Its great potential notwithstanding, Saint-Simon and Fourier were struck
by the economy's apparently unplanned and accidental character. Although

individual enterprises were being rationally organized for more efficient production, the system as a whole appeared to have a dynamic of its own which escaped understanding or control. People seemed helpless before their own creation, driven by inexorable and unknown social laws which enslaved rather than liberated them. Waste and disorder characterized social life.[62] For Fourier, society resembled a chaotic and dangerous jungle rather than the rational creation of men for the common satisfaction of their needs. The combination of commercial anarchy and predatory "free" competition was his chief enemy, and the *phalanstère* was designed to overcome the stagnation, confusion, unhappiness, suffering, and divisiveness that unrestrained market society produced.[63] Industry and commerce were destructive because they were antisocial:

> Industry embodies . . . the exact opposite of collective and individual welfare. Every industrialist is at war with the rest of society and hostile to it by personal interest. A doctor hopes his fellow citizens get sick, and a lawyer wants a good lawsuit in every family. An architect needs a good fire which reduces a quarter of the city to ashes, and a glazier would like to see a good hailstorm break every window. A tailor or shoemaker wants only that material be badly colored or that shoes be made of cheap leather so they will wear out quickly, all for the sake of commerce. A political figure thinks it necessary that Frenchmen continue to commit 12,000 crimes and misdemeanors each year to keep the criminal courts busy. Thus each individual in civilized society is in a state of intentional warfare with the mass—a necessary result of anti-social industry and an upsidedown world.[64]

Saint-Simon differed from Fourier by advocating rational state planning to allocate resources and capital and protect those who were suffering most from the prevailing unevenness. He wanted to organize capitalism, more confident than Fourier that its productive power and the experts' use of science could overcome the obsolete political and social institutions which irrationally held back the development of the economy and increased the misery of those who were already suffering.[65]

Like Fourier and Saint-Simon, Louis Blanc based much of his work on an attempt to organize the economy. He wanted to soften the effects of unrestrained competition because it led to monopoly, social antagonism, increasing polarization, and the disappearance of intermediate social strata. The "organization of work" was solution to the chaos which marked the prevailing system and described the only healthy way to eliminate the baneful effects of anarchic competition. Self-governing workers' associations would replace private capitalists in control of the means of production. These "national workshops" would be production cooperatives and would guarantee good working conditions and morale, high productivity, fair distribution of profit to the workers themselves, full employment, and industrial democracy. Initially organized by the state, they would be more productive and efficient than production based on the search for private profit because they would be democratically organized at the point of production. The money they made would be divided into three parts: one would be equally shared by all the worker-members, one would go for measures of social welfare, and one would be reinvested in the enterprise. Blanc expected that private enterprise would be gradually eliminated and that competition, now regulated and used in a socially healthy way by the state, would become an instrument for peacefully transforming the world. The state would get out of direct involvement with production when the workers were able to get along without assistance. The gradual disappearance of private industry and the transformation of the state into an agent of guidance for the working class would replace the arbitrariness and chaos of the present with measured social progress in which both the proletariat and the *petite bourgeoisie* would flourish in a system so organized as to meet everyone's needs.[66] Blanc wanted to unite the "classes populaires," the workers and the petty bourgeoisie, around a social program which would benefit them both in a frankly political and statist socialism. The "organization of work" would eliminate the major cause of social anarchy by substituting association and cooperation for the competitive and individualistic search for private profit.[67] The anarchy of the market would be replaced by public organization and regulation of the economy. Blanc's theory of association led him in a collectivist, statist, and egalitarian direction but he shared the common assumption that both the proletariat and the petty bourgeoisie could be protected from the consequences of uncontrolled economic concentration.[68]

Early social theorists were struck by the paradox that those who worked hardest seemed to remain poor while a parasitical class lived very well without having to work at all. It was tempting to regard this as an unfortunate remnant of the past, but the principle that labor should roughly correspond to distribution and consumption made it possible to begin a systematic criticism of property. Saint-Simon was certainly committed to defending the institution but at the same time he wanted demonstrated "capacity" to be rewarded, was critical of the "indolent," and denied anyone the right to live in idleness at another's expense.[69] For Fourier the fact that the idle were able to live in luxury was itself an index of social corruption and he observed that many people who had to work were wasting their time in boring and alienating labor. He was sure that work would become "attractive" as it began to fulfill human needs and provide for a reasonable level of production.[70] This would require the elimination of the parasites who had attached themselves to commerce. "By what reasoning," he asked, "have economists been able to persuade us that it was an advantage to triple or to increase tenfold the mass of tradesmen, whose intervention, far from adding to production, introduces into the distribution of goods a horde of evil-doing criminals?"[71]

Sismondi was also bothered by the deepening gulf between classes. He had a clear sense of the proletarianization of the petty bourgeoisie and the pauperization of the proletariat, seeing both as the consequence of a system which demanded the maintenance of a class of extremely poor and exploited working people.[72] Stimulated by what he had seen in England, he talked a great deal about the proletariat and attributed much of capitalism's difficulties to the fact that the workers received just enough to maintain themselves and no more.[73]

It was apparent to most of the early socialists that many hard-working people had to labor because they owned no property in the means of production and that the small property of the petty bourgeoisie was always under attack. Property seemed to be the condition of wealth, and it was largely because of its economic effects that attention was first directed to it. As social critics moved away from defining the workers in terms of their numbers or their poverty and began describing them in terms of their economic position, property moved to the center of their work. The ideological struggle against liberalism also required an examination of the institution, for defense of the right to accumulate property was extremely important to the French bourgeoisie. Property became important to the socialists because it was important to the capitalists.

Two general approaches emerged. The first tended to express the viewpoint of the petty bourgeoisie and looked to a smallscale, localized, and decentralized economy which would preserve small property. Generalizing ownership to as many people as possible was the goal, this tendency strongly influenced by a combination of romantic nostalgia for the Middle Ages and the current needs of the petty bourgeoisie. There was also a measure of genuine egalitarianism in such arguments, for as the July Monarchy developed it became clear that defense of the unrestricted, specifically *bourgeois* right to accumulate property was tantamount to defending inequality.

Sismondi was the best representative of this tendency. He desired security and protection for the small owner-cultivator above all; his desire to defend peasant agriculture led him to advocate a wide distribution of property which would be guaranteed by the state, for he had observed that the free market seemed to encourage concentration if left to itself and thus hurt the "little man."[74] He wanted a similar condition to prevail in the urban areas and is a good example of the sort of thinker who, distressed by the continuous destruction of small property, wanted to guarantee safety to as many people as possible by enlisting the state on its side.[75] Fourier shared Sismondi's antipathy to communism and complained that he was being unjustly accused of attacking property, "me, the defender of property!"[76] For his part, Saint-Simon could accept restrictions on property only if it was idle and unearned.

The second position that emerged was definitely a minority view until well after the events of 1848. It tended to express the viewpoint of the propertyless proletariat, and its opposition to private property *as such* can be taken as an important dividing line between petty-bourgeois socialism and proletarian communism. We have seen that Babeuf and the *enragés* were hostile to private property, but the most consistent advocate of socializing possession before 1848 was Etienne Cabet.[77] Convinced that people were created equal by nature and had been corrupted by the unnatural inequalities of a social order based on individual possession, he elaborated a "communist" system in which citizens would donate their labor to the community on equal terms and draw what they needed from a central storehouse based on their needs. The instruments of production would belong to the community and society would be organized according to the demands of human nature. Cabet was interested in equality first and foremost, assigning to the community the task of administering production rather than protecting property.

Cabet's advanced position notwithstanding, the dominant trend before 1848 was for social theorists to try to devise ways to protect small property, a reflection of the relatively underdeveloped state of the proletariat and the continuing influence of the petty bourgeoisie. This desire led directly to a concern with the sources and availability of credit, for small propertyowners wanted to be assured of help when they had to borrow money. Financial orthodoxy and deflation always hurt small proprietors; the tight money and deflationary policy of the *haute bourgeoisie* meant that questions of credit and interest were always central to French petty-bourgeois socialism.[78]

The fact that the economic system benefitted a small minority of the population was generally considered the most striking sign of social disorganization. This is why analyses of the productive system inevitably led to analyses of class conflict. Yet French socialism came to a recognition of the political impact of class conflict very slowly, for it had been strongly oriented to the preservation of existing classes through reform or reaction. Petty-bourgeois socialism tended to see class conflict as a mistake, a flaw in social organization which would be eliminated when production and work were established along scientific lines. Strongly influenced by its petty-bourgeois origins, "socialism, in its early days and as the term was then understood, was emphatically *not* a doctrine of class-war between Capital and Labour."[79] The desire to reform society so as to avoid the effects of class struggle manifested itself in the writings of virtually all the social theorists of the period.

Cabet was a pacifist, decried the role of violence in history, and believed that the use of force was always illegitimate. Communism would come about as the result of a gradual and peaceful transition since it was so clearly a superior form of social organization that, once people saw how well it worked and how happy they would be, they would immediately understand that it was in their interests to establish it as soon as possible. He was most interested in demonstrating how superior his ideas were compared to contemporary reality, and this is why he devoted so much energy to organizing his model communities. He was utterly confident that everyone's interests would be served by communism and never seems to have seriously considered the possibility that other people—especially big property-owners—might not be as enlightened as he. Like many others of his generation, his primary aim was to make social conflict disappear and he was convinced that the pursuit of personal interest and the power of money lay behind the contradictions of the society in which he lived; it was to eliminate these sources of conflict that he became a communist. Louis Blanc was also an evolutionist at heart, believing that cooperation and association could eliminate the antagonisms tearing France apart. Like Cabet he was a pacifist whose "greatest fear" was violence.[80]

Class peace was also Saint-Simon's goal, and his political support of the *industriels* was based on his confidence that industry's preference for peace and quiet could defeat the "warrior spirit" which had caused such suffering in the past.[81] He wanted to avoid class war at all costs and looked forward to the day when "the community . . . will be organized in such a way that will completely satisfy reasonable men of every class."[82] A reorganized society would protect the rich against revolution and simultaneously spare the propertyless from serving as cannonfodder in wars fought for the benefit of the propertied classes.[83] Disorder stemmed from the disproportionate political power of the obsolete and incompetent, and only the political rule of the *industriels* could bring social peace:

> the political tendency of the immense majority of society is to be governed as cheaply as possible, to be governed as little as possible, to be governed by the most capable men in a manner which will assure public order. Now, the only way to satisfy these different desires of the majority is to charge the most important *industriels* with the direction of public welfare. The biggest *industriels* are most interested in maintaining public order; they are most interested in controlling public spending; they are most interested in eliminating all arbitrariness. Finally, of all the members of society, it is they who have demonstrated the most administrative skill through their business success.[84]

Saint-Simon was seeking to organize a harmonious association in which everyone would occupy the position to which he or she "naturally" belonged by virtue of his or her "capacities." His Platonic theory of stability and justice arose from the demonstrable injustice of a system which rewarded inheritance instead of activity, but it imparted a conservative tinge to his writings because he seems to have expected that most people wished to remain in the social class into which they had been born.[85] His powerful desire for social peace was expressed in his hope that transferring power from the nobility to the bourgeoisie would help the workers in the long run. Politics, factories, and the banks would now be run by the same class, and life would be more rewarding and peaceful for all. Force would give way to cooperation, command would yield to direction, arbitrariness to administration. Saint-Simon wanted to change France so that bourgeois "capacity" would replace aristocratic privilege as the determinant of determine social position and political power:

> The community has often been compared to a pyramid. I admit that the nation should be composed as a pyramid; I am profoundly convinced that the national pyramid should be crowned by the monarchy, but I assert that from the base of the pyramid to its summit the layers should be composed of more and more precious materials. If we consider the present pyramid, it appears that the base is made up of granite, that up to a certain height the layers are composed of valuable materials, but that the upper part, supporting a magnificent diamond, is composed of nothing but plaster and gilt.
>
> The base of the present national pyramid consists of workers in their routine occupations; the first layers above this base are the leaders of industrial enterprises, the scientists who improve the methods of manufacture and widen their application, the artists who give the stamp of good taste to all their products. The upper layers, which I assert to be composed of nothing but plaster which is easily recognizable despite the gilding, are the courtiers, the mass of nobles, whether of ancient or recent creation, the idle rich, the governing class from the prime minister to the humblest clerk. The monarchy is the magnificent diamond which crowns the pyramid.[86]

Fourier was much more prepared than Saint-Simon to acknowledge the potentially constructive and progressive effects of social conflict.[87] His genuinely dialectical sense of history clashed with his equally strong desire for social harmony. More than most other social theorists of his time he recognized the damage that uncontrolled production and competition inflicted on the proletariat.[88] Yet he was no more an egalitarian or a democrat than was Saint-Simon, believing that "it is . . . very important that a *phalanstère* be composed of people who are unequal in wealth and in other ways."[89] The only thing special about the proletariat was the level of its suffering, and Fourier ultimately wanted all classes to be enriched.[90] "In fact, he did not desire the end of classes but only an attenuation of the conflicts which separated them from each other in the existing order, or rather the existing disorder."[91]

It was the objective reality of class struggle which stimulated French socialists to discuss social strife from a different point of view than simply wanting to eliminate it as quickly as possible. Early social theorists had tended to divide society into three classes: the landowner who lived off rent, the capitalist who made a profit, and the worker who received a wage.[92] Capitalists and workers were thought to have feudal aristocrats as a common enemy, but as the nineteenth century wore on the earlier Ricardian distinctions were dropped as conflict between employers and employees clearly became the primary force shaping French society.[93] The recognition of this conflict naturally involved a recognition of the proletariat, and if this recognition was not generally present before 1830 it was because people tended to think in terms of the "poor" rather than the "worker."[94]

Socialists began talking about class conflict because the industrialization of France forced them to. Saint-Simon had played a major role in focusing attention on the industrial proletariat[95] and by the time the July Monarchy was reaching maturity, the industrial proletariat was being presented as the direct successor of the slave, plebian, and serf.[96]

The rise of the proletariat and the increased level of class struggle soon replaced republicanism with socialism as the dominant ideology of the French left.[97] The labor movement was strongly influenced by socialism from its inception, and as it developed it talked less about legislating socialism into existence overnight and more about struggling for it, less about the state as an abstract entity and more about the class that wielded it.

From 1815 to 1848 French industry developed in great depth, although the full flowering of factory capitalism did not come until the 1860s.[98] The beginning of the July Monarchy was thus a decisive watershed for modern France, the development of industry spurring the rise of a petty-bourgeois socialism and a proletarian communism which would mature together but would diverge later. The early nineteenth-century social theorists had gone a long way toward laying the scientific and ideological foundations for both, the concerns of the petty bourgeoisie being expressed as the desire to maintain private property while peacefully smoothing out the economy's rough edges and making it possible for all classes to live together in harmony. To the extent that early social theory sought to organize a fair capitalist system which would provide credit, generalize property, organize production, and generally seek to maintain all existing classes, to that extent it tended to express the viewpoint of the petty bourgeoisie. No specific thinker can be singled out in this regard, but it is clear that the concerns of small property-owners gave general direction to much social theory and criticism in the early nineteenth century. Democracy and socialism developed under the twin pressures of petty-bourgeois demands for political power and the desire of both small property-owners and propertyless proletarians to protect themselves from the consequences of industrialization.[99]

By the middle of the 1860s, however, class distinctions were drawn much more sharply than they had been before, and so where the early socialists had spoken for a number of groups—even if they often imagined that they were speaking for everyone—specific members of the second generation tended to represent a more narrowly-defined constituency. Of all the social critics, democrats, radicals, communists, republicans, anarchists, socialists, and in-dependent leftists of the tumultuous middle of the century, almost no one spoke more clearly for the progressive wing of the petty bourgeoisie than did Proudhon. His life and works were a microcosm of the grouping for which he was speaking and, in a way, of the entire society in which he lived.

NOTES

1. Alexis de Tocqueville, *Recollections*, trans. Alexander Teixeira de Mattos and ed. J. P. Mayer (New York: Columbia University Press, 1949), 8–9.
2. Roger Henry Soltau, *French Political Thought in the Nineteenth Century* (New York: Russell and Russell, 1959), 36.
3. See, for example, the excerpt from Constant's *Cours de politique constitutionnelle*, cited by Guido de Ruggiero in his *History of European Liberalism* (Boston: Beacon Press, 1959), 161.
4. Soltau, 47–8. See also Ruggiero, 169.
5. Tocqueville, 3.
6. Albert Léon Guérard, *French Civilization in the Nineteenth Century* (New York: Century, 1914), 194.
7. *Ibid.*, 114. For a further discussion of the 'haute banque' during the July Monarchy.
8. Soltau, 61.
9. *Ibid.*, 93.
10. *Ibid.*, ch. v.
11. G. D. H. Cole, A *History of Socialist Thought*, vol. I: *The Forerunners* (New York: St. Martin's, 1965), 306–7.
12. E. J. Hobsbawm gives an interesting illustration of this process at work in England in his *Age of Revolution 1789–1848* (New York: New American Library, 1962), 58: 'The great financiers, the tight community of home and foreign "fundholders" who received what all paid in taxes ... were perhaps even more unpopular among small businessmen, farmers, and the like than among laborers, for they knew enough about money and credit to feel a personal rage at their disadvantage. It was all very well for the rich, who could raise all the credit they needed, to clamp rigid deflation and monetary orthodoxy on the economy after the Napoleonic Wars: it was the little man who suffered, and who, in all countries and at all times in the nineteenth century, demanded easy credit and financial orthodoxy. Labor and the disgruntled petty-bourgeoisie on the verge of toppling over into the unpropertied abyss therefore shared common discontents.'
13. Soltau, 108.
14. See Louis Dunham, *The Industrial Revolution in France 1815–1848* (New York: Exposition Press, 1955), 213–42 for a description of the wealth and power of the "haute banque" during the July Monarchy.
15. See the "Second Discourse" in Roger Masters ed., *The First and Second Discourses* (New York: St. Martin's, 1964), especially Part II:141–81.
16. *Ibid.*, 148.
17. See, for example, his discussion of the development of the family. *Ibid.*, 146.
18. *Ibid.*, 154–55.

19. 'C'est bien à un homme social, à un homme réel, à un consommateur, à un ouvrier qui a faim, à un paysan laborieux, à un être physique qui a *des besoins, des intérêts, qui pensent* les philosophes, à l'homme des champs nourissant des fruits de la terre qu'il a cultivé de ses mains.' Maxim Leroy, *Histoire des Idées Sociales en France* (Paris: Gallimard, 1946), 333.

20. *Ibid.*, vol. i.

21. See Celestin Bouglé, *Socialismes Français* (Paris: Armand Colin, 1951).

22. Georges Lefebvre's *The French Revolution*, 2 vols., trans. John H. Stewart and James Frigaugletti (New York: Columbia University Press, 1962–64) and *The Great Fear of 1789* (New York: Shocken, 1979) remain among the best histories of the Revolution. See also Georges Soboul, *The French Revolution 1787–1799* (New York: Viking, 1975) and *The Sans–Culottes* (Princeton: Princeton University Press, 1980).

23. George Lichtheim, *The Origins of Socialism* (New York: Praeger, 1969), 20.

24. Bouglé, 67.

25. "However attenuated," says Soltau 135, "Babouvist equalitarianism is to be found as one of the elements of virtually every manifestation of French socialism."

26. Leroy, 185.

27. E. Labrousse, *Le Mouvement ouvrier et les théories sociales en France de 1815 à 1848* (Paris: Centre de Documentation Universitaire, 1948).

28. See Engels' "Scientific and Utopian Socialism" in Karl Marx and Frederick Engels, *Selected Works* (New York: International Publishers, 1968), 399–416 for an excellent discussion of the forces at work on the early socialists.

29. Gian Mario Bravo, *Les Socialistes Avant Marx* (Paris: Maspero, 1970), 13.

30. Edward Hallett Carr, *Studies in Revolution* (London: Macmillan, 1952), 42.

31. Hobsbawm, 287.

32. Soltau, ch. 2.

33. *Ibid.*, 26–31.

34. Hobsbawn, 285.

35. Leroy, ii:64.

36. *Ibid.*, 517.

37. Ruggiero, 177–78.

38. Eugene Fournière, "La Règne de Louis-Philippe" in Jean Jaurès ed., *Histoire Socialiste* (Paris: Jules Rouff, 1909), 143.

39. Cole, 308.

40. Soltau, Introduction.

41. From "The Reorganization of the European Community" in Saint-Simon, *Social Organization, the Science of Man and Other Writings*, trans. and ed. Felix Markham (New York: Harper and Row, 1964), 40.

42. Saint-Simon, "Mémoires sur la science de l'homme" in *Oeuvres Complètes* 11 vols. (Paris: Dentu, 1868–1876), vol. xi.

43. Saint-Simon, *Catéchisme Politique des Industiels* (Paris: Ad. Naquet, 1832), 39–40.

44. Saint-Simon, "On Social Organization" in *Social Organization, the Science of Man and Other Writings*, 76–80.

45. Saint-Simon, *Catéchisme Politique*, 45–46.

46. Lichtheim, 45.

47. Saint-Simon, *Catéchisme Politique*, p. 112.

48. Footnote to 'L'Organisateur," *Oeuvres Complètes*, iv:17–26.

49. Leroy, ii:206.

50. Saint-Simon, *Catéchisme Politique*, 97–98.
51. Saint-Simon, "L'Organisateur," *Oeuvres Complètes*, iv:149–56.
52. Cole, 62.
53. See Max Poster ed., *Harmonian Man: Selected Writings of Charles Fourier* (New York: Doubleday, 1971), 151–57.
54. *Ibid.*, 160.
55. *Ibid.*, 180–90.
56. See "Le Nouveau Monde Amoreux" in Fourier, *Oeuvres Complètes*, 12 vols. (Paris: Editions Anthropos, 1966–68), 24, 33.
57. Engels, 405–6.
58. Bouglé, 119.
59. Eric Roll, *A History of Economic Thought* (Englewood Cliffs: Prentice-Hall, 1956), 235–40.
60. Fournière, 104.
61. *Ibid.*, 359.
62. See Fourier's "Extroduction" to "La Fausse Industrie," *Oeuvres Complètes*, viii:304–36.
63. See, for example, "Le Nouveau Monde Industriel et Sociétaire" in *ibid.*, vi:166–302.
64. *Ibid.*, 33–34.
65. ". . . what Saint-Simon contributed to Socialist thought was neither a distinguishable socialist movement nor a distinguishable theory, but the conception of a planned economy organized for 'full employment' and the wide distribution of purchasing power, an insistence that rewards should correspond to services rendered and that accordingly all inheritance of property was out of place in an industrial society, a recognition of the priority of economic over political forces, and a notion of the historical development of society from a political to an 'industrial' phase. In this last, he at any rate helped to suggest, though he did not hold, a Materialist Conception of History, such as was formulated subsequently by Marx." Cole, 61.
66. For interesting discussions of Louis Blanc, see *ibid.*, 169–76 and Soltau, vi.
67. Soltau, 170.
68. Ruggiero, 184.
69. This theme runs throughout his writings. See, for example, "Sur la Querelle des Abeilles et des Frelons" in his *Oeuvres Complètes*, iii:211–34.
70. "Le Nouveau Monde Industriel et Sociétaire" in *ibid.*, vi:10.
71. Fourier in Poster ed., 154.
72. Leroy, ii:301.
73. *Ibid.*, 300.
74. Cole, 80–85.
75. *Ibid.*, 83.
76. "La Fausse Industrie" in *Oeuvres Complètes*, ix:7.
77. Cole, 75–79.
78. Dunham, 68.
79. Cole, 6. His emphasis.
80. *Ibid.*, 169.
81. See "L'Industrie" in his *Oeuvres Complètes*, ii:100– 113.
82. "On Social Organization" in Saint-Simon, *Social Organization*, 77.
83. "De l'Organisation Sociale," *Oeuvres Complètes*, x:125–36.
84. *Catéchisme Politique*, 6–7.

85. Frank Manuel, *The Prophets of Paris* (Cambridge: Harvard University Press, 1962), 125–26.

86. Saint-Simon, *Selected Writings*, trans. and ed. by F. M. H. Markham (New York: Macmillan, 1952), 79–80.

87. Manuel, 222.

88. One prominent observer presents an interesting and important aspect of Fourier's thought which is not particularly important for our purposes but which is central to an understanding of his thought as a whole. "In the state of civilization class conflict has become endemic because the poor who are ungratified hate the rich who seem to be fulfilled (though in reality they are not) and the rich are fearful of the poor who might deprive them of their pleasures. The view of the class system of domination as a form of instinctual repression—which Freud hinted at in his last works—was developed extensively in Fourier." Manuel, 218.

89. "Theorie de l'unité universelle," *Oeuvres Complètes*, v:511.

90. "Fourier épreuve autant de répugnance que Saint-Simon pour un égalitarianisme niveleur. Il n'est pas disposé non plus à déclarer que tout est dû aux ouvriers, que tout valeur vient d'eux et leur doit retourner. Il proclame le Capital et le Talent aussi nécessaire que le Travail à la bonne marche des entreprises." Bouglé, 118.

91. *Ibid.*

92. When they were not being quite so precise, they often distinguished between "la classe dite très élevée, . . . la classe moyenne ou bourgeoisie, . . . le peuple." Bravo, 23.

93. Leroy, i:63.

94. *Ibid.*, 439.

95. *Ibid.*, 324.

96. Bouglé, 88–89.

97. Dunham, 203.

98. *Ibid.*, 433.

99. Ruggiero, 178.

3

Equality, Property, and Work

As the July Monarchy's contradictory pattern of economic growth and political paralysis intensified during the late 1830s, every ideological and political trend in France became stamped by the distinctive character of her industrialization. The heightened level of class conflict which accompanied the formation of a modern proletariat and its entry into national life could not find any legitimate expression within the political boundaries of an openly partisan and increasingly narrow regime, and the resulting deadlock shaped the context within which members of the second generation of French social theorists and political activists moved. Even as it became clear that a distinctly modern class of wage-workers was succeeding "the people" and "the poor" at the center of the country's economy and that comprehensive social transformation was replacing grand schemes of social reform as the centerpiece of the left's program, a strong temptation to analyze an industrializing capitalism with the theoretical tools inherited from an earlier period was clearly evident. This tendency was reinforced by the gradual changes in French class structure, for the developing proletariat was influenced by its peasant and artisan origins throughout this period and its public activity and theoretical outlook tended to reflect the perspectives of the skilled workers who initially formed its most articulate, organized and militant core.[1]

The French labor movement, whose evolution decisively influenced the independent theoretical development of the socialist intelligentsia, did not originate among factory workers but among skilled craftsmen working for wages in small-scale capitalist enterprises. Paris was a major workshop throughout the July Monarchy and had over 400,000 workers engaged in such production, while the older manufacturing centers of the Rhône valley constituted a secondary nucleus. The high-quality labor of the skilled trades affected the perspectives of the entire labor movement, for many French workers were tailors, locksmiths, jewelers, painters, shoemakers, and the like until well into the 1860s. It is no less true, however, that industrialization had been transforming the artisans from 1792 on, and they must be considered skilled workers who were being proletarianized. Throughout the century their income, skills and security were under relentless attack as the division of labor became more pronounced, foreign competition intensified, universal power machines were introduced, and mass consumption called for standardized low-quality production. The skilled trades were undergoing a decisive transition, and the initial theoretical and organizational stages of the French labor movement clearly expressed their difficulties.

A series of strikes and other labor disturbances testified to their increasingly-desperate position and willingness to organize. By the middle of the 1830s workers' association were appearing in Lyon and Paris and calls for cooperation leaned heavily on traditional forms of self-help to end the "exploitation of man by man" and replace the monarchy with a republic which would protect workers and small proprietors alike. Small capitalists and artisans became allies of a more vocal and independent workers' movement and the *haute bourgeoisie* with its July Monarchy was an increasingly isolated foe. Political and social democracy were seen as two different sides of the same coin for the moment, even if more radical plebeian and petty bourgeois concerns had always stood behind the relatively moderate demands of the liberal bourgeoisie and the proletariat showed itself ready to turn a political revolution into a social one at any time. For the moment, however, the clash between liberalism and socialism which would dominate the rest of the century was only beginning to develop.

Pierre-Joseph Proudhon, the most important representative of this second generation of French socialists and social critics, was born into a poor artisan family on February 15, 1809, grew up during the Restoration, and came to maturity under the July Monarchy.[2] Unlike most of his contemporaries on the left, he was of decidedly plebeian stock on both sides. His father was a brewer and a cooper, an honest, hardworking, and thrifty independent proprietor who tried his best to provide for his family in very difficult circumstances. His mother came from a locally-prominent republican peasant family and took great pride in her father's exploits in defense of the Revolution. She constantly encouraged her eldest son to study and saw to his education at home until Pierre-Joseph was eleven, when his father's temporarily-improved position and a scholarship enabled him to attend school in Besançon. His background set him apart from the solidly bourgeois student body, and in his later years Proudhon often recalled how he could not afford to buy books and was embarrassed by his wooden shoes. In any event, the six years he spent in school constituted the only formal education he ever received. Virtually everything he learned was self-taught, a feature of his life which reflected his self-reliance and tenacity and contributed to the often crude and unfinished character of his learning.

Proudhon spent most of the 1830s helping his entrepeneurially-minded father at a succession of unsuccessful business ventures, continuing his self-education at the Besançon library, and searching for an occupation. He moved between different printing establishments, tried his hand at editing a newspaper for a short time, and undertook the traditional *tour de France*, travelling around the country taking work where he could find it and gaining some practical experience as he did so. He tried to establish a small printing enterprise with two school friends which he hoped would provide him with a stable source of income, but after two hard years and the suicide of one of the partners the business folded and Proudhon was left with the first of a long series of debts the repayment of which burdened him throughout his life.

After several years of trying to make ends meet in a succession of futile endeavors with small businesses which could not hold their own, Proudhon got his first chance in 1838. The *Pension Suard*, a prize endowed by a wealthy businessman of Besançon which was intended to encourage young scholars of the area, was available. Saying that he wanted to study languages and philosophy in a systematic way, Proudhon applied for the scholarship—and to his surprise was chosen. He received barely enough money to go to Paris and seriously study for the first time since leaving school. Free of having to work for a while, he was delighted to be able to pursue his intellectual interests. He was expected to write the Academy of Besançon from time to time summarizing his research and indicating the direction in which he was moving. As he set out for Paris in 1838 he probably had no idea that the prize would mark a turning point in his life and enable him to research, write, and publish his first major works—one of which would permanently establish him as an important figure on the French left. His intention to share what he learned was expressed in several of his letters from this period, as well as in a revealing excerpt from his application to the Academy for the prize:

> Born and raised in the heart of the working class, still belonging to it by heart, affections, and above all by the community of suffering and desire, my greatest joy, if I gain you support, gentlemen, would be able to work without stop, with the aid of science and philosophy, with all the energy of my will and all the strength of my spirit, for the moral and intellectual improvement of those whom I call my brothers and my companions; to be able to spread among them the germ of a doctrine which I regard as the law of the moral world; and, while awaiting the success of my efforts and directed by your good judgement, to find myself, in some fashion, their spokesman to you.[3]

Several things stand out in this appeal to the bourgeois men of the Besançon Academy. Proudhon's clarity of intention, forthright style and courage were clearly expressed. He was absolutely honest when explaining his intentions to bring light and understanding to "the working class," although he sought to allay any possible misunderstanding by appealing to the Academy for help, patience and understanding and assuring it of his charitable intentions. Such a position was characteristic of most self appointed spokesmen for the poor during this period. If he intended to teach the workers what he knew about the laws of the world, we may safely assume that he did not know what they were quite yet but intended to use his time in Paris to discover and communicate them.

Proudhon was in Paris attending university classes, meeting a few people and studying philosophy, history, and linguistics at the library for several months before he was able to win some badly-needed money. The Besançon Academy announced a competition for the best essay concerning "the utility of the celebration of Sunday with reference to public hygiene, morality, and domestic and civic relations." Proudhon decided to submit a formal essay.

On the Celebration of Sunday was Proudhon's first important work. Its subject seemed trivial enough, but the essay was important for two reasons: it was his first attempt to systematically use what he had learned about social science, and it contained many themes which he would develop and refine until they became essential components of his view of social life.[4] Its tone was vigorous and declaratory, the young author trying to clarify and leave little unsaid. Yet underneath the apparent assurance one can sense a certain tentativeness, a groping for direction and a preliminary sort of involvement with new ideas.

The *Dimanche* is noteworthy because of the two related levels on which Proudhon was operating.[5] He attempted to answer the Academy's question by demonstrating that the institution of a weekly rest day was necessarily linked to a social system with equality at its foundations. A clear and unwavering commitment to equality of conditions rested at the heart of everything Proudhon tried to do for the rest of his life and was initially expressed as a criticism of the July Monarchy's dogmatic liberalism in the name of a Christian commitment to equality:

> Nature, say the sectarians, shows us inequality everywhere; draw the appropriate conclusions.—'Yes,' responds Jesus Christ, 'inequality is a law of beasts, not of men.' Harmony is the daughter of inequality. Lying fraud, harmony is equilibrium in diversity.[6]

The commitment to social equality, which was to be a central core of Proudhon's life, appeared at the very beginning of his career. His task, as he expressed it, was to "find a condition of social equality which is neither community, despotism, fragmentation, nor anarchy but *liberty in order and independence in unity*."[7] This project would lead him to establish an ideological and political identity for himself which would be independent of all existing sects, schools and tendencies and pointed the way to his entire life's work.

Proudhon had studied the Bible a good deal as a young man, and his training served him well as he developed his answer to the Academy's question. Moving from Jesus's morality to that of the ancient Hebrews, he treated Moses as an unconscious egalitarian and tried to "logically" establish an unbreakable connection between the Sabbath and social equality. Whatever Moses's intentions, claimed Proudhon, his understanding of the Sabbath establishes it as considerably more than a day of rest. It is also a public institution and serves an important social function because it enables people to fortify their social ties and thus provides an essential measure of solidarity.[8] Since it touches people from all social classes in a public manner, Sunday provides the foundation for a genuine republicanism which expresses Moses's conviction that the brotherhood of all men is the moral basis of public life:[9]

> What Moses wanted for his young nation was not public assemblies and fairs; it was not only unity in government or community of customs; all that is the consequence rather than the principle; it is the sign, not the thing. What he wanted to create in his people was a communion of love and of faith, a fusion of minds and hearts, if I may put it thus. It was the invisible bond, stronger than all material interests, that is formed between souls by love of the same God, the same conditions of domestic welfare, solidarity in their destinies, the same memories, the same hopes. He wanted, in short, not an agglomeration of individuals, but a truly fraternal society.[10]

Proudhon's attempt to draw egalitarian conclusions from Mosaic law was one thing, but his first important essay expanded his answer to the Academy's rather narrow question as it affirmed that *all* human societies tend toward equality of conditions. The Sabbath's presumption of brotherhood and equality provides the only sure basis of social stability, and any social order is henceforth to be judged on the basis of its progress toward its presumed goal. The moralism which was so characteristic of French socialism during Proudhon's lifetime derived from analysts' genuine shock at the social conditions they observed and was often expressed in the egalitarian terms that one finds in the *Dimanche*. There was a clear plebeian and petty-bourgeois cast to this sort of social egalitarianism, for it became wedded to a republic of small producers whose independence would be founded on work and whose ability to defend themselves from the bourgeoisie's concentrated capital and the proletariat's propertylessness would be founded on possession. There might be real differences between people, Proudhon admitted, but the historical tendency of man's social life is to replace them all with an equality of condition which does not deny but rests on these differences while affirming the one thing that all people share: their basic equality of needs. This understanding of equality rested at the heart of left-wing criticisms of liberalism throughout the nineteenth century and was prefigured by Proudhon. "But why should conditions be equal?" he asked. "Because the right to live and to develop oneself fully is equal for all, and because inequality of conditions is an obstacle to the exercise of this right."[11] His egalitarianism would soon point him in the direction of a systematic criticism of property, the material base of inequality and the last of the false gods.[12] If this uncompromising commitment to social and economic equality characterized Proudhon's early works, it was little more than a textually-derived assertion at this point but it would remain central to his purposes until the day he died. "Equality of conditions conforms to reason and is fused with right," he claimed; "it is in the spirit of Christianity and is the goal of society."[13]

Like many of his contemporaries, Proudhon was also convinced that the old haphazard way of approaching social questions no longer sufficed—and that people now knew enough to enable them to do better. Since equality of conditions was now the "goal" and the purpose of social life, the time had come to consciously organize and use mankind's accumulated knowledge to encourage its realization. Such knowledge must be based on an understanding of the way societies evolve rather than on the arbitrary wills of individuals.[14] He thought that the laws which govern the operations of all things in nature are external to mankind, immortal, and absolute; they are the expression not of human will but of "the nature of things." Strongly influenced by Saint-Simon and Comte, Proudhon was convinced that these laws could be expressed mathematically; his early desire was to construct an "algebra" of the social sciences, but he soon gave up the attempt. Nevertheless, he was engaged in the initial stages of what would prove to be a fruitful attempt to outline the methodological foundations of a frankly partisan social science:

> There exists a science of quantities which compels agreement, excludes the arbitrary, rejects all utopia; a science of physical phenomena which rests solidly on the observation of facts; a grammar and a poetics founded on the essence of language, etc. There must also exist a science of society, absolute, rigorous, based on the nature and faculties of man and on their relationship, a science which it is not necessary to *invent*, but to *discover*.[15]

Proudhon's insistence that the new social science be based on the observation of fact, his awareness that his work was part of a general intellectual and ideological movement, and his recognition that criticism and negation would be at the heart of the new way of dealing with the world were clearly stated in the *Dimanche*.[16] His most important conclusion, however, derived from the way he drew the two foci of the essay together as he asserted that the purpose of the new attempts to rationally understand society must be to promote the social equality which is the fundamental condition of social health. Knowledge which claims to be scientific must aim at social transformation and reorganization on lines which are in accord with the objective direction of human development. This old-fashioned

position found new life and content in Proudhon's classically left-wing argument that the proletarian and petty-bourgeois concern with equality was
a more important value than the bourgeoisie's love affair with liberty:

> How can equality of rights be proven? By the parity of judgment and of ability;
> because God, in giving them to all, did not want them to be suppressed or
> subordinated by someone else or to benefit someone else. Equality of fortune is
> an expression of the will of God, who has reserved to society the terrible punishment
> of misery. It is a question of how this equality will be realized; it is not at all a
> matter for us of its restoration, but of its establishment.[17]

The early commitment to social equality is what encouraged Proudhon
to insist that the purpose of social theory is to enable people to understand
the way the world works and provide a direction for action. If "God" rendered
the right to live and work to all men in equal measure, the *Dimanche* concluded
by directing Proudhon's initial attacks against the "exploiters of the proletariat,
aristocrats of industry," and the like, albeit in relatively primitive terms.[18]
The themes expressed in the *Dimanche* were to recur throughout his early
social analysis.

The fact that Proudhon was making equality of conditions the cornerstone of his own investigations and recommending that others do likewise
could not have escaped the conservative judges of the Besançon Academy,
and this may explain why the essay received only the bronze medal. While
praising Proudhon's vigorous style and some of his more interesting insights,
the Academy warned him not to devote too much attention to the pursuit
of dangerous or irresponsible tendencies. The warning was not heeded;
Proudhon was on his own while in Paris, and his developing sense of what
he wanted to do with himself led him to try to understand why society was
organized on hierarchical lines, how it stayed together when it was based
on so destructive a foundation, in what direction it was heading, and how
an egalitarian social system might be organized. The logic of his early
commitment to equality was to lead him in new directions, and it was
reinforced by the fact that he was living in an industrial city and daily saw
the impact of industrialization on the masses of the Parisian working class.
Their resistance made a great impression on him, as did his own poverty
and the steadily-increasing burden of his accumulated debts.[19]

THE CRITICISM OF PROPERTY

Proudhon's essay about the Sabbath had announced much of his work in
embryo; his egalitarianism, interest in social solidarity, commitment to justice
and search for a new social science had yielded some suggestive insights
but were not expressed in a coherent form. Having given up an unproductive attempt to derive a science of society through the comparative study

of language, Proudhon now turned his attention to a systematic study of social life. Convinced that scientific truth had to be discovered through observation instead of derived from logic, he now set about the task.[20]

What is Property?, still his best-known work, appeared in June 1840 and reflected his new interests even as it firmly established his reputation as France's preeminent left-wing intellectual. He had been working on the book for some time, his studies having convinced him that, as currently organized, the existing economic system was the root cause of France's intractable and escalating social chaos and that property was the most important obstacle to equality and freedom. Many early socialists took a similar position, yet a rigorous discussion of the institution had not yet appeared. Proudhon would bring his understanding of Fourier, Thomas Malthus, David Ricardo, Adam Smith, and Sismondi to bear on his commitment to equality in an analysis of a fundamental bourgeois institution.[21] The result was an altogether extraordinary work.

The importance of the *Propriété* to Proudhon's development and that of the socialist movement as a whole resulted as much from the way he analyzed property as from the specific conclusions he reached about France's existing social order. Private property was such a pillar of French society that any social analyst defending it was perforce a bourgeois apologist, while those criticizing its social effects or seeking to undermine its foundations were vulnerable to charges of sedition and rebellion. Any reasonable treatment of the problem was bound to compel a general position about the direction French society was taking. But in order to be "reasonable" an analysis had to be based upon observation, and the fact that Proudhon's work was one of the first relatively rigorous treatments of the institution is what made it so important. Starting from his basic egalitarianism and attempting to show scientifically that property as he understood it had both noxious social effects and was "impossible," a perversion of a healthy society's *raison d'être* and therefore bound to disappear as people progressed, Proudhon subjected some important bourgeois notions of property to a withering and sarcastic treatment which is still of considerable interest.

Proudhon was not attacking all property. He was opposed to the kind of ownership which permitted someone to live without working and thus stood within a well-established tradition which attacked the unearned wealth and prerogatives of the parasitical aristocracy and nonproductive rural landlords. But an ostensibly anti-feudal treatise would prove deeply disturbing to the same bourgeoisie which was consolidating its own accession to power, for Proudhon combined his attack on parasitism with the classic petty-bourgeois position that the only legitimate title to property comes from work in such a way as to call bourgeois property into question. His use of the term "property," then, was restricted to idle ownership, but he sought to preserve and even generalize the kind of ownership which was closely associated with productive work and referred to this sort of ownership as "possession."

The French Revolution had broken the formal connection between privilege and property and defined the former as an unjust usurpation even as the latter was protected as a natural right. By formally abolishing privilege, the Civil Code of 1804 had defined property as "the right to enjoy and to dispose of goods in the most absolute manner." This was Proudhon's understanding of "property," and this is what he set out to demolish. In so doing he was expressing one of the most fundamental paradoxes of France's revolutionary settlement: that even as it made private property the pivot of social life and protected it with the full sanction of the state, it simultaneously created the conditions for the all-round and comprehensive contestation of the institution as such.

"I must destroy inequality and property in a duel to the death," Proudhon announced in the very beginning of the book.[22] The egalitarianism which he carried over from his earlier work animated his initial criticism of property. Having demonstrated that people are equal in their fundamental nature and their basic needs, it followed that social and economic inequality cannot be derived from the natural differences between them and thus stand in stark opposition to the requirements of the natural order. Proudhon's distinction between "property"—which he considered illegitimate on the face of it—and "possession" left open to attack precisely that sort of property which is most characteristic of the bourgeois order: property which yields capital because it grows by gratuitously appropriating the labor of others. In exempting the possession which resulted from work, Proudhon thought that he had anchored a theory of equality on the rock of political economy. If property violated the moral law because it served as the material foundation of inequality, then it followed that "society, justice, equality *are three equivalent terms*."[23]

What is Property? was written to conform to the requirement that all winners of the Suard prize write a summary of their previous year's research and send it to the Besançon Academy. Proudhon pointed out that the basis of his approach could be found in his "declaration of faith" and added that if his investigations had led him in some unforseen directions it was because he had remained true to his original purpose and had found property to be intimately linked to inequality and the misery of the poor. He penned a warning:

> I am not constructing a system; I am demanding the end of privilege, the end of slavery, the equality of rights, the rule of law. Justice, nothing but justice; that is the summation of my work. I leave to others the care of disciplining the world.[24]

Proudhon's fundamental criticism of property is that it permits some members of society to live without working. This led to the next step—the claim that property-owners were able to live off the labor of others, and that property amounted to a "right" to deprive others of the fruits of their labor. This is what lay behind Proudhon's famous assertion that "property is theft," for in living off others the idle property-owner was stealing the material basis of another man's independence and freedom. When he called property-owners thieves, Proudhon meant that they deprived others of their very conditions of existence as he expressed the timeless complaint of both small proprietors and the propertyless.

Having shown that property violated equality and justice because it allows some to prosper from the labor of others and amounted to nothing less than exploitation, Proudhon proceeded to the second half of his criticism. In the best tradition of French rationalism, he tried to prove that property also violated logic and good sense by demonstrating that the arguments advanced to defend the institution could not be based on anything more substantial than interest. At the same time, he tried to show that traditional defenses of property could be used to prove that the institution was obsolete and would pass away. Property was not only socially harmful and hence insupportable, but was "illogical" as well. A close examination of the standard defenses of the institution was used to bring these points home.

Proudhon turned apologies for property against the institution itself by treating them as absolute and universal, a procedure which mirrored the way property was treated by its defenders. To the liberal claim that property was a natural right, he replied that the essence of natural rights was their universality and declared that if property was a natural right then it should be extended to everyone—like all rights. If property was justified because it was an extension of the personality of its holder, Proudhon responded that everyone wants to extend his personality and asked why a few should be able to do so while the vast majority cannot. To the claim that the law sanctified the institution, he declared that the law was arbitrary and opportunistic, guaranteeing rights to some while denying them to many; if it did what it should do, it would extend these rights to everyone. And finally he responded to the claim that property was justified by occupation by pointing out that everyone occupies a certain amount of space but not everyone owns the space that he occupies; why then, he asked, is the privilege of ownership extended to some but not to all?

The dilemma he was posing for property's defenders was either to admit that the justifications of property were based on self-interest by denying the claim to universal applicability that lay at the heart of bourgeois apologies for property or, admitting that bourgeois rights were universal, to acknowledge that property should be extended to all, in which case the institution was "impossible" and must be dispersed in the name of equality of conditions. Property's defenders could not have it both ways and must choose between interest at the expense of principle, in which case their argument stood exposed as self-interested hypocrisy, or must remain true to the principles they claimed to espouse, in which case property must yield.

Property thus stood condemned, first because of its harmful effects on societies and individuals, and second because its defenders had abandoned logic. The attempt to subject property to a rigorous analysis had yielded fruitful results, and the fact that Proudhon's analysis went as deep as it did is what made the *Propriété* such an important book. His conclusion was as simple as it was startling: according to the very arguments used by its most articulate defenders, property had to be universalized. Equality of conditions was the only conceivable result of social evolution, and Proudhon was confident that his discussion of property had finally settled the issue.

Driven by his egalitarianism, Proudhon was trying to universalize property and extend it to everyone even at this early stage in his career.[25] The July Monarchy's new "financial aristocracy" was particularly harmful because of its idleness and its inability to use its wealth in a socially beneficial manner; Proudhon felt that he had to mount an attack on *its* property, but he did not want to broaden it to an attack on all forms of private ownership. His egalitarian impulses conflicted to some extent with his desire for equality, security, and productivity and he never thought that socializing property was the answer to the concentration of nonproductive private holdings. Like Saint-Simon, he believed that the contradiction between idle wealth and the working mass of the French nation was primary and he wanted to remove the fetters of feudal privilege from the rural petty bourgeoisie while simultaneously protecting it from uncontrolled capitalist concentration. For the moment the bourgeoisie, petty bourgeoisie, and proletariat were united in his mind against the aristocracy and the Church even if his conclusions threatened to lead him toward a confrontation with bourgeois property itself.

What irritated Proudhon about property was that it permitted the holder to benefit without working or producing, while "possession" conferred legitimacy because no man owned more than he could use. Property was inherently antisocial, but possession guaranteed peace, justice, and stability. Proudhon felt that there was no conceivable justification for acquiring the product of another man's labor without paying him as much as his labor was worth; echoing the historical grievances of small proprietors, every moral principle he invoked led to the conclusion that the only legitimate claim to individual ownership is one's own labor. Even if he would later draw back from the implications of this position, Proudhon's position struck directly at the conditions of productive life and brought him to the edge of modern socialism:[26]

I may possess the field that I have cleared, on which I have built my home, which nourishes my family and my livestock (1) by title of first occupant; (2) by title of worker; (3) by virtue of the social contract which assigned it to me by distribution. But none of these titles gives me the right to property.[27]

"Possession" was justified since use conferred legitimacy. Use implied labor, and so we come back to the central role of the analysis of labor for all the early French socialists. It stood at the heart of Proudhon's denunciations of property, and even at this early stage in his career his claim that labor was the source of all wealth was the cornerstone of both his wider attack on the economic system as a whole and the tentative and undefined suggestions he made for improvement. It underlay his understanding of justice and equality as well, for if labor is the source of value then justice and social welfare demand that the producers have full access to what their labor creates. The notion that those who generate value should be able to appropriate the full measure of what they produce was a common theme on the left and lay behind a good deal of utopian theories for social regeneration as well.

At the heart of Proudhon's sociology of work lay his important assertion that work is collective and social rather than individual and fragmentary, an early indication that he was thinking in terms other than a peasant economy. Collective labor creates more value at less cost than does the sum of individual effort and organically links the individual to a wider social order.[28] A "collective force" lies latent in the lap of social labor, and it accounts for the high level of exploitation which paradoxically accompanies modern society's great productivity. But if workers create value socially, they are paid individually; the difference between the value created by their social labor and the sum of what they are paid individually is appropriated gratuitously by the capitalist, removed from circulation and production, and denied to those who created it in the first place. Capital has no productivity outside of human activity, and its holders unjustly enjoy the fruits of the collective labor of others. Proudhon located the "power to produce without working"[29] at the heart of the system's exploitation and difficulties very early, anticipating what Marx and Engels were later to call the appropriation of surplus value:

A force of a thousand men working for twenty days is paid as much as a single man would be for fifty-five years; but this thousand has accomplished in twenty days what one, working for a million centuries, could not accomplish. Is the exchange fair? Once again, no: you have not paid them for their collective force; consequently, there remains a right of collective property which you have not acquired and which you unjustly enjoy.[30]

Like the property-owner, the capitalist lives by his ability to take some of the value created by others. He always owes the workers more than he pays them, and this is what accounts for "the poverty of the worker, the luxury of the idle and the inequality of conditions. It is in this, above all, which consists what has so accurately called the exploitation of man by man."[31] The private appropriation by one class of the value created by the social labor of another rests at the heart of inequality and domination.

Proudhon's whole discussion of property can be interpreted as a discussion of the appropriation of surplus social labor. The position that property is theft locates a fundamental antagonism between producers and owners at the heart of modern society. If the direct producers are the sole source of the social value which the owners of capital are expropriating, then exploitation must be the root cause of the inequality which Proudhon had earlier identified as modern society's fatal flaw. When married to his provocative analysis of labor, Proudhon's distinction between property and possession struck at the heart of bourgeois political economy, for counterpoising property to equality brought one to the edge of modern socialism. Like many of his contemporaries, Proudhon tried to provide a solution for capitalism's injustice by saying that the full product of what the workers produce ought to be returned to them. Unable for the moment to push the implications of his understanding to their logical conclusion, he proposed three "reforms" which he thought would resolve the moral and economic dilemma caused by capitalism's fatal flaw:

(1) The worker should acquire things at the expense of the idle owner; (2) since all production is necessarily collective, the worker has a right to share in its products and benefit in proportion to his labor; (3) since all accumulated capital is a common possession, no one should be able to own it privately.[32]

Proudhon was confident that this solution would recognize different capacities by basing reward not on the number of hours worked but on what was actually produced. Surplus ought to be returned entirely to those who produce it in the name of justice and to guarantee that productive workers can stay alive, for "if the worker is to live, his earnings must be able to buy back his product."[33] No one deserves to appropriate a greater part of the collectively-produced social product than anyone else since no one's labor is more valuable than anyone else's. If everyone's labor is equally necessary to social health, it follows that there is only diversity in work, and difference alone cannot justify inequality. The connection between liberalism's isolated individual and the social order of which he is an unconscious part is provided by the social quality of labor. Social life makes morality possible; "liberty is the balance of rights and duties; to free a man is to balance him with others."[34] Proudhon continued his analysis as he added economic stability to morality as a criterion for judgement; the only way the economy could remain viable was to guarantee that workers' purchasing power could expand at the same rate as did their production. The private appropriation of social labor's "collective force" hurts the worker because it makes it impossible to buy back the products of his own labor, but it damages the capitalist as well because the constant attack on working peoples' purchasing power imposes a ceiling beyond which the economy cannot expand:

> the proprietor who turns his earnings into capital instead of consuming it turns it against production and thus makes the exercise of his right impossible. The more he increases the total of interest, the more he is forced to lower wages, that is, the more he cuts back on the maintenance of his machines, the more he lowers the quantity of work, and with the quantity of work the amount of production, and with the amount of production the source of these very revenues.[35]

His desire to preserve small property led Proudhon to recoil at the suggestion that the state—or any other public institution for that matter—appropriate surplus and use it for socially beneficial purposes. He shared other social analysts' skepticism about politics because he believed that the political results of the Great Revolution had to be broadened to bring social affairs into the arena of public discussion. Although he recognized that the passage from monarchy to democracy served progress because it increased the number and autonomy of self sufficient economic units and made social equality easier to organize, he was concerned that the only substantial effects of the Revolution had been that more people now had the power and the right to feed their selfish passions, amass property, and get rich at others' expense. Property— now defined as abuse—was the reason the Revolution had been short-circuited:

> Is political equality just? Some answer yes; others, no. To the former, I would recall that it appeared to be a good thing when the people abolished all privileges of birth and of caste, probably because they benefitted from it; so why don't they want privileges of fortune to disappear like those of blood and race? They say that it is because political inequality is inherent to property, and that society is impossible without property. Thus the question which we have just raised resolves itself into that of property.[36]

Proudhon never intended *Qu'est-ce que la Propriété?* to be a revolutionary work; he wanted nothing more than to apply universal scientific laws to the study of society and seems to have been shocked, frightened, chagrined— and a little pleased—at the furious reaction the book stirred up. He did not expect that what seemed to him to be self-evident scientific conclusions would be sedition and madness to others. Yet he had meant to use his criticisms of property to call the entire existing political and social order into question, for he knew that property rested at its very center and was the material base of the inequality whose eradication was his most important project.[37] But he never intended to become the "homme-terreur" of the bourgeoisie and attempted, without success, to set the record straight by explaining to the learned gentlemen of the Besançon Academy what he had in mind when he wrote the already-famous work, at the same time apologizing for any inconvenience he may have caused them:

> With regard to the book itself, I could not support the course which I seem to have embraced; I have no desire to appear before you as an adversary or an accuser; my conviction, or rather my certainty, is that the truths I have discovered are unavoidable, and I respect your views enough, gentlemen, not to want to combat them directly. But, if I put forward some unheard-of paradoxes about property, this foundation of the existing order, does it follow that I am an implacable revolutionary, a secret conspirator, an enemy of society? No, gentlemen; in reading my opinions completely, all that one could conclude and what I have concluded myself is that there exists a natural, inalienable right of *possession* and of work, to the enjoyment of which the worker must be prepared, much like the *Negro* of the colonies, before receiving the freedom which no one contests as his right, must be prepared for it. This education of the proletariat is the mission conferred on every influential man by intelligence and fortune, under penalty of being overwhelmed sooner or later by an inundation of those barbarians to whom we have come to give the name of *proletarians*.[38]

Apology and a tendency to appeal to well-intentioned members of the upper classes dominate this letter and give us a clue to Proudhon's state of mind at the time. He had written a book which had honestly investigated a fundamental bourgeois institution and had been vilified for his pains. At the same time, he wanted to have his cake and eat it too. His analysis called the most basic conditions of bourgeois life into question and took Proudhon to the outer limits of bourgeois ideology. Yet he was reluctant to recognize just how radical his analysis was and he consistently avoided pursuing its criticisms of property to their logical conclusions. He would define his task as generalizing ownership and guaranteeing autonomy for his entire life, convinced—even in the face of increasing evidence to the contrary— that the problems he diagnosed so accurately did not call for a fundamental break with private appropriation. At the same time, however, it is important to remember that Proudhon was alone in Paris, dependent on the Besançon Academy for his welfare, and a little frightened at the reaction to his first major work even if, like many of his generation, he was beginning to come to positions which involved a clear break with his own past and with most of "respectable" society.

The promising thing about the young social critic was that the direction in which he was moving was clearly full of promise. Yet he intended to do no more than correct some or property's most glaring abuses and prepare the way for the universalization of possession, convinced that this was the way the individual could be connected to the society of which he was a part and a just social order be organized. "Justice makes each of us feel individual and collective at the same time, alone and in a family, a citizen and part of the people, a man and part of humanity," he thought.[39] Liberalism's ancient problem was its failure to provide an adequate foundation for social and moral life from its individualistic epistemological and market assumptions, and Proudhon thought that if right is "the antithesis of egoism"[40] then it followed that a theory of justice might complement his trenchant criticism of property and provide the foundation for a new understanding of modern society. The elaboration of such a theory lay in the future, and for the moment Proudhon had to be satisfied with being the most notorious man in France, the enemy of property and civilization.

PROBLEMS OF METHOD

Qu'est-ce que la Propriété? made Proudhon famous but not rich; the subject-matter, the audience for whom the book was written, and its scholarly tone limited sales to a relatively small circle. His family's declining fortunes and the expiration of the Suard prize forced him to seek a steady income, and in 1843 he took a job with some school friends whose business in Lyon transported goods and arranged paperwork for small manufacturers in the Rhône valley. His new job got him into practical economic life and enabled him to acquire some concrete experience to supplement his book-learning. Since he was working as a clerk, secretary, and bookkeeper for a small middleman he was able to learn both the internal operations of such an enterprise and gather the experience which helped him understand how it fit into the commercial network of an economically active part of France which was undergoing rapid and unsettling industrialization. He learned a good deal about keeping accounts and filling orders, the impact of the state on a business such as Gauthier *frères*, the dynamics of business life, and the pressures operating on small commercial establishments. He also came into direct contact with the city's skilled workers who were being squeezed by the progress of modern industry and were trying to defend themselves.

The fact that his job kept him in Lyon a great deal was as important to Proudhon's development as was the nature of the work, for the city was an early battleground in the transformations which were beginning to change the entire society.[41] As the traditional center of the French silk and clothing industry, Lyon had formerly been dominated by small *ateliers* with a few employees and owners who had to work. As French capital began to concentrate and English competition became more pronounced, the small enterprises of the Rhône valley began to suffer. The slow and painful decline of the companies which had traditionally supported the people of the area subjected the old artisan classes to enormous pressure and gave birth to many kinds of political and social movements.

Proudhon saw much of this developing, and what he learned at Lyon stamped him for the rest of his life. The struggle of small proprietors to stay afloat and the attempt by isolated groups of workers to defend their standard of living and retain their independence deeply impressed him. He also learned a great deal from the organizations that spontaneously sprang up in Lyon during this period—especially a wide variety of mutual-aid societies and cooperative organizations.[42] The skilled workers of the area turned to different kinds of producers' associations and cooperatives in an attempt to free themselves from what they were starting to call "the wage system," but these traditional forms of mutual assistance took a new and more militant form as industry began to decisively change the economic environment. Forming and defending these associations proved to be an important priority for the French labor movement, and the area's skilled workers increasingly looked to association as a way to halt the erosion of their status, skills, security, and incomes. Ancient *campagonnages* stood alongside the newer mutual-aid societies, and many of the mutualist ideas which Proudhon would later incorporate into his social theory originated in his observation of the Lyonnais workers' attempts to defend their autonomy and independence.[43] The state remained implacably hostile to any and all expressions of worker discontent throughout the July Monarchy, and the associationism of the early trade union movement often merged into a classic republicanism.

Much of what Proudhon learned during his stay in Lyon did not manifest itself until the late 1840s, when he began trying to develop a systematic view of social and economic forces. His efforts during the early years of the decade tended to focus on methods of social analysis. He had devoted a fair amount of attention in his early works to this problem, and now he tried to summarize and develop his methodological views.

His intentions notwithstanding, *De la Création de l'ordre dans l'humanité* was badly planned, unclear, and disorganized. It is difficult to follow what Proudhon was trying to say, and he and his friends later agreed that he had wasted his time. But many of his future purposes, plans, criticisms, and suggestions can be seen in the rambling pages of the "lost" work, and they merit some attention because they became so basic to his later thinking.

Proudhon spent a good deal of time trying to master the basic principles of political economy because, like most of the other socialists of this period, he had become convinced that understanding the objective laws of social development was necessary for meaningful social reform. His effort to come to a scientific analysis of social conditions was bound to involve him in a confrontation with the prevailing wisdom, for the economic, social, and political corruption that marked the July Monarchy had become part of the "established" way of doing things. He expressed his contempt for the regime's political and ideological decay in a letter to a friend:

monarchical reaction, ecclesiastical reaction; both assisted by the connivance of the big bourgeoisie, big commerce, big property and the gathering legitimists: in two words you have the character of our present politics.[44]

Political corruption made it all the more imperative that he learn the principles of political economy and social science, for only reason and observation could triumph over the arbitrariness and senselessness of the existing state of affairs. But where Proudhon had earlier limited himself to appealing to enlightened and progressive bourgeois intellectuals, his recent experiences in Lyon led him to address a different audience. This was a most significant development which, although it never became the exclusive focus of his life, did help him attract a substantial following among the French proletariat and petty bourgeoisie, contribute to the political education of the "lower classes," and play an important role as propagandist, journalist, and teacher in later years:

> If you want to know where you are and in what direction the world is turning, believe me, don't ask those in power. Don't listen to sermons or believe the rich egoists. Don't trust proclamations, programs and bulletins, don't read academic harangues. Inquire into the state of the muffled propaganda which is spontaneously developing among the people, without a spokesman, without a catechism, without a well-developed system, and try to understand its meaning and import; that is the real gauge of politics.[45]

As he continued to study political economy, Proudhon became more convinced that the best he could do was to communicate his knowledge to those who could best use it. The early works on property were left behind and would serve as a foundation for his later effort to arrive at as scientific an understanding of society and government as was possible.[46] For the moment he remained convinced that the basis for such a "science of society" must be the study of real conditions rather than the repetition of sterile formulas, a position he had held since he had begun to turn his attention to social affairs. The new book's purpose was as basic as it was arrogant: he would reformulate all human knowledge and base logic on its "true foundations." Science was the key to a just and legitimate social order and Proudhon set about organizing it.

Before people could begin to organize their world in accordance with their needs they had to learn how to think scientifically, and for this the dead weight of the past had to be discarded. In an important break with many of his contemporaries on the French left, Proudhon implicated the Church as one of the obstacles to modern thought, with its emphasis on faith, its empty incantations, and its self-serving teaching that the truth was mysterious and external to man. Proudhon occupied a very special place among nineteenth-century French socialists in this respect, his consistent attacks upon the Church—both for its socially regressive activities as an institution and for the way of thinking it encouraged—standing in marked contrast to almost all other progressive individuals and groups. Whether they themselves were believers or were afraid to attack the Church because of public opinion, most French socialists were reluctant to confront religion. Saint-Simon, Pierre Leroux, Edgar Quinet, even Louis Blanc—most of the important figures on the left either embarrassedly ignored or enthusiastically embraced religious faith. Proudhon's overt hostility to the Church was probably based on old-fashioned French rationalism and the legacy of the Enlightenment rather than on the Revolution's anticlericalist tradition, but he stood apart from most self-described leftists by openly attacking it in the name of progress, equality, justice, and morality.

The *Création de l'Ordre* saw Proudhon broaden his attack on religion as he tried to overcome the influences of the past which he felt were holding back the advance of science. He increasingly came to feel that the main characteristic of the old way of thinking (which he called "philosophy") was that it restricted itself to the examination of causes rather than facts, to attempts to explain why things existed rather than what they were and how they interacted with each other. He was sure that so long as philosophy refused to plant its feet on the ground in an examination of real events, it would retard man's ability to understand and control the social world which he had constructed. He had expressed this view many times,[47] but never in so coherent a form as appears in the writings between the criticism of property and his attempts to summarize his understanding of economic theory. He was reading German philosophy in translation during this period, and his early positions that religion represented a kind of false consciousness were strongly influenced by Kant's formulations about the limits of human knowledge:[48]

> According to me, *religion* and *philosophy* are specific and transitory states of consciousness and of reason and must dissolve into pure science. Nevertheless, my negation does not bear upon the *objective reality* of religion and philosophy, but on their speculative forms. That is to say, I admit the legitimacy of the questions which they raise, the reality of the object which they seek; but I reject their solutions. Dogmatically and scientifically, religion and philosophy are nothing.[49]

Social science must be based on the objective laws which govern the way nature works, the manner in which people understand the world, and the way they act. It cannot restrict itself to political economy but must also examine the nature and functions of government, for social laws are universal in scope and the reorganization of society must touch all spheres of social life. Once these immutable laws are understood they can be used to transform society along egalitarian lines. Politics had to be studied in the same way that one would study the economy:

From the government to the governed and back to the government, everything is reciprocal service, exchange, salary and reimbursement; in the government, everything is direction, distribution, circulation, organization; so why should Political Economy exclude the government from its investigations? Government is the direction of social forces toward social well-being or usefulness; isn't Political Economy's goal also well-being, usefulness, and justice? Isn't one of its characteristics to distinguish what is useful from what is unproductive? Aren't the economists subtitled *utilitarians?*[50]

This equation of politics and economics, which Proudhon adopted from Saint-Simon and Comte and which came to characterize a good deal of nineteenth-century European social thought,[51] became more important to his thinking as time went on and reflected the materialism of the age, the relentless search for the universal underlying laws which governed all aspects of social life, and the widespread disillusionment with political solutions to social and economic problems. But the search for unifying principles was not enough, for Proudhon also recognized the importance of being able to make distinctions and engage in analysis. Fourier's "serial method" seemed to permit simultaneous classification and differentiation and make it possible to grasp both the unity and the diversity in nature and in society. His own declamations notwithstanding, however, he was never able to systematize his own innate sense of dialectics and contradiction. Fourier's scheme of an ascending spiral whose elements were linked together in a never-ending and always-changing "series" proved too vague for him. He discarded it because he felt that it flew in the face of his understanding that "the determination of a point of view, no matter how subjective it might appear, must always follow from the nature of things and never have anything of the arbitrary."[52] Nevertheless, Comte's positivism and Fourier's method were clearly the two most important influences shaping the *Création de l'Ordre.*[53]

Proudhon seriously believed that society had to be "organized" before it could accomplish the satisfaction of needs for which people live together, but it also appears that he occasionally forgot the realities of the world in which he was living. Still committed to social equality, he was trying to find a balance between opposed elements. Since he was looking for stability and equilibrium during a period of intensifying conflict, his method of analysis increasingly began to appear static and dull, a vulgar characterization of what Fourier had been trying to do. His desire for clarity notwithstanding, he was largely unable to look beyond what he saw in front of him because the future was unclear and the limitations he consciously and unconsciously imposed on himself tended to hold him back:

It is by a series . . . that political economy will bring about the transition of our anarchic and subversive society to one which is correctly organized. Then we will see how, without departing from established legality, it is always possible to insert a series of partial reforms into a governmental structure, no matter how arbitrary and tarnished by privilege it is, which will enable us to arrive rapidly and smoothly at a perfect equality.[54]

Equality was still the goal, but Proudhon wanted to get there "smoothly." This commitment to peaceful harmony stayed with him all his life. At this point he tended to return to the necessity of "organizing" work so as to arrive at equality through what he called the "equivalence of capacities."[55] What he meant by "organizing work" was as vague to him as it was to most other socialists of the period, but the fact that he emphasized it so much placed him solidly in the mainstream of left wing critiques of capitalism's anarchy. Much of his desire to "organize" work stemmed from his continuing attempt to preserve the independence of the small producer:

his status as a worker irresistibly pushes man to become an individual, the more so as he perfects his skills; the exercise of the right to property, such as our legislatures have defined it, is nothing more than nature's constant effort to assume this individualization. It is the task of the organization of work to create civic equality from individual freedom alongside domestic equality.[56]

The "organization of work" would encourage social equality because it would enable workers to buy back what they had produced. If "justice consists in giving to all workers the means to attain equal welfare from their products"[57] and the market makes this impossible because of its chaotic anarchy, Proudhon's task was to show how each producer's autonomy could be safeguarded in a more rationally-organized system. If society was being deprived of socially-produced capital, his goal was to find a way to return to it, by a peaceful economic reorganization, the value which capitalists arbitrarily remove. He seemed to feel that the division of labor, competition, exchange, and mechanization which capitalism had introduced to production should lead to equality of conditions. But they cannot do so because the workers are not paid for the collective value of their labor. An "erreur de compte" was at fault and Proudhon conceived his mission to be the rectification of this error, a task he would take up later.[58] Capitalists' ability to appropriate socially-produced value for their private benefit must be curtailed, but his problem was to find a way to peacefully accomplish this lofty aim without interfering with the "possession" which rested at the center of his world-view.

Proudhon's oft-repeated claims that the analysis of work was essential to the new social science stands alongside a distinctly idealist view concerning the source of the knowledge which was to organize society. Materialism and idealism stood together throughout his life, and its initial expression was heavily influenced by his reading of Kant:

... political economy, like the science of numbers, is the sequel of abstract propositions which are susceptible to development and systematization independent of practice ... Thus, technology or technique is the result of manual labor or execution; general laws of the production and distribution of wealth is political economy.[59]

Proudhon was also trying to reconcile Fourier's "serial theory," which was frankly materialistic at its core, with Hegel's idealistic dialectics. He hoped that the *Création de l'Ordre* would articulate a comprehensive and scientific methodology but was clearly not yet up to the task he had set himself:

> When the series lets itself be seen after a long agitation of ideas and prolonged research into innumerable possibilities, this appearance is always sudden, instantaneous and complete. The series does not at all manifest itself successively or in parts; it breaks loose, sudden, pure, clean, and like the sun piercing the clouds fills the soul with its sudden glare. Often this manifestation occurs when it is least expected ...[60]

A self-taught and still-unformed young man trying to make a contribution to social criticism was doing his best to bring his own understanding of social life to the attention of the public. Conservative and radical themes stand side by side and marked his thinking during this brief hiatus, all the way from the private thoughts he expressed in his diary toward the end of April 1846 about the desirability of generalized ownership of property[61] to a clear indication that for the moment at least he was unable to follow through on many of the strongest and most provocative lines of his thinking:

> Political Economy is essentially beneficent and conserving; ... in proclaiming the most radical ideas that have ever been stated, we have the right to say that we want to turn nothing upside down; ... equality should result from the steady development of existing institutions, ... it is the necessary consequence of all possible legislation.
>
> We need only legal avenues to change property: lowering the rate of interest, extending the public domain, administrative supervision, centralization of agriculture, of commerce and of industry with appropriate police measures;
>
> To strengthen our political system, we request only legal measures: division, specialization, coordination and responsibility of powers according to economic laws.[62]

If Proudhon could not penetrate to the heart of what was wrong with contemporary society despite his real and important insights, it is because he was not yet able to analyze what he saw in terms of social structure and social class. He held back from such a course for most of his life, for he badly wanted to believe that a harmonious solution to France's problems could be found "without disruption." This happy hope was to be replaced by a bitter cynicism as French society proved incapable of resolving its contradictions in so civilized a manner, and Proudhon, like many of his predecessors, would conceal some of the important failures of his own approach by concluding that his ideas were too advanced for his time.

ECONOMICS AND POLITICS

If Proudhon had been spending most of his time trying to discover the laws of political economy and explain how they manifested themselves in social life, it now remained for him to put his conclusions together in a coherent manner. He had been feeling the need to summarize his research for some time. As soon as he finished the *Création de l'Ordre* he set to work.

Système des contradictions économiques, his attempt to organize his knowledge in an organized way, appeared on October 5, 1846, after more than two years of preparation. The last work he published before the Revolution of 1848, it stands as the summary of his early investigations into political economy and provides a valuable indication of the direction in which his thinking was leading him. It was also strongly influenced by his continuing study of German philosophy, for he had begun to read Hegel in translation soon after the appearance of the *Création de l'Ordre* and the book represents his effort to apply his limited understanding of Hegelian dialectics to a study of the economy.[63] Yet Hegel was not the only influence on Proudhon during this period, and his attempt to derive a dynamic understanding of social life suffered from the confusing interaction between Fourier's series, Kant's antinomies, and Hegel's dialectics.[64] David Ricardo, Saint-Simon, Comte, Adam Smith, Sismondi, and the Bible were also important influences on him.[65]

Ever since the appearance of *Qu'est-ce que la Propriété?* Proudhon had been considered France's arch revolutionary. His notoriety made it difficult to find a publisher despite his evident intention to put social science to work to find a basis for conciliation and compromise. It was at this point in his career that he began his life-long attempt to reconcile his deeply-held egalitarianism with his cautious reformism. Convinced that there was no contradiction between them, he tried to explain the aims of his new work in a letter to a bookseller who he hoped would be willing to take a risk. He portrayed the project as a purely scientific endeavor to set things right:

> I am involved in a work whose fundamental goal is to apply known and admitted principles, the hitherto irrefutable laws of political economy, to the solution of several contemporary social questions, as well as to an examination of our constitutional system and our laws. You understand, sir, that I do not and can not have the hope of reforming all this by myself; that's enough work for a hundred economists working together. It's only a matter of opening the path and taking a first step.[66]

His desire to popularize political economy by "putting it into action" led him to try to demonstrate that all the "givens" of social science, legislation and morality were "essentially contradictory, contradictory, I say, not just *between* each other but *internally,* and yet completely necessary and irrefutable."[67] He intended to subject the categories of political economy to careful analysis by using his well-developed sense of paradox, the method he had employed in his earlier works, and what he had learned from Fourier and Hegel to pinpoint the underlying contradictions inherent in all the laws of social life. He was convinced that his work was so important that "I will have begun the most vast, radical and decisive revolutionary movement which the world will have seen."[68]

Still a reformer at heart, however, Proudhon was sure that, by analyzing the contradictions inherent in social life, he could contribute to revolutionizing man's understanding of the forces which had molded the past and would shape the future. Although pleased at his fast-growing notoriety among the bourgeoisie, he sought to reassure his more timorous associates by disclaiming any destructive intentions. When his publisher wrote to express his anxiety about some of the more scandalous attacks on God, religion and the state which are scattered throughout the book, Proudhon advised him in the following terms:

> Don't be afraid of the prosecutor. I insult no person, no social class, no religion. I have the right to discuss every principle, to combat them, to restore them, etc.; and if I've chosen a thoroughly dramatic form, that's nothing but a matter of literature and of taste.[69]

Proudhon considered himself an economist at this point in his career but was also aware that at some point he would have to examine "the practical or governmental problem whose solution is necessary in order to realize all possible syntheses."[70] His political desire to conciliate drove his analysis of the eleven "categories" of political economy: division of labor, machines, competition, monopoly, taxation, balance of trade, credit, property, community, competition, and population. He proposed to examine those aspects of each which were "positive" because they tended toward equality, those aspects which were "negative" because they reinforced inequality, how these aspects interacted with each other within the category itself, and finally how the categories interacted with each other. He was confident that such an analysis might make it possible to derive a "formula" which would strengthen the positive aspect at the expense of the negative and turn both political economy and the economic system itself into agencies of progress and equality.

Proudhon had concluded earlier that the direct producers' inability to buy back what they produced was the root of capitalism's difficulties. His task was to find a measure of value which would accurately reflect the labor-time spent in the production of a given commodity, and his desire to find a way to return the full value of their labor to the producers—a view which was very common on the French left—would drive his criticism of political economy:

the price of each thing is the work which is required for its production; and since each worker is individually paid according to his product, the product of one must be able to pay for the labor of the other; the only difficulty is discovering the comparative measure of value.[71]

If commodities should be valued according to the labor they embody and all producers' labor is equal in social value, then "constituting" the value of commodities on the basis of labor performed would make possible the equal exchange of equivalents as a first step toward the substantive equality of conditions whose realization rested at the heart of Proudhon's work. Exchange based on the equality of different producers' labor and a scientific appraisal of a commodity's value would end the anarchy and arbitrariness of the uncontrolled market. The private appropriation of socially-produced value would now be impossible and unnecessary, since the entire surplus would be appropriated by those whose work had created it in the first place.[72] The "proportionality of values" could be scientifically determined since it would be based on what all commodities have in common, namely, that they are all produced by human labor:

It is work, and work alone, which produces all the elements of wealth and which combines them down to their last molecule according to a law of proportionality which is variable but certain.[73]

Proudhon was confident that, the contradiction between use and exchange-value having been resolved by "constituting value" according to labor time, arbitrariness and accident would be replaced by equality and justice and the "proportionality of values" would become the foundation of order and progress.[74] The social order as a whole would guarantee this arrangement by making sure that products be valued in such a way that producers could buy back the equivalent of what they produce. If a just price could be established, the unearned income and exploitation of the capitalist would end. Everything depended on controlling the irrationalities of a market which was badly organized and socially harmful because it worked on "impossible" premises. His goal was a modified market in which the exchange of products would take place according to the unhampered circulation of the products of equally-valuable labor-time. All autonomous and independent producers would have equal rights and would be equally protected.

Having uncovered the root problems of modern economics and indicated the general direction of desired change, Proudhon now turned his attention to a scientific discussion of the contradictions at work within and between the standard categories of bourgeois political economy. The "positive" side of the division of labor, for example, encourages more production and specialization, links the producer with his customers, and prepares the conditions for social equality by making possible the "proportionality of products" and the "equilibrium of exchange."[75] At the same time, however, the division of labor encourages economic and political inequality by debasing the quality of work, lengthening the working day, lowering wages, destroying the independence of the worker, and creating a hierarchy of jobs which violates the principle that everyone's labor is equally valuable.[76] Its internal contradictions guaranteed that the division of labor produced social effects which constantly acted in contradiction to the wealth which it made possible:

> The problem of the division of labor is not simply realizing the greatest quantity of products; it is also realizing this quantity without physical, moral, or intellectual prejudice for the worker. Now, it has been proven that the worker's intelligence is inclined toward idiocy the more labor is divided.[77]

Like the division of labor, machinery simultaneously favors equality and holds it back. It allows for a free expression of human creativity, lessens the burden of labor, and facilitates the conquest of nature. At the same time, it enslaves and degrades the laborer, intensifies his exploitation, increases unemployment, worsens economic crises, and exacerbates inequality.[78] In a similar vein, competition can encourage more efficient production and help establish an accurate gauge of price; on the other hand, it can increase misery, exploitation, and theft.[79]

Having subjected the division of labor, machinery, and competition to what he thought was a scientific analysis, Proudhon wondered how the contradiction within and between these categories could be resolved. He explicitly rejected Sismondi's reactionary proposal to abandon industry and return to family centered production, saying rather vaguely that the solution was to "organize" society by "organizing" work.[80] He always tried to avoid the implications that would flow from a recognition that the only way capitalism can "organize" work is through the labor market but would not get more specific about what he meant until the Revolution of 1848 forced him to.

All the other economic categories were subjected to the same analysis: an examination of the good and bad aspects of each was followed by an attempt to indicate how a "solution" could be found and equality result from the suppression of the bad by the good. Monopoly and community, taxes and the balance of commerce, credit, property: all had good and bad effects, and the problem was to find a way in which the good aspects could overcome the bad by "constituting" work in accordance with the labor theory of value. His proposed solution was the same in each case: to "organize" work. After discussing competition's destructive effects, for example, he concluded that

> The remedy for competition, we say, is to make it universal. But in order for competition to be universal, everyone must have the means to compete; we must

destroy or modify the dominance of capital over the worker, change the relation of the boss to the worker, resolve, in a word, the antinomy of the division of labor and of machines; we must *organize labor*.[81]

In subjecting the categories of political economy to this sort of criticism, Proudhon was himself caught in a contradiction because he was trying to draw egalitarian conclusions from a market system which irresistibly tended toward inequality. He had tried the same sort of thing in the *Propriété* and it had worked well there, but that was because he had been trying to logically show that the defenders of property had to extend their arguments to their limits or drop them altogether. He attempted to resolve his dilemma by holding that the economic categories were themselves independent of human experience and could be resolved and understood mathematically by scientifically organizing work. Proudhon shared with the utopians whom he derided so caustically the conviction that "errors" and disturbances stem from a failure of knowledge and understanding, and once ideas were set right everything else will fall neatly into place. Like them, he was never able to clearly understand the role of material interest in the formation of ideology and the direction of politics.

The *Système des contradictions économiques* accelerated the criticism of politics and the state which Proudhon had first advanced in his discussion of property. Observing that political power had always served to protect the strong from the weak, he had become convinced that political activity as such could play no role in freeing mankind from the irrationalities of an unstable economy. Politics was arbitrary by definition and Proudhon drew a sharp distinction between society, the self-directing source of all progressive and egalitarian innovation, and politics, retrograde and hierarchical to its core. He was convinced that the state was nothing more than an external and parasitical excrescence, the major force retarding social development. To take it for society, he said, was to take "the mask for the man."[82] Politics was anti-social because of its intimate association with power:

> power, instrument of the collective force, created by society to mediate between work and privilege, finds itself entangled with capital and directed against the proletariat. No political reform can resolve this contradiction, since even the politicians admit that such a reform would only result in giving more energy and extent to power, and that unless hierarchy is reversed and society is dissolved, power cannot touch the prerogatives of monopoly. For the working classes, therefore, the problem is not to conquer but to vanquish power as much as monopoly, which is the same as calling forth, from the bowels of the people and from the depths of work, a greater authority, a more powerful fact which would envelop and subjugate capital and the state. Any suggestion for reform which does not satisfy this condition is nothing but another plague which threatens the proletariat.[83]

Proudhon took his distance from socialists like Louis Blanc who looked to a reformed state to reorganize society and was sympathetic only to the attempt to find the appropriate "formula" which would make possible the peaceful resolution of all the "antinomies" and contradictions of social life by harmonizing economic categories and organizing work.[84] He often waxed most eloquent and sounded most revolutionary when denouncing politics, power and the state:

> This is the war which you have to support: a war of labor against capital; a war of freedom against authority; a war of the productive against the unproductive; a war of equality against privilege ... we must find an agricultural and industrial combination by means of which power, which dominates society today, can become its servant.[85]

His attack on politics and the state served as the backdrop for Proudhon's famous attack on communism. As dangerous to individual freedom as capital and "industrial feudalism," communism subordinated the freedom of the individual to the dictates of the state, destroyed the family, and substituted the tyranny of the many for the tyranny of a few. Lumping capital and the state together as arbitrary tools of privilege and inequality, Proudhon declared war on both and remained a confirmed anticommunist until the end of his life.[86] If both the communists and the economists are wrong, then it follows that the categories of political economy and the market system which gave rise to them must be controlled. Since they cannot be eliminated and should not be surrendered to, the market must be disciplined so as to utilize its "good" side and eliminate its "bad."[87] Association and mutuality would replace the vague exhortations to "constitute" value and "organize" work in a few years, but for the moment Proudhon's antiauthoritarianism was strongly influenced by his developing anarchism. "Whoever appeals to power and capital to organize work has lied," he asserted, "because the organization of work must be the downfall of capital and power."[88]

Proudhon's protests against communism were made in the name of an individual freedom which has always been at the center of petty-bourgeois democratic thinking.[89] The proletariat's communism was arbitrary and utopian, but the bourgeoisie's political economy reinforced hierarchy, based itself on egoism, and lacked any purpose beyond trying to convince people that all was well when everyone knew better.[90] Proudhon explicitly declared his independence of both schools, convinced that each dogmatically negated the human experience and ignored mankind's aspirations as it degenerated to the level of rank class apologetics. Each school, taken by itself, was unable either to ask the questions or provide the answers that humanity was seeking.[91] Yet both had their strong points, and Proudhon's method of conserving his independence lay in his attempt to combine the insights of socialism and political economy in one approach. Convinced that "truth lies in a formula which would conciliate these two terms: conservation and movement," he summarized his position as follows:[92]

> since the goal which socialism and political economy pursue is the same in the end, namely liberty, order and human welfare, it is obvious that the conditions to fulfill, in other words, the difficulties to vanquish to attain this aim, are the same for both, and that it is only a matter of bringing the solutions attempted for one to bear on the other.[93]

Proudhon's entire approach was now based on his explicit desire to stand between political economy and socialism. He thought he could engage in a scientific analysis of the two dominant schools of economic thought as well as the economic categories, separate out the "good" and "bad" aspects of each school, and figure out a strategy which would combine the positive aspects of both. It was in this way that he thought he could help overcome the disorganization of economic life. It was becoming difficult to combine market considerations and social egalitarianism, however, and to escape from this dilemma Proudhon resorted to an increasingly metaphysical methodology which removed social life from the world of humans and placed it in the sky.

The categories were considered to be independent, living forces. They were presumed to have their own history, their own purpose, their own dynamic, a movement which was independent of the world of men. The motion of the categories themselves, considered in isolation and apart from their real source in the human world, moved history forward. When it came to the category with which he was most familiar, property, Proudhon held that "the establishment of property among men has had nothing to do with choice or philosophy . . . its origin, like that of royalty, language and cults, is spontaneously mystical, in a word divine."[94]

If Proudhon had been abstracting from history or human relations he might still have been able to analyze real life with some measure of accuracy; but because the categories of political economy were now timeless and eternal, he was left with a set of propositions which only betrayed his own confusion because they were little more than emanations of his own mind. The categories were logically linked together in his own head and his analysis ultimately rested on little more than logic. "Everything that has happened since 1789 and 1830 was predestined by the eternal laws of logic,"[95] he said, holding that what was now needed was to find the appropriate resolution of the contradictions in and between the categories:

> Equality develops among people according to the rigorous and inflexible law of work, by the proportionality of values, the sincerity of exchanges and the equivalence of functions; in a word, by the mathematic solution of all antinomies.[96]

Although Proudhon thought that he was examining logical and timeless categories, the economic framework within which he was operating was that given to him by classical political economy. Unable to make a break with private property and the market, he was doing the same thing that all the bourgeois economists he was attacking so violently for being apologists were doing. As Marx pointed out, he was making bourgeois life, the material underpinning of bourgeois economics, as holy and unchangeable as the categories themselves:

> Indeed he does what all good bourgeois do. They all tell you that in principle, that is, considered as abstract ideas, competition, monopoly, etc., are the only basis of life, but that in practice they leave much to be desired. They all want competition without the lethal effects of competition. They all want the impossible, namely, the conditions of bourgeois existence without the necessary consequences of those conditions. None of them understands that the bourgeois form of production is historical and transitory, just as the feudal form was. This mistake arises from the fact that the bourgeois man is to them the only possible basis of every society; they cannot imagine a society in which men have ceased to be bourgeois.[97]

Proudhon's inclination to accept the "givens" of the world and seek their organization within the existing social structure imposed by capitalist production was stronger than the subversive implications of his analysis. Prior to 1848 his basic orientation was reformist and critical. Holding that "the world, humanity, capital, industry and the conduct of business exist; it is only a matter of seeking their philosophy, in other words of organizing them,"[98] he combined his refusal to break with the market with an orientation which denied social movement and sought to establish social peace at all costs:

> everything in political economy having a true and a false side, the product resolves itself into combining the economic elements in such a way that their harmony doesn't present any more contradiction.[99]

This truncated view of Fourier's series and Hegel's dialectics and a clear desire to conciliate and harmonize the conflicting elements of social life were reflected in Proudhon's own vacillation with respect to class antagonisms themselves. He was able to criticize the proletariat and the bourgeoisie alike for their alleged selfishness,[100] but he shared with other social reformers a tendency to regard class conflict as a sad manifestation of an unorganized economy, an "error" which, like all the other contradictions with which he was concerned, would disappear when work was organized in accordance with the appropriate formula.[101]

This reluctance to deal concretely with class conflict stemmed from Proudhon's fear of being caught in the middle, a fear which was central to the views of the small proprietors whose welfare was so important to him. He seemed to have sensed that his attempt to find a middle ground between proletariat and bourgeoisie would be threatened if the two antagonists could not peacefully conciliate their differences and he wanted to forge an alliance between them so they could pursue their joint struggle against the "new feudalism." "I am sincerely attached to the working and progressive bourgeoisie," he confided to his diary.[102] He had expressed the same stand in a letter to his friend Maurice somewhat earlier; for him, "it is a matter of cementing the alliance between the working bourgeoisie and the working class in our century; everything else must disappear or pass away."[103]

Proudhon's desire to establish an alliance between the proletariat and the petty bourgeoisie was by no means unique. Neither was his hope that it would be led by the latter, since the conditions for a fully-independent proletarian movement were not yet in place. For the moment he was primarily interested in the benefits such an alliance could bring to the petty bourgeoisie:

> There is no help for finance, the parliamentary bourgeoisie, the peasant; nor for the day-worker, the republican, the fourierist, the legitimist, . . .
> There is help for only the factory worker, the journeyman, the artisan, the small industrialist.[104]

Proudhon's attacks on the concentration of capital, the destructiveness of "free" competition, idle property, the Church, and the aristocracy were all motivated by his deeply-held conviction that, in threatening small business, they threatened the material basis of security and freedom. Heavily influenced by what he had seen of the disintegration of the Lyonnais silk industry, he badly wanted to maintain a balanced economy marked by the independence and security of autonomous centers of production.[105] His conviction that justice demanded that the worker be able to buy back the equivalent of his contribution to the value of a commodity was a reflection of the social arrangements prevailing within many small French *ateliers* in which the owner was simultaneously a worker, resisted the introduction of machines and did not make much more money than did his employees. Based on the labor of all who worked there, Proudhon's workshop was society's basic productive unit, a school for the intellectual, moral, and technical instruction of the workers.[106]

Proudhon's main concerns at this time—outlets, exchange, credit, taxes, mechanization, and the like—were those of small manufacturers. His work-based egalitarianism was based on a handicraft and small peasant economy. His denunciations of middlemen, idle property, and big capital alike coincided with the economic concerns of small business and expressed a desire to preserve and generalize small property which reflected the concerns of the beleaguered petty bourgeoisie.[107] The purpose of the *Système des contradictions économiques* was to understand how the new forms of production would affect those for whom he was speaking.

Increasingly preoccupied by the difficulty of maneuvering between political economy and socialism and trying to find a middle ground between contending schools and contending classes, Proudhon tended to see the solutions to society's problems in the logical formulations of his own mind. At the same time, he recognized the self-serving hypocrisy which rested at the center of bourgeois defenses of property. His fierce commitment to equality and his hatred of oppression in any form interacted with his native sense of contradiction to strengthen his concern for all those who were being hurt by industrialization. He clarified many of the issues which the beleaguered petty bourgeoisie and proletariat would have to confront after 1848. Dominated as it was by the social and political concerns of small proprietors, the French left of the 1840s found one of its early spokesmen in Proudhon. Whether his view was clear enough to navigate a period of intense political struggle and theoretical reorientation remained to be seen.

NOTES

1. Bernard Moss, "Producers' Associations and the Origins of French Socialism: Ideology from Below," *Journal of Modern History* 48 (March 1976), 69–89.
2. George Woodcock's *Pierre-Joseph Proudhon* (London: Routledge and Kegan Paul, 1956) is one of the best sources for information about Proudhon's life available in English. There are many French sources as well, the most noteworthy of which are Edouard Droz, *P.-J. Proudhon* (Paris: Librarie de 'Pages Libres,' 1909); Armand Cuvillier, *Proudhon* (Paris: Editions Sociales Internationales, 1937); Daniel Halévy, *Proudhon d'après ses carnets inédits* (Paris: Sequana, 1944); Charles Sainte-Beuve, *Proudhon: sa vie et sa correspondance* (Paris: Costes, 1947); Edouard Dolléans, *Proudhon* (Paris: Gallimard, 1948); Georges Gurvitch, *Proudhon: Sa vie, son oeuvre, avec un exposé de sa philosophie* (Paris: Presses Universitaires de France, 1965); and Pierre Ansart, *Naissance de l'anarchism* (Paris: Presses Universitaires de France, 1970).
3. "Profession de foi," from the *Candidature à la pension Suard* (Paris: Rivière, 1926), 15–16. It was written on May 31, 1838.
4. *De la Célébration du dimanche considérée sous les rapports de l'hygiène publique, de la morale, des relations de famille et de cité* (Paris: Rivière, 1926) was first published in 1839. An earlier philological piece, the *Essai de grammaire generale*, had appeared in 1837 and is no longer of any interest.
5. Daniel Halévy, "Introduction," *ibid.*, 24.
6. *Ibid.*
7. *Ibid.*, 61. His emphasis.
8. *Ibid.*, 33.
9. *Ibid.*, 49.
10. *Ibid.*, 41.
11. *Ibid.*, 90.
12. *Ibid.*, 60.
13. *Ibid.*, 59.
14. See *ibid.*, His remarks about Rousseau.

15. *Ibid.*, 89. The emphasis is Proudhon's.
16. Halévy, *ibid.*, 24.
17. *Ibid.*, 90.
18. *Ibid.*, 55.
19. Woodcock, 43.
20. *Dimanche*, 77, 89.
21. Aime Berthod, *Proudhon et la propriété, un socialisme pour les paysans* (Paris: V. Giard et E. Brière, 1910), 61.
22. *Qu'est-ce que la propriété? ou recherche sur le principe du droit et du gouvernement* (Paris: Rivière, 1926), 28; exactly the same words appear in a letter to Ackermann of Feb. 12, 1840, *Correspondance* (Paris: Lacroix, 1875), i:185.
23. *Ibid.*, 181. Proudhon's emphasis.
24. *Ibid.*, 134.
25. See, for example, Berthod and Celestin Bouglé, *La Sociologie de Proudhon* (Paris: Armand Colin, 1911).
26. Maurice Dommanget, *Les grands socialistes et l'éducation* (Paris: Armand Colin, 1970).
27. *Qu'est-ce la propriété?*, 180.
28. *Ibid.*, 212.
29. *Ibid.*, 245.
30. *Ibid.*, 215.
31. *Ibid.*, 217.
32. *Ibid.*, 218.
33. *Ibid.*, 270.
34. *Ibid.*, 242.
35. *Ibid.*, 288–89.
36. *Ibid.*, 153.
37. *Ibid.*, 131.
38. From his *Correspondance*, i:22. The letter was written on August 3, 1840, less than two months after the publication of *Qu'est-ce que la propriété?* The emphases are Proudhon's.
39. *Qu'est-ce que la propriété?*, 216–17.
40. *Ibid.*, 234.
41. See, for example, Eugene Fournière, "Le Règne de Louis-Philippe" in Jean Jaurès ed., *Histoire Socialiste* (Paris: Jules Rouff, 1907), viii:142–63.
42. Woodcock, 74.
43. See Ansart; Moss 1976; Sanford Elwitt, "Politics and Ideology in the French Labour Movement," *Journal of Modern History* 49:3 (1977), 468–80; Mary Lynn McDougall, "Consciousness and Community: the Workers of Lyon, 1830–1850," *Journal of Social History* 12:1 (Fall 1978), 129–45; and Michael Hanagan, "The Politics of Proletarianization," *Comparative Studies in Society and History* 21 (April 1979), 227–30.
44. Letter to Maurice, August 13, 1844. *Correspondance*, ii:126.
45. *Ibid.*, 136–37.
46. Proudhon had published *Qu'est-ce que la propriété?* in June 1840. Four months later he responded to the friendly criticism of the book by the famous economist Blanqui (the brother of the conspirator) in *Lettre à M. Blanqui*, known more formally as *Qu'est-ce que la propriété?*, *2e memoire*. The *Avertissement aux propriétaires*, which appeared early in 1842, completes the list of his early writings about property.

47. See, for example, the letter to his friend and associate Antoine Gauthier of May 2, 1841. *Correspondance*, i:325.
48. Henry Michel, *L'Idée de l'état* (Paris: Hachette, 1896), 411. See also Henri de Lubac, *The Un-Marxian Socialist: a Study of Proudhon* (New York: Sheed and Ward, 1948), ch. vi.
49. Letter to Bergmann, December 26, 1842. *Correspondance*, ii:65–66. The emphases are his.
50. *De la Création de l'ordre dans l'humanité, ou principes d'organisation politique* (Paris: Rivière, 1927), 294. The emphasis is his.
51. Sheldon Wolin, *Politics and Vision: Continuity and Innovation in Western Political Thought* (Boston: Little, Brown, 1960), ch. x.
52. *De la Création de l'ordre*, 187.
53. Lubac, 139.
54. *De la Création de l'ordre*, 174.
55. *Ibid.*, 247–48.
56. *Ibid.*, 181–82.
57. *Ibid.*, 347.
58. *Ibid.*, 201–2.
59. *Ibid.*, 294.
60. *Ibid.*, 191.
61. "Ce n'est pas une *dispossession* que je veux; c'est un nouveau mode de *possession*, qui rendra le cultivateur plus heureux, plus possédeur et moins ppre." *Carnets* (Paris: Rivière, 1960), i:240.
62. *De la Création de l'ordre*, 427.
63. See his letter to Ackermann of October 4, 1844. *Correspondance*, i:158.
64. Armand Cuvillier, "Marx et Proudhon" in Auguste Cornu et al, *A la lumière du Marxisme*, vol. 2: *Karl Marx et la pensée moderne* (Paris: Editions Sociales Internationales, 1937).
65. See Proudhon's summary of his own intellectual development in *Les Confessions d'un révolutionnaire pour servir à l'histoire de la Révolution de février* (Paris: Rivière, 1929), 193. The book first appeared in October 1849.
66. Letter to Guillaumain of August 15, 1844. *Correspondance*, ii:138.
67. Letter to Bergmann, October 24, 1844. *Ibid.*, 166. His emphasis.
68. Letter to Ackermann, July 2, 1846. *Ibid.*, 208.
69. Letter to Guillaumain, November 21, 1846. *Ibid.*, 228.
70. Letter to Bergmann, October 24, 1844. *Ibid.*, 167. This position stands in some contradiction to his earlier statement that 'la solution des antinomies ne peut se resoudre par les moyens politiques, qui sont eux-mêmes des antinomies; . . .' *Carnets*, i:96.
71. *De la Création de l'ordre*, 322.
72. *Système des contradictions économiques, ou philosophie de la misère* (Paris: Rivière, 1925), i:97.
73. *Ibid.*, 108.
74. *Ibid.*, 109.
75. *Ibid.*, 174.
76. *Ibid.*, 140.
77. *Ibid.*, ii94.
78. *Ibid.*, i:194.
79. *Ibid.*, 212, 223.
80. *Ibid.*, 196.

81. *Ibid.*, 266. The emphasis is his.
82. *Ibid.*, ii:101.
83. *Ibid.*, 345.
84. *Ibid.*, 141, 348.
85. *Ibid.*, 344.
86. Although he had Cabet in mind during this period before Marxism came to dominate European socialism, Proudhon would have been unhappy with Marx and Engels as well.
87. *Système des contradictions économiques*, i:239, 247–48.
88. *Ibid.*, ii:310.
89. *Ibid.*, i:293.
90. *Ibid.*, 68.
91. *Ibid.*, 391.
92. *Ibid.*, 86.
93. *Ibid.*, 72.
94. *Ibid.*, ii:237.
95. *Carnets* (Paris: Rivière, 1961), ii:2.
96. *Système des contradictions économiques*, i:256.
97. Karl Marx, *The Poverty of Philosophy* (New York: International Publishers, 1963), 190.
98. *Système des contradictions économiques*, i:283–84.
99. *Ibid.*, 344.
100. See, for example, *ibid.*, 359, 366.
101. Cuvillier *1937*, 75.
102. *Carnets*, ii:66. This note was written on March 23, 1847, five months after *Philosophie de la misère* appeared.
103. *Correspondance*, ii:214. The letter was written on August 27, 1846.
104. *Carnets*, ii:90.
105. His *Carnets* of this period are a testament to the influence of Lyon's small and decentralized silk industry.
106. Eugene Fournière, *Les Théories socialistes au XIXe siècle de Babeuf à Proudhon* (Paris: Alcan, 1904), 388.
107. *Philosophie de la Misère*, ii:199.

4

Revolution, Politics, and the State

Turning Points

"I'm moving from criticism to action," Proudhon wrote his friend Bergmann in August 1847;[1] he had grown tired of theoretical investigation and institutional criticism and was thinking of becoming a journalist so he could disseminate his views and have an influence in public affairs.[2] He arrived in Paris from Lyon on December 15, 1847, and immediately began looking for a newspaper which would be willing to publish his opinions. The sheerest coincidence had brought Proudhon to a turning point in his life just as the Revolution of 1848 burst upon France and decisively changed nineteenth-century European political history.

The increasing size and influence of the modern proletariat—now understood to mean the growing class of propertyless industrial wageworkers—was becoming an important factor in French public life, and the events of 1848 served notice that a distinctly modern set of social and political problems now confronted the country. The failure of the Great Revolution to eliminate the economic roots of inequality and oppression had aroused intense interest in "the social question" for some time, and as property came to dominate the left's discourse it became clear that the workers' urgent social demands were forcing themselves to the front of the political stage. The social content of the Revolution of 1848 was much more pronounced than earlier, and so was the impact of its distinctly proletarian current. If a defensive labor movement had confined itself to intermittent agitation against hoarders and merchants, tax rebellions, and attacks on machinery during the 1830s, an increasingly aggressive movement characterized the decade which followed. The demonstrations, strikes and insurrections of the 1840s were accompanied by a heightened level of class consciousness and assumed an increasingly militant political expression. The development of a modern market, modern state, and modern culture served to broaden the scale and extent of working-class politics—all the more so because the uniquely pure

79

French case was relatively uncomplicated by extraneous factors like the national question. An openly partisan political regime tended to politicize economic struggles and enlarge the scope of the labor movement from the immediate issues at hand to more general matters of state and politics. A combination of the growing intensity and scope of economic and social matters and a rigid and unyielding political regime compelled the developing labor movement to turn to systematic political activity.

There were really two revolutions at work during this period, and the relationship between them shaped the environment within which every important actor moved—Proudhon among them. On the one hand, the "pure" republicans and democrats fought for a revolution whose goal was to replace the July Monarchy with a classical bourgeois republic whose task and structure would be shaped by the gradual development of market relations. On the other hand, many "social" republicans, socialists, and communists began to call private property in the means of production into question and found support in the ranks of an impoverished working class whose propertylessness lay at the root of all social misery and corruption. The Revolution of 1848 was a watershed because it raised the possibility of using political power to systematically interfere with or abolish existing property relations on a national level for the first time. It did so only briefly and unsuccessfully, but few observers doubted that it anticipated the shape of future politics.

The radical character of the Revolution's social content was shaped by a proletarian-based socialist movement which began to emerge from the matrix of the general-democratic movement within which it had previously been contained. No matter how it was defined, socialism now meant something considerably more than a radicalization of the petty-bourgeoisie's democracy. The bourgeoisie's liberalism was counter-revolutionary and anti-democratic from the very beginning of the revolution, a revolution whose success now depended on the relationship between the democratic small proprietors and the smaller but strategically-located socialist workers. The bourgeoisie, petty bourgeoisie, and proletariat were beginning to separate themselves out in classically modern fashion, and the ideological reflection of this development was the increasingly problematical relationship between liberalism, democracy, and socialism.

The ideological struggles of nineteenth-century France evolved in close connection to the Revolution's political fallout. All the sects and schools which had characterized the 1830s and 1840s began to die out, and the utopian expectation that social renewal could be accomplished by this or that would-be Savior of Humanity slowly yielded to the understanding that there was no substitute for patient theoretical and practical work among the workers. There were many saint-simonians, fourierists, babouvists, jacobins, "pure" republicans, and democrats after the Revolution was defeated, of course, but it was increasingly clear that there was a big difference between a *coup de main* and a revolution and that more was needed than an elegant demonstration of the self-evident need for social reform. The slow decay and eventual disappearance of almost all the pre-1848 schools of thought was paralleled by new and more sophisticated understandings of "the people," "democracy," "socialism," and the like. Eighteen forty-eight was a watershed because it simultaneously expressed and precipitated fundamental changes in the way people thought about and acted in political affairs.

The Revolution's velocity, scope, and thrust forced Proudhon to make important personal and political choices time and time again. As the political crisis deepened, came to a head, and was finally resolved, the positions he took revealed the tensions, strengths, and weaknesses of his approach to public affairs with a clarity which "normal" periods tend to conceal. They also revealed the shifting ground upon which the petty bourgeoisie tried to maneuver and illustrated the complexity of its politics. The Revolution of 1848 and its aftermath clarified some important things about Proudhon because the press of events compelled him to clarify them for himself.

Bad harvests in 1845 and 1846 and the resulting commercial industrial crisis of 1847 underlay the events of the following year. Peasants and workers suffered more than any other segment of the population, but the scope of the crisis was revealed by the extent to which much of the petty bourgeoisie was ruined. This served to accentuate the usual difficulties of its social position. Marx pointed out how it was propelled into the struggle against the July Monarchy by an intensification of the same trends which had formed the backdrop to Proudhon's own political education:

> In Paris the commercial crisis had, in particular, the effect of throwing a number of manufacturers and big traders, who under the existing circumstances could no longer do any business in the foreign market, on to the home market. They set up large establishments, the competition of which ruined the *épiciers* and *boutiquiers en masse*. Hence the innumerable bankruptcies among this section of the Paris bourgeoisie, and hence their revolutionary action in February.[3]

Chronic economic weakness, an intensified social crisis, and the constant political exposures of the "banquet campaign" combined to produce a spontaneous revolution in Paris which swept away the entire political structure of the July Monarchy in three February days and resulted in the proclamation of the Second Republic.[4] Largely driven by the activity of the Parisian workers, the new bourgeois republic would permit a wider measure of popular sovereignty than had the bourgeois monarchy and might make possible a more active interference with the market in the name of the public good than had been possible under the political domination of the financiers. But the new Provisional Government, drawn as it was from the moderate parliamentary and journalistic opposition and the very functionaries and institutions which had made up the previous organization of state power, was very careful to keep within narrow boundaries.[5] The urgent social and economic demands of the workers, who had made the revolution possible and whose militancy had pushed events faster than the "legal" opposition had contemplated, came into conflict with the liberal bourgeoisie's desire to go no further than changing the personnel at the head of the state and opening up some political institutions to a wider debate about the country's future. In a *reprise* of the events of the Great Revolution, the "right to work" was proclaimed (though it would take more than proclaiming it to make it a reality), the National Guard was filled with young republicans, press censorship was ended, universal suffrage was proclaimed, and slavery was abolished in French colonies. An advisory commission established to recommend methods to improve the condition of workers—called the Luxembourg Commission after its meeting-place—was headed by Louis Blanc but quickly degenerated into an impotent debating society.

For the Revolution's moderate bourgeois leadership the overthrow of the July Monarchy and establishment of a republic would permit a wider, more open and more efficient political structure for debating and organizing the common affairs of its landed, commercial, financial, and manufacturing wings than had been possible earlier. But the political, economic, and intellectual freedom for which the bourgeoisie, petty bourgeoisie, and proletariat had fought together in February had dramatically different meanings to each of the Revolution's participants. For the liberal bourgeoisie, freedom must facilitate and not interfere with the social relations of capitalist accumulation.[6] For their part, the "pure democrats" who drew their strength from the massive petty bourgeoisie sought a series of reforms which would help them protect their smallholdings from the twin threats of the bourgeoisie's concentrated property and the workers' inclination to do away with the institution altogether. Finally, the proletarian-based socialist and communist left wanted to use state power to transform and organize the economy so as to satisfy the social and economic needs of the laboring population. The clash between the bourgeoisie's right to property, the petty bourgeoisie's right to security, and the proletariat's right to life shaped the split between those who wanted to stop at establishing a "democratic republic" and those who wanted to push on to a "social republic." This, the Revolution's most basic contradiction, appeared at the proclamation of the Second Republic and was an important early expression of the struggle between the bourgeoisie and the proletariat. Caught in the middle and pulled in two directions, the *petite bourgeoisie* would split, vacillate, and act. Its motion determined the limits beyond which the Revolution would not go and at the same time illustrated some of the fundamental political tensions of contemporary politics. At all times it would be responding to the political expression of a distinctly modern form of the class struggle:

> The February republic finally brought the rule of the bourgeoisie clearly into prominence, since it struck off the crown behind which Capital kept itself concealed.
>
> Just as the workers in the July days had fought and won the bourgeois monarchy, so in the February days they fought and won the bourgeois republic. Just as the July monarchy had to proclaim itself a monarchy surrounded by republican institutions, so the February republic was forced to proclaim itself a republic surrounded by social institutions. The Parisian proletariat compelled this concession, too.[7]

Proudhon himself played a small role in the February events, helping to distribute the proclamation which demanded Louis-Philippe's abdication and aiding in the construction of at least one barricade.[8] He may have joined Barbès' political club for a short time, but his participation in the revolution was considerably less than one would expect judging from his reputation.[9]

He was cautious and suspicious about the men who were coming forward to assume political leadership of the movement and justly feared that the revolution would once again be contained within the established limits of bourgeois politics. He worried that the social and economic needs of the laboring poor would be lost in the tidal wave of well-intentioned, empty-headed, and self-serving pomposity which swept over the country in the aftermath of Louis-Philippe's fall. He was sure that the Provisional Government did not understand the issues facing the country and if he placed more emphasis on its collective ignorance than on its class character, his initial distrust proved to be well-founded indeed:

> The Republic is under the protection of several honest men and some first-rate but bumbling fools. February 24 was made without an idea; now it's a matter of giving the movement a direction, and I can already see it losing itself in a wave of speeches. I wouldn't want to be too pessimistic, particularly since I took part in the events; but now, with the excitement over, I am giving myself over to reflection. While the intriguers, who were thinking of nothing three days ago, share the victory, I—who foresaw everything—regret that things couldn't be arranged differently. France will certainly move forward, with the Republic or in another way; but it could have accomplished as much with the former government such as it was, and would have cost much less.[10]

His distrust of the Revolution's leadership and his annoyance that the Provisional Government was not seeking his advice left him undecided about February, and he chose to stay out of public life until the new regime's intentions became clearer. He was not convinced that the Revolution represented a sufficiently sharp break with the past to merit his support.

Considering that its leadership and the composition of its first Provisional Government was drawn from the ranks of the July Regime's loyal opposition, he was not far off the mark. "I'm going to remain in my solitude and try to orient myself," he said. "The times are bad for studying, and I don't have time for foolishness. Maybe I'll be useful to the new order; who knows? Maybe I'll end up in the opposition; again, who knows?"[11]

Proudhon's reluctance to endorse the February Revolution was rooted in the way his thinking had developed during the 1840s and had been shaped by the development of the "banquet campaign" during the summer of 1847. He was concerned about the exclusively political tone of the "legitimate" parliamentary and journalistic opposition, worried that another section of the bourgeoisie was trying to share in the Revolution's spoils at the expense of the people[12] or that failure to understand that "political reform will be the effect and not the cause of social reform" would leave France's most important social questions unanswered.[13] He was worried about both greed and ignorance, and his insistence that social reforms take precedence over political changes lay at the heart of almost every important position he came to during this period. It was his way of expressing the acute struggle between the bourgeoisie and the proletariat which would dominate the political life of the entire country as the revolutionary crisis matured during the spring and came to a head in June.

Proudhon was equally sure that the republicans, saint-simonians, fourierists, and communists had nothing to offer France except a continuation of the opposition's most retrograde and self-destructive tendencies, and a good deal of his activity during this period was driven by his desire to conduct uncompromising ideological struggle against "obsolete" approaches to politics.[14] His campaign against what he called "statist socialism" has been described as "the great preoccupation of his life" and lay behind his consistent refusal to cooperate with other socialists.[15] His truculent independence would get him in a good deal of trouble and provide him with genuine opportunities for leadership at the same time.

The other side of his certainty that no one knew anything was his equally strong conviction that only he could provide the solutions to France's problems.[16] "La Révolution, c'est moi," he declared in his diary, and his occasional flashes of arrogance stemmed from his knowledge that 1848 was an ideological watershed for the French left.[17] Proudhon may have been wrong about the power of his own theories, but he did understand that the approaches which had dominated the left for decades were no longer adequate to the social and political tasks at hand. His contemptuous dismissal of the empty posturing which characterized the traditional left pointed to the Revolution's near-universal discrediting of all socialist reform projects. Whether it was the "republic one and indivisible," the "organization of work," the "association," or any of the other shibboleths of the reformist opposition, all the schemes of the traditional left were dashed on the reality of the open class struggle between the bourgeoisie and the proletariat. Ironically enough, this would turn out to be as true of much of Proudhon's work as it was of the established opposition he so emphatically and tellingly criticized. His desire to remain independent of the "crowd" reinforced his equally strong intention to continue his attacks on the traditional left.[18] "I adore humanity, but I spit on people," he confided to his diary.[19] Although he was sure that "I am the voice of the people . . . the spontaneous and reflective reason of the proletariat," he also understood the price his self-imposed isolation was forcing him to pay:[20]

> Maybe I'm badly placed to judge accurately. My body is in the midst of the people, but my thoughts are elsewhere. As a result of my ideas, I have come to have almost nothing in common with my contemporaries and I would much rather believe that my point of view is false than accuse them of stupidity.
> . . . I am lazy, disgusted, loafing around, and already dreaming of getting out of this confusion.[21]

Proudhon remained convinced throughout the spring that his ideas would have to be implemented before France's problems could be solved.[22] As the elections of April 23 for the Constituent Assembly approached without any substantial change in social conditions, he decided to offer himself to the voters of his home department of Doubs. He was breaking out of his self-imposed isolation during March and April, having previously agreed to serve as a contributing editor of the new paper *Le Représentant du Peuple*, established by old school friends as a journal of progressive criticism and action. His decision to run for a seat in the Constituent Assembly was surprising for such a prominent anti-political socialist and can be understood only in terms of his conviction that he could help rescue France from chaos and impending civil war.

Indeed, the declaration he issued to the voters of the Doubs[23] clearly expressed his desire to find a way to harmonize the interests of all classes. Such a wish was not new; during the previous winter he had expressed his conviction that "social health will come from only a reconciliation between the conservative party and the working class, between labor and capital."[24] In the fall he had felt that "the proletariat's interests are identical to those of the middle class, since everyone must become middle class."[25] Caught between the social demands of the workers and the more limited political aims of the bourgeoisie, Proudhon echoed the petty-bourgeois desire to stay out of trouble by denying that there was any. Such a stance worked well enough during the spring but broke down as June approached and would prove utterly untenable during the reaction which followed the workers' historic defeat.

Proudhon was conciliatory throughout the Declaration, repeatedly pointing out that every class stood to gain if "the social question" could be resolved. He accused the Provisional Government of ignorance and inefficiency, holding that its first priority should be narrowing the gap between the bourgeoisie and the proletariat. To this end he presented himself as the representative of the radical as well as the conservative "spirit."[26] He wanted to get as many conservative as radical votes in the election, hoping that this would make it possible for him to "conciliate the principle of social reform with the principle of bourgeois conservation,"[27] and his final bit of advice to both classes echoed this orientation. "Workers," he urged, "hold out your hand to your bosses; and you, employers, don't reject the overtures of those who were your workers."[28]

The bourgeoisie's desire for the sort of compromise Proudhon sought could be gauged by the Provisional Government's effort to solve "the social problem." Given the insistent demands for work and security coming from the workers and the beleaguered petty bourgeoisie, this came to mean reorganizing the economy so as to lay the basis for full employment, economic stability, and the gradual narrowing of class distinctions. No one expected or demanded that these goals be accomplished overnight, but much depended on whether the Provisional Government showed any sign of even being interested in the plight of the working and non-working poor.

Two major concessions had been forced out of it in the days immediately following the Revolution. The Luxembourg Commission headed by Louis Blanc had been constituted to study and recommend ways in which "the social problem" could be solved. Initial hopes notwithstanding, it was never more than an advisory body and what recommendations it did make were never taken seriously by either the Provisional Government or the Constituent Assembly. It quickly degenerated into a disorganized debating society which tried to patch up disputes between employers and workers and occasionally issued vague warnings of an impending political crisis. Louis Blanc himself soon came to realize that the only way the bourgeoisie can "organize" work is through the labor market, and as the Luxembourg Commission became more and more paralyzed, attention shifted to the National Workshops.

The *Ateliers Nationaux*, allegedly the concrete embodiment of Blanc's proposals in *Organisation du Travail*, were supposed to "organize" and "guarantee" work. Blanc had originally intended them to be state-organized workers' production cooperatives which would gradually outperform private enterprises and thus replace the anarchy of the market with a stable and long-term public regulation of the economy. Their establishment was virtually the only concrete step the Provisional Government ever took to address the overwhelming social needs of the Paris workers, but they had almost nothing to do with Blanc's thinking and did little more than provide meaningless and humiliating labor for tens of thousands of unemployed workers. Nevertheless, they were virtually the only source of income in the spring of 1848 for many of the unemployed. Unsatisfactory as they were, they were all the workers had, and an attack on them was tantamount to an attack on the workers themselves. Their abrupt dissolution was a declaration of open war on the proletariat and precipitated the desperate rising of June.

In the long run, the Luxembourg Commission and the *ateliers* were used to embarrass Louis Blanc and discredit socialism.[29] The increasingly independent political activity of the workers and the growing popularity of socialist ideas during the spring worried the Provisional Government, and part of the rationale behind establishing a twisted caricature of Blanc's proposals was to "demonstrate the emptiness of the 'inapplicable theories' (of Louis Blanc), discredit and weaken the socialist theorist and, beyond this personal goal, diminish socialism."[30] The failure of the *ateliers* served to drive a wedge between the proletariat and the petty bourgeoisie and contributed to the workers' political isolation as June approached. Marx commented:

> In their title, though not in their content, the National *Ateliers* were the embodied protest of the proletariat against bourgeois industry, bourgeois credit and the bourgeois republic. The whole hate of the bourgeoisie was therefore turned upon them. At the same time, it had found in them the point against which it could direct the attack, as soon as it was strong enough to break openly with the February illusions. All the discontent, all the ill humor of the petty bourgeoisie was simultaneously directed against these National *Ateliers*, the common target. With real fury they reckoned up the sums that the proletarian loafers swallowed, while their own situation became daily more unbearable. A state pension for sham labor! they growled to themselves. They sought the basis of their misery in the National *Ateliers*, the declarations of the Luxembourg, the marches of the workers through Paris. And no one was more fantastic about the alleged machinations of the Communists than the petty bourgeoisie who hovered hopelessly on the brink of bankruptcy.[31]

Proudhon did not fall into the trap Marx described. He had been suspicious of the Provisional Government's motives in establishing the *ateliers* from the beginning,[32] and the fact that he had some direct contact with Parisian workers undoubtedly helped him understand why the laborers hated them as well. The failure of the National Workshops was apparent to all classes of French society,[33] but Proudhon opposed the increasing demands from the bourgeoisie that they be abolished.[34]

The first issue of *Le Représentant du Peuple* appeared on February 27. Proudhon's public positions can best be understood from an examination of his newspaper articles, for it was as a journalist that he exercised most of his considerable influence on public affairs during the next two and a half years. The paper called itself the "Journal des Travailleurs" on the masthead, stated its critical support for the Provisional Government, and declared, "we have conquered freedom; now on to the organization of work."[35] Proudhon did not begin contributing articles until April, and from that time the paper could best be described as "Proudhon's journal, widely read because of his articles."[36]

BOURGEOIS REPUBLIC OR SOCIAL DEMOCRACY?

The economic crisis which provided much of the basis for the February Revolution continued through the spring of 1848. The economy was stagnant, unemployment remained high, and a shortage of credit was strangling the *petite bourgeoisie*.[37] Proudhon's first priority was reviving the economy in the interest of small proprietors, for he was coming to believe that only the free and equal exchange of products between autonomous centers of production could provide a stable foundation for a harmonious social life.[38] His initial appraisal of the February Revolution was shaped by the relationship between its social content and the political emphasis of its 1789 predecessor. "In proclaiming freedom of opinion, equality before the law, sovereignty of the people and the subordination of power to the country," he observed, "the Revolution made the society and the government into two incompatible things, and it's this incompatibility which is the cause of our enslaving concentration."[39] Echoing a rather common theme on the left, Proudhon asserted that the time had come to organize the social reconstruction which would supplement 1789's earlier political transformation and reintegrate man's fractured social life. His prior fame made him an influential journalist and he put forward a series of observations and suggestions for the organization of the economy in his first series of articles, more commonly known as the *Solution du Problème Social*.

A subtle and important shift had occurred in his mind, and it lent a markedly different emphasis to his work during the Revolution of 1848 from that of the more "orthodox" left. Where he had formerly placed primary importance on the organization of work, he was now thinking of the organization of credit and exchange; where he had previously made an attempt to articulate the needs of the proletariat, he was now demanding help for the petty bourgeoisie. This line of thought had been developing for some time; he had summarized it in his *Carnets* during the fall of 1847 by writing, "my power is neither the Bastille's cannons nor July's paving-stones; it's exchange."[40] The organization of credit and circulation was now taken to be the basis of social reconstruction, and the distribution of the means of consumption was now considered independent of and primary to the question of property in the means of production. Because he was trying to assure an ample supply of cheap credit and a stable market for its goods to the beleaguered petty bourgeoisie,[41] Proudhon proposed a series of reforms which stopped far short of changing the system of production but presented socialism and the solution of the social question as turning on distribution.[42] Organizing the "right to work," whose subversive core implied social control over the labor market, now yielded to a reformist call for democratizing access to credit.

Proudhon was convinced that a "Banque d'Echange" would "constitute" value along the lines he had suggested in 1846, making it possible to exchange products against products in proportion to the amount of labor embodied in them. The Bank would unclog circulation by providing a central institution where labor-notes based upon time spent in production would link production, exchange, and credit.[43] These "exchange notes" would circulate in lieu of money or gold and would facilitate exchange without extracting any value from the process. Because the notes would be based on the actual value of the commodities they represented, prices could now be expressed in terms of the actual social effort required for production rather than by the erratic and unstable relationship between supply and demand.[44] The connections between all productive members of society could now be set on a "real" foundation of individual work and reciprocal exchange, and equality would be more substantial than the empty legal pronouncements of an untrustworthy and necessarily partisan state. If small producers could be freed from the tyranny of the "financial aristocracy" and organized in a program of mutual financial cooperation, the interest which would normally flow to parasitical investors could now enable a producer to make what he wanted and exchange for what he needed without taking "irrelevant" matters into account. Inequality and injustice would disappear because the market would finally be able to reward real work. Social conflict and the state would both die out because they would have lost their *raison d'être*.[45] Proudhon was confident that capitalists and proletarians would disappear as well and that everyone would have equal access to the means of production and consumption. Everyone would be a small producer, a petty bourgeois.

The proposal that the Revolution organize an Exchange Bank, which Proudhon would repeat in various forms and at various times for the rest of his life, grew out of his desire to harmonize capital and labor by combining them and thus eliminating the source of political conflict which was undermining the February Revolution. This was a common enough theme in early French socialism, but the fact that Proudhon proposed it in a period of intense class struggle indicated a strong desire to stand between and above contending classes:

> It's by the same principle of reciprocity that we should arrive, without communism, without the agrarian law, without terror, out of the free will of all the citizens, at the satisfaction of the bourgeoisie and the proletariat, and by constantly

increasing the public wealth and the wellbeing of families, at the *transformation of property*, at *positive anarchy*, in a word at the realization of the republican slogan *Liberty, Equality, Fraternity*.[46]

Proudhon was confident that he was proposing a universal solution which would lay the foundations for social stability and peace because it reflected the universal laws he had set out to discover at the beginning of his career. His theory of an Exchange Bank started from the familiar proposition that interest lies at the root of capitalism's tendency to destroy equality because it rewards unearned income. It follows that to suppress interest and eliminate the market in money is to strike a blow at inequality. If all producers could borrow money gratuitously, they could consciously control it instead of being forced to rent it. It would be impossible to make money without working and every producer would be compelled to contribute to social progress. Exchange would be reciprocal, each producer would be rewarded in direct proportion to his work, and justice would replace coercion as the basis of social life. It was some time before Proudhon's anarchism became sufficiently developed to permit a more complete discussion of social reconstruction, but his early hope that free distribution, exchange, and circulation could be guaranteed through minor changes in an economic system which would retain the private ownership of the means of production is the theoretical expression of his overwhelming desire to safeguard small property at this stage of the revolution.[47] His aim was still to equalize the private ownership of the means of production and transform France into a network of interrelated small producer-consumers.

Even though the Luxembourg delegates were inclined to agree with Proudhon and were disposed to provide free credit to small proprietors, they differed from him in seeing it as an opportunity to organize monopolies in each trade. The workers' collectivism would clash with Proudhon's preference for petty-bourgeois autonomy throughout his life, and the different interpretations given to the People's Bank mirrored the simmering conflict which lay at the heart of the relationship between the Revolution's two core classes. Proudhon wanted to protect the petty bourgeoisie by universalizing it, thus preserving the seed-bed of the problems whose final solution he imagined he understood.[48] His proposals should be seen as part of a well-established tradition among petty-bourgeois critics of large-scale production:

From the post-Napoleonic Radicalism in Britain to the Populists in the USA, all protest movements including farmers and small entrepreneurs can be recognized by their demand for financial unorthodoxy: they were all 'currency cranks.'[49]

The need to inject some life into the economy and defuse the workers' demands was as apparent to the Provisional Government as to Proudhon, even if its motivation was dramatically different from his. It had quickly repaid all its obligations to its creditors among the upper bourgeoisie well in advance of the due date, and to put state finances on a sound basis it now decreed a forty-five percent increase in the land tax. The "forty-five centimes" drove another wedge between the proletariat and the peasantry because it appeared that the Republic's social program was forcing the latter to shoulder the burden of the former's unemployment. The tax contributed to the increasing isolation of the Paris workers and helped turn the bulk of the petty bourgeoisie and peasantry against their social demands as the spring wore on. It fell heaviest on the peasants, and it seemed that they were being forced to pay to keep the workers idle—even though they were really financing the enrichment of speculators and government creditors.[50]

The ultimate cause of the workers' isolation from the rest of the country, however, was the fear of all the property-owning classes that satisfying the "right to work" might endanger property.[51] The upper bourgeoisie carefully nurtured this fear, and the Revolution's fate was decided when their desire to protect their smallholdings drove the bulk of the petty bourgeoisie and peasantry into the arms of the bourgeoisie.[52] The Revolution's uneven course posed distinctly modern challenges to the mass of France's smallholders, and if things worked out badly for the workers there was a portent of future victories in their present defeat:

> it soon became obvious that Paris had far outrun the rest of France. The dense mass of petty shopkeepers, small manufacturers, independent artisans, and peasant proprietors, whose small capital represented years of toil and self-denial, saw nothing in socialism but the equal division of property, and shuddered at the thought. The rift between the victors of February soon became irremediable.[53]

The elections of April 23 resulted in a very conservative Constituent Assembly. The political consolidation of a counterrevolutionary bourgeois republic was now possible, after which it would be necessary to eliminate the threat from the capital's workers.[54] Revolt was in the air from the elections on, fed by the Constituent Assembly's refusal to guarantee work and its ever-clearer desire to rid itself of the National Workshops.[55] The intense criticism of them appearing daily in the bourgeois press was preparing the mass of public opinion for the government's action,[56] and the Executive Commission of the Assembly secretly decided to abolish them as early as May 13.[57] The February Revolution's failure to break up the existing organization of political power guaranteed a basic continuity between the July Monarchy and the bourgeois republic which replaced it, and the two regimes' roots in private property proved far more important than the relatively trivial structural and personnel differences between them.

The Provisional Government was well aware that the dissolution of the National *Ateliers* would be taken as a declaration of war by the Parisian workers, and Proudhon himself came to this understanding as he assessed the disastrous elections of April 23.[58] He had expressed his fear before the elections that the gains of the February Revolution were in danger because the bourgeoisie was unwilling to deal with labor on any terms other than its own. The proletariat's demand that the elections be postponed to permit the opposition enough time to organize had attracted more than 200,000 demonstrators on March 16, but the Provisional Government had refused to even consider rescheduling the elections. Warning that France was falling into the "mystification of universal suffrage," Proudhon observed that "the surest way to make the people lie is to establish universal suffrage. Voting by head, as a fact of government and as a means of determining the national will, is exactly the same thing that a new division of the land would be in political economy. It's the agrarian law moved from the land to authority."[59] He knew that the left had suffered an enormous defeat in the election, raised the specter of civil war and suggested that the workers might have no alternative but to rise in revolt, although he cautioned them against such a step.[60]

Proudhon's sympathies were clearly with the workers but he wanted peaceful, intellectual debate above all, convinced that the truth could emerge only in a struggle of ideas.[61] "Killing people is the worst method for combatting principles. It's only through ideas that we can triumph over ideas," he advised the workers as late as May 4, echoing many of the sentiments he had expressed in his declaration to the voters of the Doubs two months earlier.[62] He was still looking for a "third term" between and property and communism, bourgeoisie and proletariat,[63] and he summarized his hopes for France with extraordinary clarity as civil war approached. The tensions of a *petit bourgeois* who wanted social peace at any cost were driving his politics, and it was sadly ironic that they would combine to paralyze him in the revolution's hour of maximum danger:

> What we want to abolish in capital is its preponderance over labor: the separation of the workers and the capitalists into two categories of people whose interests are contradictory, one of which is necessarily oppressive of the other. The worker and the capitalist are only one; they can no more be separated than the soul can be separated from the body. To separate them from the other, the soul from the body, is to simultaneously destroy both, to kill the man; similarly, to separate the worker from the capitalist is to plunder the first and bankrupt the second, to destroy production. Whatever precaution one takes or combination one imagines, from the moment the worker and the capitalist become two distinct figures, it is absolutely and mathematically certain either that the capitalist will crush the worker or that the worker will damage the capitalist.[64]

Proudhon's desire to solidify the "unity" of workers and capitalists stemmed from his conviction that society could not stand the shock of their separation. He still believed that increased production within a reformed capitalist framework could conciliate their interests and he continued to try to locate himself between and above both contending classes. Considering how fatal the impending divorce between the workers and the bulk of the petty bourgeoisie would be to the progress of the February Revolution, his concerns were well-founded. A deadly counter-revolution was taking shape, and the workers were alone.

Proudhon's decision to run for the Assembly on April 23 had come as a surprise, and when he ran again in a partial election on June 4 the contradiction between his antipolitical bias and his candidacy was again brought to the fore.[65] He was elected this time with 77,094 votes along with Victor Hugo, General Cavaignac, and Louis-Napoleon Bonaparte "thanks to proletarian discipline."[66] He was popular in Paris, and it is possible that he still hoped to induce the government to adopt his policies as a basis for action. But his desire to reconcile the interests of antagonistic classes soon came into conflict with political developments.

The Assembly's open war against February's social content took shape on June 21 as it decreed the abolition of the National *Ateliers*, ordered those workers in Paris for less than six months to go home, mandated the dismissal of any worker who refused work offered him, and scattered the others into the army or on rural public works projects. Troops had been moved into Paris to deal with the expected reaction, and two days after the decree the workers of the capital rose in a desperate and hopeless insurrection. Abandoned by their allies of February, they held out against cannon and terror for four days.[67] The entire proletariat was involved,[68] yet it was the ferocity of the bourgeoisie's response which determined the radical nature of the insurrection, for the workers' original demands were rather mild; they wanted the continuation of the inadequate National *Ateliers*, the removal of the army from Paris, the release of all their leaders imprisoned since May 15, and the assurance that "the people" would write the Second Republic's constitution.[69]

The June Days marked the highest level of class conflict yet reached in France: open massive armed combat between labor and capital. The brutality of the bourgeois counter-revolution put an end to most of the work begun by the February Revolution, and the thousands of dead and deported marked the definitive abandonment of democracy by the entire bourgeoisie as it organized itself into the "Party of Order."[70] The revolution's progress had boiled down to a one-sided struggle between the bourgeoisie and the proletariat for the allegiance of the small proprietors, but the bourgeoisie's momentary victory could not change the fact that every subsequent democratic movement would be driven by the social demands of the laboring poor. The split between its liberalism and the workers' socialism would dominate a good deal of French politics from June on. Democracy had begun to make possible the political expression of the workers' social demands, and the French bourgeoisie's abandonment of "its" principles when they threatened property was part of an 1848 trend so general that it continues to shape contemporary politics:

> On every side it was the liberal and democratic *bourgeoisie* that excited the revolutionary movement and attempted to limit its operation, but was overwhelmed by the action of the masses which it had itself set in motion, and which were resolved to profit by it on their own account even at the expense of their allies. Confronted by this unforeseen outburst, the liberal *bourgeoisie*, terrified by the specter of Communism, demanded a reaction. This it brought about at first by means of the National Guard, which took the field against the revolted masses in the towns and the country; but, this weak barrier proving insufficient, it joined hands with the ancient forces of reaction, the lately detested tyrants where they still existed, or new tyrants where they could be improvised.[71]

Proudhon blamed the Assembly for provoking the workers' rising and was horrified by the brutality with which the insurrection was repressed. If "there was both in the struggle and in the repression an element of implacable ferocity which had been absent in French history since the darkest days of the Terror,"[72] the *Représentant du Peuple* was fairly mild in public, obliquely attacking the Assembly and commending the insurgents' bravery. Proudhon himself did little more than indicate a willingness to mediate in a declaration he signed with Raspail, Leroux, Considerant, Greppo, and Blanc. Appearing as it did when the cannons of the army had reduced the workers to the Faubourg Saint-Antoine, the declaration was noteworthy because it indicated the limits beyond which even the most progressive members of the Assembly could not go:

> If we are chosen, we will enthusiastically go where the struggle is most intense but to bring only words of peace, convinced that the best way of reestablishing order and saving the Republic is to remember the slogan inscribed on the republican flag and invoke the sentiment of brotherhood.[73]

Despite this surrender to the same Assembly which was crying for the blood of the workers and the extirpation of socialism, Proudhon himself figured on some of the workers' lists for proposed new governments along with Blanqui, Barbès, Raspail, Cabet, Louis-Napoleon, Leroux, and Louis Blanc.[74] And, although he believed some of the bourgeoisie's propaganda during the June Days (for which he later professed himself later "deeply ashamed"),[75] it was also true that "the only place in the whole city where families of insurgents could go for relief was the office of Proudhon's newspaper."[76] So thorough was the reaction that even this modest measure made Proudhon stand out.

REACTION AND RESISTANCE

Proudhon was in a delicate personal and political position after the June Days. A target of the reactionaries for allegedly having fanned the revolt with his attacks on property, he was also violently criticized by the left for his vacillations and waverings since February. It was a position he had made for himself, and his reactions to and analysis of the June Days continued to illustrate the dilemma confronting him.

His first public statement about the insurrection came in a letter published on July 6 in the *Représentant du Peuple*. The paper had escaped being closed down by Cavaignac because of its relatively mild reaction to the June slaughter, and Proudhon carefully adopted a middle position. He was trying to decide whether the June rebellion had been "legitimate" or not, presumably because he wanted to decide whether it was worthy of his belated support. Since the Provisional Government had not violated the "republican principle" when it dissolved the National Workshops, the June insurrection was illegitimate; but then again, the rising was a reaction to real misery and hence was legitimate. He appealed to the Assembly for mercy, calling the June Days a tragedy in which both sides shared right and wrong. Since neither was completely responsible, neither should be condemned.

He continued this line of thinking in an article published two days later, suggesting that the June Days were caused by "history" to support his claim that no single party was responsible for what had happened. He was trying to convince the Assembly to be merciful with the insurgents, but he was also expressing his desire to protect the entire bourgeoisie from the consequences of its own victory. "It is not a matter of saving the proletariat; the proletariat doesn't exist any more, they've thrown it into the gutter," he declared. "We must save the bourgeoisie: the petty bourgeoisie from hunger, the middle bourgeoisie from ruin, the upper bourgeoisie from its infernal egoism. The question for the bourgeoisie today is what it was for the proletariat on June 23."[77]

His public position coincided with his privately-expressed sense of his role after June. He was appalled by the brutality of the reaction and planned to use *Le Représentant du Peuple* to help prevent further damage:

Le Représentant du Peuple
> Support the government.
> Its personnel is republican: only in politics, it's true, not in political economy.
> No faith in its ideas, much faith in its instincts.
> The majority of the Assembly is republican. Well-intentioned, like the middle bourgeoisie it represents.

But fearful, frightened by the noise of the reaction. Support it,
encourage it, give it some guarantees.[78]

Proudhon's attempt to maintain his neutrality soon broke down because
the offensive by the right did not abate as he hoped it would. As it became
clear that even the most modest gains of February were under attack he
started slowly moving to the left. His famous and courageous speech to the
Assembly of July 31, 1848, resulted from this motion.[79]

The speech was the occasion of Proudhon's second formal suggestion that
the state establish a "Banque" to organize credit and circulation and stimu-
late the economy. Yet it was only partly a defense of his favorite project,
for he was surely under no illusion that a rabidly counter-revolutionary
bourgeoisie would be more willing to entertain such a suggestion after its
June victory than it had been before. The speech's importance lay in
Proudhon's suddenly open support of the workers, socialism, and the original aims of the February Revolution, of which "the right to work" remained
central. Declaring it essential that the workers have jobs and attacking the
outraged Assembly for its brutality, arrogance, and ignorance, Proudhon
repeated his demand for free credit, linked it to an attack on property and
again claimed that only a reorganization of the economy along the lines he
had been suggesting for years could solve France's social problems. He was
not really proposing anything new here, but in the atmosphere following
the June Days his repetition of the "real" aims of February and his earlier
proposals for reform were acts of genuine courage. It took an uncommon
degree of fortitude to tell the bourgeoisie that "the Revolution" would like
its cooperation as it continued its inexorable march toward "social liquidation," but that it would proceed even in the face of its bitter opposition.

The speech marked a certain departure from Proudhon's earlier tendency
to bridge over differences and seek to conciliate the interests of workers
and owners, for he was trying to enlist the support of the petty bourgeoisie
for the social content of the workers' February program.[80] Like many Frenchmen, he appears to have been genuinely horrified by the bourgeoisie's brutality and its evident intention to completely destroy any possibility of social
reform. His declaration that he stood by the stricken proletariat was a strong
challenge to the Assembly, and he drew a line between the bourgeoisie and
the proletariat and threatened the former with class war because he was
trying to frighten its political representatives into adopting his ideas.

The speech was courageous but it left him vulnerable. His legislative proposal
was rejected by 691–2 with only his friend Greppo joining him, and the
Assembly then passed a motion censuring him on five counts: harming
public morality, violating property, encouraging revolt, appealing to peoples' lowest passions, and insulting the February Revolution by trying to

use it to support his "antisocial" theories. He was now under constant attack from all directions, and on July 10 Cavaignac temporarily suspended the *Représentant du Peuple*. Proudhon remained in the Assembly for the moment despite having been censured.

The first article he wrote after the paper's suspension was lifted was an attack on the measures taken against the press by Cavaignac and the Assembly. The article was a strong defense of freedom of speech and accused the reaction of being antisocial, since freedom of speech was a necessary condition of social health.[81] The next day an article attacking Malthusianism appeared; it was timely, because the view that poverty and starvation were caused by the ignorance and intemperance of the poor was popular among those anxious to defend bourgeois behavior since February. Mounting an aggressive, clear, and effective attack, Proudhon claimed that bourgeois society's disorganization was responsible for widespread suffering and pointed to the self-serving nature of the theories being advanced: "they are courageous and stoic, the malthusians, when it comes to sacrificing millions of workers."[82]

Proudhon got bolder as the summer progressed. Yet the reaction was gathering strength throughout this period, and he was clearly involved in a losing struggle to salvage what was left of February's social revolution from a triumphant bourgeoisie intent on obliterating it. Like everything else associated with the workers, he was under continuous and hysterical attack from the right-wing press and the bulk of the Assembly and had time to issue only one more article defending the workers and attacking the reactionaries.[83] On August 24 the Assembly voted to permanently suppress the *Représentant du Peuple* on General Cavaignac's recommendation.

Proudhon's reactions to the June Days were a crystallization of the tensions at work within him and the small proprietors whose defense lay at the heart of what he was trying to do. His desire to protect the petty bourgeoisie and avoid political confrontation were mixed with defiance, courage, and a defense of the proletariat. There were two contradictory forces at work, forces which had been present in his more abstract early writings but which were now revealed in his reactions to the twists and turns of political affairs. These two tendencies were themselves linked, both being called into play by the nature of his basic project.

On one hand, Proudhon was deeply suspicious of the bourgeoisie's motives and knew how important it was to defend the workers. He assigned primary responsibility for France's social crisis to its shortsighted greed and believed that subjecting property to some sort of democratic control had become an essential condition of social health. He understood that the peasantry, petty bourgeoisie, and proletariat had to stand together and support one another against common antagonists.[84] The Revolution of 1848 had raised the issue of the specifically proletarian struggle against property, and Proudhon knew that, in "affirming the authority and preponderance of labor, we recognize only one sort of right, the right to work, one class of producers, the working class, one interest, that of production."[85] The confusion of an uncommonly complicated period did not prevent him from defending the workers in the interests of all who labored.

At the same time, however, Proudhon's desire to defend and universalize small property led him to look to the bourgeoisie for leadership and try to escape from the unsettling and potentially dangerous influence of the proletariat. This tendency dominated his development from February to June and was first manifested in his letter to the electors of the Doubs.[86] Although personal considerations doubtless played a role in shaping his position, political and social forces were of determining influence.[87] His criticisms of property notwithstanding, Proudhon was never tempted to become a communist. Before 1848 "socialism" had described a school of thought which placed "the social question" at the center of its analyses of public life. After 1848 it came to describe those who were committed, to a greater or lesser degree, to the limitation or abolition of private property in the means of production. Proudhon's ambiguity about this matter reflected the fact that he stood at a transitional moment in the development of modern European socialism and this is what ultimately shaped his reactions to the events of 1848.

Yet this does not mean that he was incapable of change as the social forces set in motion by the February Revolution continued to develop. Indeed we might expect him to swing to the left as France moved right, becoming once again the critic and "homme-terreur" as the bourgeoisie moved to consolidate its June victory. When the proletariat had been in motion Proudhon, like the rest of the petty bourgeoisie, had moved toward the bourgeoisie. As the victors of June moved against the petty bourgeoisie, he moved toward the proletariat. In this respect his own development faithfully mirrored that of the petty bourgeoisie itself. Hostile to the concentrated property of the bourgeoisie but equally frightened by to the propertylessness of the proletariat, Proudhon's twists and turns were driven by his desire to mitigate or eliminate "extremism" and construct a safe area within which France's millions of small proprietors could find safety from revolution and reaction alike. The independent political activity of the workers during the Revolution of 1848 made things very difficult for him, and his immediate reaction was to try to right the scales after the class struggle had tipped them in one direction or another.

CONSOLIDATION

The June massacre had definitively tipped the political scale toward the *haute bourgeoisie* which, emboldened by its decisive victory, moved quickly to eliminate all significant opposition from below, establish the political structure of its rule, and settle the differences between the parties which composed it. The threat of revolution had not completely disappeared even after the June Days, and the violent repression which swept over the country was a measure of the bourgeoisie's awareness of potential danger.[88] In the absence of a political framework within which it could rule as a united class, the "parti d'ordre" exercised power through Cavaignac and the army, and a series of political and economic measures were borrowed from the Restoration to organize the counter-revolution.[89]

Cavaignac ruled France through a permanent state of siege until October 12. All political clubs were dissolved, the citizenry was disarmed, thousands of workers were imprisoned and deported, and 50,000 troops were kept in reserve in and around Paris. The working day was lengthened to twelve hours, wages were slashed, imprisonment for debt was reintroduced, and the government started extending large interest-free loans to the *haute bourgeoisie*. A 24,000-franc deposit for newspapers appearing in Paris strengthened a strict censorship of virtually all publications and silenced the democratic and socialist opposition. Freed for the moment from the immediate fear of proletarian revolution, the bourgeoisie quickly moved to establish its exclusive political domination and break its tentative alliance with the petty bourgeoisie.[90] With the necessity to compromise now eliminated by the completeness of its June victory, it no longer had to retain the illusion that the bourgeoisie spoke for anyone but itself. As Marx observed, "thus, after the democratic representatives of the petty bourgeoisie had long been repulsed by the bourgeois representatives of the bourgeoisie within the National Assembly, this parliamentary breach received its civil, real economic meaning, when the petty bourgeois as debtors were handed over to the bourgeois as creditors. A large part of the former were completely ruined and the remainder were only allowed to continue their business under conditions which made them virtual serfs of capital."[91]

The *petite bourgeoisie* had turned itself over to the bourgeoisie in the spring because of its fear of the proletariat, but it now found itself under attack by its former ally. When the proletariat had pushed "the social question" close to its logical conclusion of an assault on private property, the small proprietors had sided with the bourgeoisie; now, with the workers eliminated from the stage, it was left alone against the bulk of the *haute bourgeoisie* organized in the "parti d'ordre." Had this situation persisted it would have been easy for the victorious upper bourgeoisie to finish off its former ally and dispense with its democratic pretensions after June. But the bourgeoisie was split into republican and monarchist factions. This provided the bulk of the democratic petty bourgeoisie with a new ally in the republican bourgeoisie, for both parties were anxious to preserve the last political remnant of the February Revolution. It turned out that the remaining political forms were empty and irrelevant, for the "pure" republicans had organized the repression of the workers, were utterly unable to offer a coherent alternative to the extremism of the reaction, and were easily pushed aside when the monarchists had no further need of them. The bourgeoisie as a whole had definitively abandoned democracy after its decisive June victory, and the petty bourgeoisie found itself in the paradoxical position of taking its lead from the declining republicans during the fall and winter of 1848.

Proudhon's own motion mirrored the political evolution of the *petite bourgeoisie* during this period of intense reaction. He was struck by the ferocity of the repression after June[92] and continued to experiment with projects for preserving France's small proprietors.[93] He and his former collaborators on the *Représentant du Peuple* were hard at work raising the deposit for a new paper and his second attempt at political journalism allowed him to join the debate about a proposal for a new constitution which had been put before the Assembly by the *Parti d'Ordre*.

A specimen copy of *Le Peuple* appeared on September 4.[94] In it Proudhon declared that since France was in the grip of the counter-revolution the newspaper would continue the work of expressing "la pensée ouvrière" begun by the *Représentant du Peuple* and would defend what little remained of the February Revolution.[95] Saying even that took some courage in the fall of 1848, and the ferocity of the reaction is illustrated by the fact that Proudhon was assuming a political position he would never have taken in the spring. "The February Revolution," he claimed, "which had to satisfy all the people's wishes betrayed in July, is no longer, like that of 89 and 92, only one stage in our emancipation; it will be the last."[96]

Proudhon did not enter the political struggle to defend the existing constitution and brutally reactionary Assembly with great enthusiasm, for he remained deeply convinced that "it's politics which is the source of all mischief. It alone distracts us from economic questions, from the real revolution."[97] Despite his misgivings, however, the contradictory motion of the counter-revolution forced him to defend the republic against the monarchists.

Proudhon's reentry into political life was capped by a speech he delivered at an October 15 banquet to unite all the parties and individuals who wanted to defend the February Revolution. Two thousand democratic and socialist Parisians were there,[98] and his *Toast à la Révolution* summarized his thoughts about February's significance.[99] He suggested that human history had been marked by one central revolutionary trend which had taken different forms in four different historical periods, a theme he would later develop in some detail. The Christian revolution had freed the heart from law and ritual, the Enlightenment's philosophic revolution had liberated reason from theology, and the French Revolution had laid the foundations for political freedom in place of medieval prejudice and particularism. He defined the completion of this single revolution as mankind's great task: "after having been religious, philosophic and political in turn, the Revolution has become economic."[100] Social transformation was now on humanity's agenda. Proudhon's speech served both as a summary and as a foundation on which he would continue his attempt to understand current events in a historical perspective.

Two weeks later, he addressed himself to the proposed new constitution.[101] He was against it, he said, because it was a constitution, because any attempt to "solve" France's problems politically could only exacerbate them. He was opposed to the establishment of universal suffrage in the absence of substantial economic equality because it would substitute a sham, formalistic equality for a real, substantive one. He was opposed to the proposed constitution's most important feature, fearing that in dividing sovereignty and creating a strong executive the constitution was institutionalizing a permanent threat to freedom. He articulated a clear preference for parliamentary rule, the first indication that he would soon be moving to defend an utterly reactionary Assembly against an even more dangerous president. Finally, he said, he was against the constitution because public discussion of it had taken place under the shadow of a state of siege and a near-total censorship.

He voted against the constitution on November 4, but that did not stop the Assembly from accepting it by the lopsided margin of 739–30.[102] The vote indicated the extent to which the bourgeois republicans dominated the Constituent Assembly, and it placed Proudhon on record as initially opposing the same constitution he would later take many risks to defend. In this he mirrored the dilemma of the petty bourgeoisie in the fall of 1848, a dilemma whose outlines were completed with the election of Louis-Napoleon Bonaparte as President of the Republic.

The new constitution established a strong presidential power to fill out the institutional framework of the republic and the Assembly had set December 10, 1848, as election day. The monarchical fraction of the bourgeoisie needed a candidate and, unable to settle the split between its own Orleanist and Legitimist wings, selected Prince Louis-Napoleon Bonaparte, the Emperor's mysterious nephew.[103] He had been in England during the June Days and throughout the summer and so was not associated with the repression carried out by the "pure" republicans. No one knew very much about him, but he had been elected to the Assembly a second time in a tremendous personal triumph on September 17, receiving 300,000 votes in the five departments in which he ran.[104] His advantage was precisely that he was unknown except for his famous name, everyone else available to the "parti d'ordre" being unacceptable because of their public association with the reaction. The problem was that he was a known anti-republican adventurer, had a seedy and disreputable reputation, appeared to be an imbecile, and was deeply in debt. Yet he soon became the candidate of the monarchist bourgeoisie, helped no doubt by his friend Persigny's successful effort to convince the "parti d'Ordre" that its interests lay in backing him:

> I am no more republican than you; the republic is a calamity for France; your best chances, if you look objectively at the situation, is not at all where you stubbornly insist on looking, at Claremont or Wiesbaden; they are at the Elysée and nowhere else. If those who possess want to continue to possess, only a consular or imperial dictatorship will dependably permit it; its name—Napoleon—will suffice to dazzle the proletarians; they will accept as a 'crowned democracy' any regime where Louis Bonaparte will be the master. You, royalists, will have the satisfaction of living, in fact, under a new monarchy: a new monarchy, but a monarchy all the same; and to all of you proprietors, the concentration of power in Louis Bonaparte's hands will bring the most concrete of realities instead of a shadow: the security of your interests and the absolute triumph of order.[105]

Louis-Napoleon won an overwhelming victory on December 10, gaining 5,434,266 votes out of nearly 7,000,000 total ballots.[106] Persigny's extraordinary private condor notwithstanding, the peasantry voted for Napoleon because he represented sweet revenge on the republic and its "forty-five centimes."[107] Those workers who could vote cast their ballots for him because they could not bring themselves to cast their ballots for the "pure republican" Cavaignac, the "butcher of June."[108] For the petty bourgeoisie the defeat of some of their creditors brought satisfaction and some hope of change, and for the *haute bourgeoisie* Napoleon was the victory of the monarchists over the republicans. For everyone it was the end of the hated, reactionary, and brutal bourgeois republic, and the meaning of the vote would soon become clear to all:

> Napoleon III, in after years, always claimed that his true title to power was neither heredity nor the coup d'etat, but the popular election of the 10th of December. There could be no doubt as to the sincerity of the vote or its meaning. In choosing Louis-Napoleon simply because he was a Bonaparte, the people did certainly not express their wish for a parliamentary republic. On December 10th, the Empire was virtually made.... The coup d'etat, the 'crime' of 1851, was but the natural consequence of the presidential election.[109]

Louis-Napoleon did not fool Proudhon, who was implacably hostile to the Prince throughout the campaign. Upon his return to France, Bonaparte had requested interviews with many prominent political figures, and Proudhon had jotted down his initial impressions in his diary:

> This man *appears* well-intentioned to me with his chivalrous head and heart, more full of his uncle's glory than of an active ambition, yet a mediocre soul. I doubt that when viewed closely *and well known he can make himself acceptable.* Be careful—every pretender begins by stroking the heads of parties.[110]

Proudhon was concerned that a strong presidency was a threat to the republic, and he repeatedly warned that Louis-Napoleon should not be trusted. He was worried that the long-term effects of the election of December 10 because it confirmed his suspicion of the ballot as the exclusive or accurate gauge of the popular will. He worried that people would tend to vote for their "natural superiors," that their attention would be diverted from the social and economic roots of their problems, that an impotent and irrelevant opposition could justify its inactivity by invoking the empty formalities of political liberty, and that the oppressive and dictatorial rule of small propertied minorities could be legitimized through elections. His suspicions about the presidency and the president could not bring him to support Cavaignac,[111] and he expressed his dismay at Louis-Napoleon's popularity in the pages of *Le Peuple*:

> Come then, Napoleon, take possession of this race of hypocrites, of these fawning courtiers. They say that you're nothing but a cretin, an adventurer, a fool. You have been a policeman and played at comedy; you have all the stuffing, with a ferocity which is not of this age, of Nero and Caligula. Come, I tell you, you are the man we need. Come bring these bourgeois to order; come take their last child and their last centime.... Come end our disagreements and take our freedom! Come consummate the shame of the French people. Come, come, come...[112]

While advising his readers to vote because "politics demands it," Proudhon urged them not to participate in the undermining of democracy that the election of a president—any president—implied. Declaring that "I protest against existing society and I search for science; in this double sense, I am a socialist,"[113] Proudhon endorsed Raspail's protest against both the constitution and the presidency despite his communist views. By the end of 1848 Proudhon was being read by 40,000 working-class readers.[114] And, his hostility to politics notwithstanding, his endorsement of Raspail certainly reserved considerable supervisory authority to a democratic state which would encourage and protect the "social liquidation" he had begun to outline earlier:

> We want the mines, canals and railroads turned over to workers' associations which would be democratically organized and would work under state supervision. We want these associations to be models for agriculture, industry and commerce, first nuclei of the vast federation of companies and associations reunited on the common ground of a democratic and social republic.[115]

If he was critical of anyone on the left, it was of Ledru Rollin and the petty bourgeois democrats for really trying to win the election.[116] That Proudhon was thinking of little more than defending the republic was clear in his recommendations to the proletariat:

> We say that the proletariat must be careful to avoid any attack, direct or indirect, financial or other, against capital and property because such an attack, no matter what one calls it, would only be a way of recognizing the preponderance of capital, a contradiction. It is in working on itself and by itself, through association, mutual guarantee and spontaneous organization, that labor can triumph over capital.
>   In 89, the Revolution's goal was the displacement of power and property; that's why that Revolution was a battle. In 1848, the Revolution's goal is the democratization and reorganization of property; that's why this revolution is a fusion. Now, one can organize or fuse only with principles; force and fraud are unable to conciliate or organize.[117]

As Louis-Napoleon was forming his first cabinet, Proudhon urged that the left adopt a minimum strategy of trying to hold the president to his oath of office—especially his pledge that he would respect the constitution, serve only one term, and turn power over to his duly-elected successor.[118] Having suggested this line of defense, he sat back with the rest of France to gauge Louis-Napoleon's intentions. He was not kept waiting for long.

Louis-Napoleon's first ministry was assigned the twin tasks of restoring political "order" and dismantling virtually everything that had happened in France since February.[119] The attempt to organize a joint dictatorship of all factions of the bourgeoisie having failed, the new governmental apparatus for consolidating the counter-revolution was clearly a reflection of the tasks set for it by the president. Its personnel and policy reflected the basic continuity of all bourgeois politics in this age of nascent social revolution, for "the ministry was principally composed of former left orleanist parliamentarians, those who would have formed the government in February if the revolution could have been avoided."[120]

The contradictory motion of the counter-revolution meant that Louis-Napoleon's attack on the republic and the constitution took the form of an attack on the reactionary Assembly and its republican majority. At the president's instigation, a Representative Rateau introduced a "proposition de loi" on January 6 that the Assembly dissolve itself. The monarchist bourgeoisie's demand that the republicans go home was finally defeated on January 29, and the Assembly seemed to have won the first round of its struggle with the Elysée. It was during these battles that the *petite bourgeoisie* in the Assembly, led by the "democratic-socialist party" but including several independents such as Proudhon, became little more than an appendage of the republican bourgeoisie. Its attempt to protect the constitution from the Prince president's obvious intention to install himself *en permanence* would be its first—and last—attempt to protect what little remained of February. The Revolution's failure to break the political structure of bourgeois rule guaranteed the generally smooth development of counter-revolution and France's unobstructed descent into reaction.

Proudhon was sufficiently notorious by the end of 1848 to be the subject of ridicule in at least one popular reactionary play, but he outdid himself in his attacks on Louis-Napoleon during the "January crisis."[121] Three days before the Assembly was to vote on Rateau's motion Proudhon submitted a violent attack on the president to *Le Peuple*.[122] The next day a more extreme article appeared, Proudhon calling Louis-Napoleon the incarnation of the counter-revolution and demanding that the Assembly remove him from office. Contending that the legislature and the constitution were now the expressions of February, Proudhon launched a bitter and violent attack on the "bastard of universal suffrage":

> Bonaparte, elect of the reaction, instrument of the reaction, personification of the reaction, Bonaparte is the entire reaction at the moment; whoever opposes Bonaparte is unquestionably a revolutionary; with Bonaparte fallen, the whole doctrinaire, legitimist, orleanist, imperialist, capitalist and jesuit conspiracy will collapse with him.[123]

The edition of *Le Peuple* carrying this call was immediately seized, and the next day the Procurator General accused Proudhon of three major political crimes before the Assembly: "attacking the President, exciting hate or contempt for the government, and seeking to trouble public order by setting citizens against each other."[124] The government indicated its desire to bring Proudhon to trial and asked the Assembly to lift his parliamentary immunity. A commission was established to study the matter.

The threat of jail did not bother Proudhon, for he was convinced that the president fully intended to destroy even the hollow political shell of February and had become the major threat to freedom.[125] He urged the Assembly to defend itself and the constitution in several more articles at the end of January, and if he was following in the wake of the republicans his bravery at this time was unquestionable. His concerns were primarily political because Louis-Napoleon's demagoguery disturbed him, but personal considerations played a role as well.[126] "It is in my nature to always contradict authority," he had written to a friend earlier; now he could be a rebel and be sure that he was defending freedom at the same time.[127] Yet he was irritated that the Assembly was even considering lifting his immunity,[128] and when it did so on February 14 he discovered to his chagrin that its bourgeois nature and commitment to property were more important than its republicanism and connection to February.[129]

If Proudhon was in a difficult position in the Assembly, he remained popular with his proletarian and petty-bourgeois readers. The circulation of *Le Peuple* was 25,000 per day in the middle of February 1849, and since its working-class readership passed the newspaper around it is likely that well over 50,000 people read his long commentaries and were familiar with his thinking.[130] He wanted to place his real position in its proper light at this time, and a discussion on the necessary conditions for a healthy revolution affirmed that it must be peaceful, legal (based on established law), and "legitimate" (growing out of some sort of previous social organization).[131] Unable to contemplate a decisive break with the existing order, Proudhon was trying to separate himself from any attempt to remove Louis-Napoleon by force of arms, and he continued his retreat when he tried to explain his real desires to a conservative correspondent:

> I did not provoke the February Revolution; I wanted slow, measured, rational and philosophic progress; events and human foolishness, especially from those teasing and mediocre bourgeois of whom you are a part, made things work out differently. I promised myself that, to the extent that it would depend on me, the results of the February Revolution would not be lost; I said to myself that one would have to make a century's progress in a year unless one wanted to be doing nonsensical things.[132]

Despite this disclaimer, the Seine Assizes found Proudhon guilty of the charges brought against him on March 28, 1849. He was condemned to three years in jail and a fine of 3,000 francs. The bourgeoisie and its government wanted order, and Proudhon knew that he had become one of its victims. Refusing to accept the sentence, he went underground but was recognized and jailed on June 5. *Le Peuple* was suppressed in the reaction which followed the abortive demonstrations of June 13 called to protest the government's intervention to protect the Pope from the Roman Republic.

POLITICS AND ANARCHISM

Even while jailed, Proudhon remained an influential figure in Paris and his words continued to carry weight. As a political prisoner he was deprived of his ability to directly influence public affairs but the facilities at Sainte-Pélagie were reasonably comfortable, he had all the books he wanted, and he was able to write and publish.[133] Because the history of the Revolution of 1848 had suddenly become contested terrain he began a project to set the record straight and explain his own role in the momentous events of that year. Still shocked by the disastrous consequences of the workers' political isolation in June and trying to figure out a way to convince the bourgeoisie that its long-run interests lay with "the revolution," he had a reasonably clear sense of how he wanted to proceed:

Work with the bourgeoisie. Make it see that socialism is in its interests, that it has to happen in *the people* to begin with; that we are sure of them. A bourgeois, liberal, voltarian, anti-jesuit and anti-papal socialism: that's what we want.
    Take care of the bourgeoisie; treat it as the first victims.[134]

Proudhon's continuing attempt to construct an alliance between the workers and small proprietors which would anchor a "liberal bourgeois socialism" would be shaped by his leftward drift as the political reaction deepened. The history on which he was working illustrated this motion, as did the articles he wrote for *La Voix du Peuple*, a new newspaper financed by his friend and admirer Alexander Herzen.[135] Its first number appeared on September 25 and was immediately popular, Proudhon retaining considerable influence with his working-class readers. He described the paper as a "journal of discussion" rather than a "journal of combat" (his characterization of *Le Peuple*),[136] but he was soon attacking Louis-Napoleon for the overthrow of the Roman Republic, his alliance with the Church, and his moves against the Assembly.[137] Proudhon certainly wanted peace and quiet after the Revolution's drama and instability, but he was one of the most prominent ideological representatives of the popular movement and felt compelled to defend as much of the legacy of 1848 as he could.

His *Confessions d'un révolutionnaire* was meant to "serve as the history of the February Revolution."[138] It appeared at the end of October 1849 and is the most coherent Proudhonist explanation of the February Revolution's historical significance. Despite the speed with which it was written, it stands with the work of Marx and Tocqueville as one of the best contemporary accounts of the events of 1848. It also provided Proudhon with the opportunity to systematize many of the conclusions to which he had come since February.

The *Confessions* opened the period of his strongest "antigouver-nementalisme," and it is during this period that Proudhon became the "father of anarchism." He grasped the Revolution's central truth that France's social and economic problems could no longer be addressed unless the existing distribution of property was changed. Even if he wanted to protect the bourgeoisie, petty bourgeoisie, and workers from one another, he also knew that political liberalism could not provide a credible framework for ordering the market relations which were at the root of France's social chaos. The social content of "the revolution" was coming into violent conflict with its political form, and Proudhon's anarchism represented his response to this contradiction.

His earlier conviction that politics could not be used to address social problems was expanded to the position that politics and government were harmful and negative by definition. In a period when the executive power of the state was growing in importance every day and was clearly in the service of the counter-revolution, Proudhon looked to the absorption of the government into "l'organisation industrielle" and counterpoised the initiative and spontaneity of the masses to the rigidity and immovability of the state. "A revolution," he held, "is an explosion of organic force, an evolution of society from the inside out," and[139] in fact "what the government does is by nature immobilist, conservative, resistant to all initiative, even counter-revolutionary, while a revolution is an organic thing, a *creative* thing, and Power is mechanical or executive."[140]

If the Revolution's goal is to liberate society from the state and eliminate the "artificial" restrictions on social initiative that any organization of public power represents, it follows that any hierarchical concentration of power is an enemy of liberty and freedom. A mechanical sort of materialism was advanced to prove Proudhon's contention that if the state is rooted in the social relations of the economy, then political power is inherently unable to change the property relations on which it is based and from which it draws sustenance.[141] The state is now the alienation of the "force collective" that Proudhon had identified earlier and its inherent tendency to grasp power and enlarge its scope of activity always came as an attack on the social spontaneity whose preservation was the revolution's *raison d'être*. "No authority, no government—even a popular one; that's where the revolution is," Proudhon declared.[142] Social vitality cannot be organized from a central place, and it is of the state's essence that it try to centralize everything, appropriate to itself, aggrandize its influence. "In matters of revolution, initiative is as repugnant to the state as work is repugnant to capital."[143]

Any government, regardless of its form, the individuals occupying its key positions, or the class it serves, is now an enemy of social health. Driven by the basic continuity between all the bourgeois governments he had seen come to power, try to organize themselves, and yield to their successors, Proudhon's anarchism now rejected any political formation and reaffirmed the "être collectif" whose spontaneity is inherently opposed to any state formation. Capital, religion, power, Church, and state were collapsed together, all founded on the "fatal" proposition that the people cannot legislate for themselves but must represent their sovereignty to self-appointed spokesmen. Social order and the state are now mutually incompatible; at the bottom of Proudhon's rapidly-developing anarchism is a criticism of authority which holds that political power is a usurpation, a theft of the people's "force collective." Fundamentally despotic, the state strives for monopoly and can develop only as it stifles the autonomy of its constituent parts.

Proudhon's hostility to Rousseau was expressed in his conviction that there can be no single, identifiable, and unitary general will which can express the best interests of any group of people. His pluralistic vantage point led him to argue that "the people" can never consist of more than a number of reasoning, morally independent individuals whose wills can be expressed or represented only in social interactions. Inherently hierarchical, political rule is based on antagonism, competition, arbitrariness, and false claims to universality. No conceivable state can express or organize popular interests, and Proudhon attacked what he thought was Rousseau's effort to impose an arbitrary and metaphysical political yoke on a vibrant and dynamic social order.

His most significant argument with the classical left derived from a criticism of Rousseau which was rooted in his rejection of the view that political power can be an instrument of social reconstruction. He bequeathed to anarchism both its major point of agreement with classical socialism—the criticism of the state—and its major disagreement with what became Marxism's core position that political power can serve social revolution.[144] Proudhon's theory of liberty and order was coming to rest on the decidedly nonpolitical foundation of equal exchange between substantially equal contracting parties, and the revolution's goals must now be to "dissolve, immerse and make the political or governmental system disappear into the economic system in reducing, simplifying, decentralizing and suppressing the entire machine which we call the government or the state."[145] Society is an intricate web of differentiated personal relations which spontaneously express and organize the connections between independent wills. Individual conscience and voluntary mutual agreement are the only durable foundations of social peace. Law should aim at encouraging and regularizing exchange, not at imposing uniform, general, and necessarily arbitrary rules. If Rousseau favored the Republic One and Indivisible, Proudhon's preference was clearly for a network of associations and private groupings in which "each individual would be equally and simultaneously producer and consumer, citizen and prince, ruler and ruled."[146] This point of view is what lay behind his famous denunciation of the state:

> To be governed is to be watched over, inspected, spied on, directed, legislated at, regulated, docketed, indoctrinated, preached at, controlled, assessed, weighed, censored, ordered about, by men who have neither the right nor the knowledge nor the virtue. To be governed means to be, at each operation, at each transaction, at each movement, noted, registered, controlled, stamped, measured, valued, assessed, patented, licensed, authorized, endorsed, admonished, hampered, reformed, rebuked, arrested. It is to be, on the pretext of the general interest, taxed, drilled, held for ransom, exploited, monopolized, exhorted, squeezed, tricked, robbed; then at the least resistance, at the first word of complaint, to be repressed, fined, abused, annoyed, followed, bullied, beaten, disarmed, strangled, imprisoned, machine-gunned, judged, condemned, deported, whipped, sold, betrayed and finally mocked, ridiculed, insulted, dishonored. That's government, that's its justice, that's its morality![147]

If this stage of Proudhon's development represents one of the high points of nineteenth-century antipolitical socialism, his attacks on the state formed the basis of his charge that Leroux, Blanc, Ledru-Rollin, and all the other leaders of 1848 had betrayed the people through their statism. Blanc was singled out and violently attacked as an enemy of freedom, a "man of power."[148] Proudhon may have wanted to solidify the unity of the bourgeoisie, petty bourgeoisie, and proletariat, but he was not prepared to cooperate with any individual or political sect which ignored the lessons of history and stood in the way of progress:

> In the nineteenth century, the revolution has a double aim:
> 1. In the economic order, it aims at the complete subordination of capital to labor, the identification of the worker with the capitalist by democratizing credit, annihilating interest and reducing all transactions which involve the instruments and products of work to equal and true exchange. From this point of view, we have been the first to say that there are only two parties in France, the party of work and the party of capital.
> 2. In the political order, the Revolution aims at absorbing the state into society, that is, moving to the elimination of all authority and to the suppression of the entire governmental machine by abolishing taxes, simplifying administration, and separately centralizing each functional category, in order words by organizing universal suffrage. From this point of view, once again, we say that there are only two parties in France: the party of freedom and the party of government.[149]

Driven by his conviction that only he knew what was best for France, Proudhon's attacks on the traditional left were as strong and as uncompromising as they had ever been. He considered soliciting help from Louis-Napoleon so his campaign could continue[150] and yet refused to assign responsibility for the June Days to any particular party or class. He remained convinced that his *Banque du Peuple* would have begun the reorganization of society if it had gotten off the ground.[151] The *Banque* was the instrument of social liquidation and the true answer to the left's false faith in the state. "To destroy the government is to replace administrative or political unity with economic unity. There is liberty and equality only with political decentralization and economic unity. This is the central idea of the People's Bank," he asserted.[152] The explicit antigovernmentalism might have been expressed in new ways but it sprang from old roots, and Proudhon's position that the immediate abolition of the state is the essence of the socialist project would be the important theoretical divide between anarchism and socialism from then on.[153]

His hostility to the state led to important short-run errors of judgement which would get him in a lot of trouble. He was impressed that Louis-Napoleon belonged to no established party and seemed hostile to all political groupings. Proudhon hoped that he represented the end of organized political power, and the *Confessions* contain some hopeful and ultimately naive speculation that the president would lead France to the "république démocratique et sociale."[154] He apologized for his past attacks against Louis-

Napoleon, suggesting that he had been a "reactionary" in opposing the Prince.[155] This position was in direct contradiction to what he had said before and would say later of the president, about whom his opinions remained ambiguous. He also acknowledged that he had believed the Provisional Government's propaganda during June that secret communist societies were misleading the workers with the aid of mysterious foreigners, admitting his "irreparable fault" and disgustedly calling himself an "imbecile."[156]

Proudhon was surprised in retrospect that he had run for political office in the spring and was even more surprised that the workers had taken his candidacy seriously enough to vote for him. At the same time, he wondered why the bourgeoisie had taken him for an ogre:

> When I think about all that I've said, written and published for ten years on the role of government in society, on the subordination of power and the revolutionary incapacity of the government, I'm tempted to think that my election in June 1848 was the result of popular misunderstanding. These ideas are as old as my first thoughts; they are contemporaneous with my vocation as a socialist . . . it is strange that . . . I could have appeared for an instant as a fearful agitator to a society which I take as a judge and to a Power which I do not covet.[157]

His evident hostility to politics notwithstanding, Proudhon continued to hold many positions which were characteristic of petty-bourgeois democracy throughout this period. Unable to break with property or abandon his hope that the bourgeoisie could be won over to "the revolution" and save France further agony, he continued to develop a highly idiosyncratic and increasingly utopian version of socialism which remained oriented toward the needs of the petty bourgeoisie even as he thought it provided the most comprehensive solution to France's problems:

> socialism is not simply the elimination of misery, the abolition of capitalism and of wage-labor, the transformation of property, the decentralization of government, the organization of universal suffrage, the effective and direct sovereignty of the workers, the equilibration of economic forces, the substitution of the contractual regime for the legal regime, etc. It is, in the most rigorous meaning of the term, the establishment of middle fortunes, the universalization of the middle class.[158]

Proudhon still regarded the organization and equilibration of economic forces as the foundation of any meaningful social reorganization. If he was convinced for the moment that the state could play no positive role in solving "the social problem," he would have to think through how he proposed to organize "free and mutual credit." The "mutualism" of his later years would replace the radical-sounding anarchism of the immediate post-revolutionary period and reserve a somewhat amplified role for politics, but Proudhon would remain convinced that only if it were afforded a chance to become a small proprietor could the proletariat break the chains which bound it, become its own master and attain "la dignité bourgeoise."[159]

When the "democratic-socialist party" scored a stunning victory in the partial parliamentary elections of March 10, 1850, the guerilla war the president had been conducting against the Assembly came to an abrupt stop. The "spectre rouge" had surfaced once again, and the election of the pseudo-socialist Eugene Sue on April 28 only increased the terror of both political branches of the counter-revolution. Universal suffrage was becoming a risk to the rule of the *haute bourgeoisie*, and so on May 31, 1850, the Assembly abolished it. Since it was guaranteed by the constitution and both Louis-Napoleon and the monarchists were claiming to defend the republic, abolition was carried out "legally" by establishing a three-year residency requirement. One-third of the eligible voters, most of them proletarians, were eliminated at one stroke.[160] Sixty-four percent of the Parisian working class was disenfranchised.[161] A series of extremely harsh laws followed which furthered the alienation of the "parti d'Ordre" from the rest of the country. The press was muzzled, open political meetings banned, clubs suppressed, deportation reintroduced for political crimes.

As the monarchical party began to split into its legitimist and orleanist factions during the summer of 1850, only the desire to maintain the repression encouraged decisive action in the Assembly. Throughout 1851 rumors of a presidential *coup* coincided with the increasing paralysis of the legislative branch. The bitter struggle between Bonaparte and the Assembly centered around the president's demand that the constitution be revised so he could run for a second term in 1852.

Presidential elections were scheduled for the second Sunday in May 1852, and the political confusion of the period coincided with an economic slump to generate a call for peace at any price from the mass of the French bourgeoisie. Petitions calling upon the Assembly to revise the constitution began circulating in mid-April 1851; when 1,123,625 signatures were placed before the Assembly on May 31, it stood warned that bourgeois France wanted an end to trouble.[162] Marx's description of the situation is as classic now as when it was written:

> Now picture to yourself the French bourgeois, how in the throes of this business panic his trade-crazy brain is tortured, set in a whirl and stunned by rumors of *coups d'état* and the restoration of universal suffrage, by the struggle between parliament and the executive power, by the Fronde war between Orleanists and Legitimists, by the communist conspiracies in the south of France, by alleged *Jacqueries* in the Departments of Nièvre and Cher, by the advertisements of the different candidates for the presidency, by the cheapjack solutions offered by the journals, by the threats of the republicans to uphold the Constitution and universal suffrage by force of arms, by the gospel-preaching emigre heroes *in partibus*, who announced that the world would come to an end on the second Sunday in May 1852—think of all this and you will comprehend why in this unspeakable,

deafening chaos of fusion, revision, propogation, constitution, conspiration, coalition, emigration, usurpation and revolution, the bourgeois madly snorts at his parliamentary republic: '*Rather an end with terror than terror without end!*'[163]

Persistent rumors and threats of a presidential *coup* accompanied the Assembly's increasingly pointless debate about whether the constitution should be revised. When revision was rejected on July 19, active preparations began at the Elysée.

The political stage was set when the Assembly reconvened on November 11, 1851, and Louis-Napoleon demanded the restoration of universal suffrage. Warning that "le menace rouge" still hung over "good" France, he watched as the Assembly defeated the government's proposition to repeal the law of May 31, 1851. With its subsequent refusal to lower the residency requirement from three years to one, the "parti d'Ordre" had completed its work of declaring itself against the people.

The only substantial opposition to Louis-Napoleon's *coup d'état* of December 2, 1851, came from some Paris workers and groups of advanced peasants.[164] The Assembly was dissolved, universal suffrage was reestablished, and a wave of arrests and deportations removed all potential leaders of an anti-Bonapartist struggle from the scene. The work of the February Revolution was over,[165] yet in many ways the *coup* was but another step in an established historical process, for the bourgeoisie's failure to rule France as a whole did not mean that a fraction of it could not continue the essential work of the Days of June:

> It is often asserted that in December, 1851, Louis-Napoleon strangled the harmless, generous, idealistic Republic of 1848. As a matter of fact, political and social reaction began immediately after the Days of June. The true character of the following twenty years was determined before their political form. Had the Republic survived, it would, for many years, have been as conservative as any Empire, and possibly more cruel.[166]

Proudhon's war with the socialists gradually yielded to a campaign against the government as the president moved toward a Bonapartist solution to the bourgeoisie's inability to organize its political rule. His newspaper articles were climaxed by warnings appearing in the *Voix du Peuple* of February 5 that Louis-Napoleon was preparing an anti-republican, anti-constitutional and anti-Assembly coup.[167] His tone was sarcastic and scornful, and he was quickly in trouble; on February 7 the *Voix du Peuple* announced that Proudhon was in solitary confinement with all the normal privileges of a political prisoner suspended. The paper itself was seized several times during February for correctly accusing the Elysée of preparing a *coup*.

No articles from Proudhon appeared in the *Voix* until March 25, more than two weeks after the left's stunning victory in the partial election which

precipitated the Assembly's abolition of universal suffrage. Suddenly an article was printed in which it became clear that he had been badly frightened and isolated during the punishment he received in prison. He had
written an abject letter to the "prefet de police" on February 21 offering to
limit himself to discussions of "scientific questions" and nonpolitical issues
in return for better prison conditions.[168] Now he informed his readers that
he would not be writing about politics in the future. He would adopt a
neutral position with respect to relations between the proletariat and the
bourgeoisie, he would stop attacking the government, and to prove his change
of heart he referred to the left's important electoral victory of March 10 as
an unmitigated disaster:

> The government's desperation is a calamity for the people. You say that in pre-
> paring for the elections of March 10 you only wanted to give power a warning;
> you've thrown it into a state of terror. And since one never insolently attacks
> power, your electoral triumph has become a dirge for freedom. . . . It would be
> dangerous at the moment, for the Revolution and for humanity, to foment a
> conflict between the government and the people. Instead of overpowering, as
> you are doing, people who, believing themselves to be obeying a presidential
> mandate, suddenly and unexpectedly find themselves in open hostility with the
> people, the source of providence, think of reassuring and enlightening them in-
> stead.[169]

Seldom did Proudhon indicate so complete a collapse before the same
authority that he had so loudly attacked. He was exposed to be sure and
was afraid that he would lose what remained of his personal freedom if
there was any more strife.[170] He simply could not cope with having lost
some of his prison privileges, and his fear of increased repression forced a
stunning retreat.

Three days later the second part of the article appeared. February 1848
had raised the social problem with respect to the proletariat, said Proudhon,
but the Revolution must now deal with the suffering bourgeoisie as well.
Social reconstruction must not grant the worker full title to the product of
his labor at the expense of the capitalist's right to a secure market for his
goods and the safety of his capital. Still confident that the interests of both
classes could be guaranteed simultaneously, Proudhon went on to explain
that both the bourgeoisie and the proletariat had an interest in a "revolution"
which would establish "socialism," his understanding of both these terms
becoming progressively more idiosyncratic. He was still hoping for the fusion
of all classes, and his desire to make everyone a petty bourgeois remained
central to his work:

> Reconciliation of the bourgeoisie and the proletariat means today, as always, the
> emancipation of the serf; offensive and defensive alliance between the *industriels*
> and the workers against the aristocratic capitalist or noble; solidarity of interest

between the journeyman and the master; guarantee for the worker to become the boss and a bourgeois after an appropriate period of apprenticeship and service.

At bottom, the bourgeoisie is liberty and, more, the right to control and to govern.[171]

Proudhon's efforts to allay the bourgeoisie's fears and prevent the further consolidation of an already-organized counter-revolution continued during the six weeks between March 10 and the elections of April 28. He addressed several appeals to the workers to take a step toward the bourgeoisie, simultaneously urging the latter to vote for Sue to avoid a new popular rising.[172] Caught between proletariat and bourgeoisie, appealing to and warning both at the same time, and desiring peace at all costs, Proudhon was pleased when Sue beat his monarchist opponent. The day of reckoning had been put off again—or so he thought.

As the attack on universal suffrage developed, Proudhon urged his readers to protect the institution if possible and prevent its abolition if necessary—but under no circumstances was anything more than legal peaceful resistance legitimate.[173] The *Voix du Peuple* defended universal suffrage as best it could until, crushed by fines and police harassment, it was driven from the newsstands on May 14. Deprived of a newspaper, Proudhon could do no more than record his private thoughts. He was angry and depressed about another defeat but was too frightened of civil war to go beyond recommending civil disobedience and non-payment of taxes, adding his hope that such acts might precipitate the end of government after all.[174]

On June 15, 1850, *Le Peuple de 1850* appeared for the first time. Proudhon wrote a few articles for it, mostly repeating the themes that had appeared in his earlier writings.[175] He continued to recommend that the paper enlist the bourgeoisie and the petty bourgeoisie in the cause of socialism, pointing out several times that the economic developments which were exposing the petty bourgeoisie to disaster and the political repression which was depriving it of democratic rights made an alliance between it and the proletariat both possible and necessary.[176] But the paper folded on October 13, 1850, unable to pay a fine of 6,000 francs. Proudhon's career as a journalist was at an end, but he had been working on *L'Idée générale de la révolution au XIXème siècle* for several months and the book's publication closed this middle period of his life, his political direction changing dramatically with the appearance of his next work.

Proudhon tried to summarize the important lessons to be learned from February 1848 once again while simultaneously raising "the social question," reviving the "spirit of February," and combatting the left's "governmental spirit." His discussion of "the revolution" was similar to what he had put forward in the *Toast à la Révolution* and in many newspaper articles. He still wanted to forge a political alliance between the proletariat and the working petty bourgeoisie. He was still hopeful that the revolution was about to take a big step forward and thought that it might be possible to complete the work begun in 1789 by equilibrating economic forces.[177] He was still sure that the prevailing disorganization could be overcome only with a thorough-going change in social structure accomplished through a National Bank which would assure ample amounts of free credit to all.[178] Credit remained the moving force for him: "the first problem, that of exchange and conciliation, resolved, all the others will resolve themselves."[179]

A society founded on voluntary contract rather than the anarchic market, the arbitrary government, or the unstable principles of political democracy would be able to solve all of France's interrelated problems. Contracts would replace laws; "companies of workers," assured of free credit and grouping workers as producers independently of the state, would be largely responsible for the operations of the economy.[180] Every economic unit would be guaranteed its autonomy because economic inequality and governmental authority would have been eliminated. The germ of the third period of Proudhon's life is contained in the *Idée Générale*, although it was not until his last years that he clearly and definitively linked the contractual organization of the economy to the defense of small property. For the moment the desirability of such an arrangement was summed up in the light of positions he had already reached:

> Capitalist and landlord exploitation halted everywhere, wage-labor abolished, equal and dependable exchange guaranteed, value constituted, cheap prices assured, the standard of protectionism changed, the world market open to producers of all nations: thus barriers fallen, the ancient right of people replaced by commercial agreements, the police, justice and administration returned to the *industriels* everywhere; economic organization replacing the governmental and military regime in colonial possessions as well as in the metropolis; finally, the free and universal interpenetration of all races under the exclusive law of contract: that's the Revolution.[181]

The Revolution of 1848 was as important a turning point for Proudhon as it was for France and the European left. By the time he was released from jail on June 4, 1852, much of his complete doctrine was already in place. Tempered by his observations of the February Revolution, anarchism emerged as central to his thought and would establish Proudhon as one of the foremost representatives of pre-Marxian nonpolitical radicalism. The third period of his life would see his continued theoretical development and the organization of a fully developed, integrated scheme to universalize the petty bourgeoisie.

The concrete demands Proudhon presented to the French bourgeoisie during the Revolution and its immediate aftermath stood as a testament to the pressures under which the petty bourgeoisie was functioning. His calls for the regulation of the budget, the organization of work, secular public education, free credit, the abolition of the state, and the like covered the *ensemble* of social and political issues over which the upper and the lower bourgeoisie struggled after June. Many of these issues were expressed in sharpened political terms because the it took the Revolution of 1848 to pave the way for the creation of the modern bureaucratic and parliamentary state which is so characteristic of contemporary political life.

Even if it had a certain historical logic, the process was a deeply contradictory and uneven one. Reluctant to rule directly and rooted in the market processes of civil society, the bourgeoisie proved unable to organize a viable political framework for its joint rule after its overwhelming June victory and had to hand over power to a shameless adventurer so its social position could be protected. Proudhon understood this, and yet he was no more able than anyone else to help organize a consistent political struggle against Bonapartism because his limited worldview paralleled that of the petty-bourgeois left described by Marx:

> From . . . bourgeois socialism, to which, as to every variety of socialism, a section of the workers and petty bourgeois naturally rallies, specific petty bourgeois socialism, socialism *par excellence* is distinct. Capital hounds this class chiefly as its creditors, so it demands credit institutions; capital crushes it by competition, so it demands associations supported by the state; capital overwhelms it by concentration, so it demands progressive taxes, limitations on inheritance, taking over of large works by the state, and other measures that forcibly stem the growth of capital. Since it dreams of the peaceful achievement of socialism—allowing, perhaps, for a second February Revolution lasting for a brief day— naturally the coming historical process appears to it as the application of systems, which the thinkers of society, whether in companies or as individual inventors, devise or have devised.[182]

The elimination of the Paris proletariat left the petty bourgeoisie no alternative but to try to assert its own leadership or fall under the influence of one or another fraction of the upper bourgeoisie. Proudhon's activities illustrated the limits of this dilemma, a dilemma for which there was as yet no solution. The major social formation for which he spoke and which proved most receptive to his views were independent artisans in an environment of rapid industrialization and political instability. Anarchism and other schemes of social reorganization reflect the Janus-like character of the petty bourgeoisie, and Proudhon's violent hostility to the state reflected the small proprietors' inability to articulate an independent political position in the absence of a coherent proletarian movement. The elimination of the workers after June guaranteed that the social relations of bourgeois society would work their will sooner or later, and Proudhon's inability to break with the market exposed the limits of his perspective. His occasional support for the workers, his frequent attacks on "capitalist feudalism," his constant demolition of "doctrinaire socialism," and his general commitment to a more equitable distribution of wealth expressed one side of his dilemma, the side that looked to the workers. On the other hand, his drive to stand between classes, his inability to see further than a reformed capitalism, and his desire to universalize a relatively backward form of production made it difficult for Proudhon to clearly articulate a credible alternative to the liberalism he so articulately denounced.

As a leading spokesman of the petty bourgeoisie, Proudhon vacillated between the proletariat and the bourgeoisie. Drawn to and repelled by both, he was never able to gain an independent position but attached himself to one of the antagonists of the day. Both the content of his theories and the manner in which they were expressed mirrored the theoretical and practical dilemma of the petty bourgeoisie during a period of acute class struggle and civil war. The third period of Proudhon's life would see further developments and refinements of the class stand which he had adopted long before his release from prison.

NOTES

1. Letter to Bergmann, August 24, 1847. See P.-J. Proudhon, *Correspondance* (Paris: Lacroix, 1875), ii:271–72.
2. See, for example, his letters to his friend Maurice in May 1847, Bergmann of June 4, 1847, and again to Maurice on August 16, 1847, in *ibid.*
3. Karl Marx, *Class Struggles in France 1848–1852* (New York: International Publishers, 1964), 38.
4. The popular character of the revolution impressed many observers, the conservative Tocqueville among them. See his *Recollections*, ed. J. P. Mayer and trans. Alexander Teixeira de Mattos (New York: Columbia University Press, 1949), 64–65.
5. The timorous politicians and journalists took their lead from the popular movement during these days. Yet even Tocqueville, himself a prominent conservative member of the Chamber, had no idea how the Provisional Government came to be chosen. He described how, at the height of the Revolution on February 24, "Lamartine began to read out a list containing the names of the different people proposed by I don't know whom to take a share in the Provisional Government that had just been decreed, nobody knows how." See his *Recollections*, 56 and Priscilla Robertson, *Revolutions of 1848: A Social History* (New York: Harper and Row, 1952), 28.
6. Robertson, 24.
7. Marx, 41.
8. Letter to Maurice, February 25, 1848. *Correspondance*, ii: 282.
9. Jean Dautry, *1848 et la Deuxième République* (Paris: Editions Sociales, 1957), 90.
10. Letter to Maurice, February 25, 1848. *Correspondance*, ii: 280.
11. *Ibid.*, 283–84.

12. He offered the following observation on the banquet campaign during the fall of 1847, *Carnets* ii:227: "Celle qu'on propose aujourd'hui et pour laquelle on fait des banquets, ne regarde pas le peuple. Il y a une bourgeoisie, petite, envieuse, tracassière, corrompue, pire que la haute, qui veut sa part des intrigailleries parlementaires . . ."

13. *Ibid.*, 154.

14. See, for example, his immediate reaction to the Revolution in the *Carnets* (Paris: Riviere, 1968), iii:23.

15. Georges du Rostu, *Proudhon et les socialistes de son temps* (Paris: Giard et Brière, 1913), 80.

16. See, for example, the writings in his *Carnets* from this period, especially iii:12.

17. *Ibid.*, 39–40. Such sentiments also appear in the *Carnets* during the fall of 1848, for example: " . . . les Saint-Simoniens, les fourieristes, les communistes, les républicains, ne sont rien, ne peuvent être rien, et . . . attendent une théorie pour etre quelque chose." *Carnets*, ii:201 and "Il n'y a pas d'autre vérité que ma doctrine," *ibid.*, 243.

18. Rostu, 27.

19. *Carnets*, ii:56.

20. *Ibid.*, 91.

21. Letter to Maurice, February 25, 1848. *Correspondance*, ii: 284.

22. See the following claim in his letter to Haguenot of March 15, 1848, in *ibid.*, 291–92: "J'ai, je peux le dire en ce moment, le monopole des idées dont on a les plus besoin, des idées économiques. Les faiseurs d'utopies sont à bout de science; ils ont le pouvoir, ils taillent, ils tranchent et ne produisent rien. Tout le monde rit des ateliers nationaux; M. Louis Blanc est sifflé; M. Considérant est impuissant. On s'aperçoit enfin que tous ces charlatans du socialisme n'ont rien dans la tête, et nombre de gens viennent à moi. J'attends. Je suis sûr de mes idées, plus sur que jamais. L'argent se cache, je me passserai de lui; le crédit est mort, je le ferai sans violence ressusciter. Mais il faut attendre; le moment approche pour moi, il n'est pas venu."

23. "Déclaration aux électeurs du Doubs," *ibid.*, 299–304.

24. *Carnets*, ii:299.

25. *Ibid.*, 211. He had earlier expressed the view that "notre société doit être une société de petits ppres., petits bourgeois, paysans aisés. Notre industrie n'existe que par mesure de précaution." *ibid.*, 172.

26. "Déclaration aux électeurs du Doubs," *Correspondance*, ii:300.

27. *Ibid.*, 299.

28. *Ibid.*, 304.

29. Robertson, 67. Blanc was put on the Luxembourg Commission largely to embarrass him.

30. Georges Bourgin, *1848: Naissance et mort d'une république* (Paris: Les Deux Sirènes, 1948), 71. Dautry suggests similar intentions on the part of the Provisional Government in *1848 et la Deuxième République*, 108.

31. Marx, 51–2.

32. See, for example, his *Carnets*, ii:32–6.

33. Robertson, 72–3.

34. *Ibid.*, 43 and *Le Représentant du Peuple*, May 5 and June 6, 1848.

35. *Le Représentant du Peuple*, April 10, 1848.

36. Dautry, 93.

37. Robertson, 65.

38. He expressed this view many times during the fall and winter of 1847–1848. See, for example, the *Carnets*, ii:262.

39. *Idée Générale de la révolution au XIXe siècle* (Paris: Rivière, 1924), 151.

40. *Ibid.*, 156.

41. *Représentant du Peuple*, April 10, 1848.

42. Laurent Labrusse, *Les conceptions proudhiennes du crédit gratuit* (Paris: Jouve, 1919), 21.

43. *Ibid.*, 42.

44. *Carnets* (Paris: Rivière, 1960), i:95.

45. "Organisation du crédit et de la circulation," part III of *Solution du problème social*, appeared in the *Représentant du Peuple* on March 22, 26, and April 6, 1848.

46. *Représentant du Peuple*, April 12, 1848.

47. "Le communisme utopique est un communisme de répartition des biens, non un communism des moyens de production." Dautry, 43n.

48. See *Le Représentant du Peuple* from April 7 and April 12, 1848.

49. E. J. Hobsbawm, *The Age of Revolution 1789–1848* (New York: New American Library, 1962), 58n.

50. Robertson, 66.

51. Tocqueville asked in his *Recollections*, 79–80, "How should the poor and humbler and yet powerful classes not have dreamt of issuing from their poverty and inferiority by means of their power, especially in an epoch when our view into another world has become dimmer, and the miseries of this world become more visible and seem more intolerable? They had been working to this end for the last sixty years. The people had first endeavored to help itself by changing political institutions, but after each change it found that its lot was in no way improved, or was only improving with a slowness quite incompatible with the eagerness of its desire. Inevitably, it must sooner or later discover that what held it fixed in its position was not the constitution of the government but the unalterable laws that constitute society itself; and it was natural that it should be brought to ask itself if it had not both the power and the right to alter those laws, as it had altered all the rest. And to speak more specially of property, which is, as it were, the foundation of our social order—all the privileges which covered it and which, so to speak, concealed the privilege of property having been destroyed, and the latter remaining the principal obstacle to equality among men, and appearing to be the only sign of inequality—was it not necessary, I will not say that it should be abolished in its turn, but at least that the thought of abolishing it should occur to the minds of those who did not enjoy it?"

52. Tocqueville, among others, was very clear on this point. See *ibid.*, 93–104.

53. Albert Leon Guérard, *French Civilization in the Nineteenth Century* (New York: The Century Co., 1914), 201.

54. Dautry, 41.

55. Tocqueville's description of his impressions of Paris after his return from his successful electoral campaign in Normandy is worthy of attention. "One thing was not ridiculous but really ominous and terrible," he said, "and that was the appearance of Paris on my return. I found in the capital a hundred thousand armed workmen formed into regiments, out of work, dying of hunger, but with their minds crammed with vain theories and visionary hopes. I saw society cut in two; those who possessed nothing, united in a common greed; those

who possessed something, united in a common terror. There were no bonds, no sympathy between these two great sections; everywhere the idea of an inevitable and immediate struggle seemed at hand." *Recollections*, 107.

56. Dautry, 179.
57. Robertson, 85.
58. Bourgin, 74.
59. *Représentant du Peuple*, April 20, 1848.
60. *Ibid.*, April 29, 1848.
61. Auguste Cornu, "Utopisme et Marxisme" in Auguste Cornu et al, *A la lumière du Marxisme*, iv: *Karl Marx et la pensée moderne* (Paris: Editions Sociales Internationales, 1937), 137–40.
62. *Représentant du Peuple*, May 4, 1848.
63. *Ibid.*, May 8, 1848.
64. *Ibid.*, May 26, 1848.
65. See Celestin Bouglé, *La Sociologie de Proudhon* (Paris: Armand Colin, 1911), ch. v.
66. Dautry, 172. Louis-Napoleon's election was challenged by some members of the Assembly because of his past participation in anti-republican conspiracies and adventures. He declined to take his seat when challenged and returned to England to await a more propitious occasion for entering legitimate political life.
67. There are many descriptions of these days. Tocqueville's is particularly vivid, the more so because he showed little sympathy for the insurgents. See his *Recollections*, 150–85.
68. *Ibid.*, 157.
69. Robertson, 95.
70. Tocqueville, *Recollections*, 184.
71. Guido de Ruggiero, *The History of European Socialism* (Boston: Beacon Press, 1959), 193.
72. Guérard, 126.
73. *Représentant du Peuple*, June 27, 1848.
74. Dautry, 191.
75. Robertson, 96.
76. *Ibid.*
77. *Représentant du Peuple*, July 8, 1848.
78. *Carnets*, iii:76.
79. The speech was printed in *Le Moniteur Universel* of August 1, 1848.
80. Pierre Ansart, *Socialisme et anarchisme* (Paris: Presses Universitaires de France, 1969).
81. "La société est un être moral, ou elle n'est pas. Comme être moral, elle ne subsiste, elle ne vit qu'une part les conditions qui ont fait la vie de l'homme même: la liberté, la qualité, la sécurité, la pensée, la parole et l'action." *Représentant du Peuple*, August 10, 1848.
82. "Les Malthusiens," *Représentant du Peuple*, August 11, 1848.
83. The last issue appeared on August 14, 1848.
84. This view was suggested in his article "Qu'est-ce que la propriété?" which appeared in the *Représentant du Peuple* on April 26, 1848.
85. *Ibid.*, June 18, 1848.
86. Sudan, 34.
87. *Ibid.*, 17–18.

88. Guérard, 202.
89. Bourgin, 93.
90. See Marx, 60–95, for an excellent description of this process.
91. Ibid., 65.
92. Letter to Maguet, June 28, 1848. Correspondance, ii:337.
93. See, for example, the Carnets, iii:98–99, 118.
94. See the letter to Abram of September 2, 1848, Correspondance, ii:348, where Proudhon discusses his plans for the new paper.
95. Le Peuple, September 2, 1848.
96. Ibid.
97. Carnets, iii:129.
98. George Woodcock, Pierre-Joseph Proudhon (London: Routledge and Kegan Paul, 1956), 138–39.
99. "Toast à la Révolution," Le Peuple, October 17, 1848.
100. Ibid.
101. "La Constitution et la Présidence," Le Peuple, October 31, 1848.
102. Woodcock, 138.
103. Thiers and Montalembert were instrumental in arranging the compromise between their respective parties, the Orleanists and Legitimists. Confident that they could use Louis-Napoleon, both were rudely awakened later. Robertson, 127.
104. Dautry, 215.
105. Quoted in Henri Guillemin, Le coup du 2 décembre (Paris: Gallimard, 1951), 111. The Duc de Clarement was the Legitimist pretender; the Orleanist branch of the royal family lived at Wiesbaden.
106. The final results were as follows:

Louis-Napoleon	5,434,266
Cavaignac	1,448,107
Ledru-Rollin	307,119
Raspail	36,920
Lamartine	17,910

See Guérard, 128; Robertson, 102; Dautry, 231.
107. Marx, 71. "[T]he republic had announced itself to this class with the tax collector; it announced itself to the republic with the emperor."
108. Guérard, 204; Maxime Leroy, Histoire des idées sociales en France (Paris: Gallimard, 1954), iii:259; Dautry, 232.
109. Guérard, 128.
110. Carnets, iii:111.
111. See, for example, Le Peuple, no. 3, from the beginning of November 1848.
112. Ibid.
113. Voix du Peuple, December 4, 1848.
114. Daniel Halévy, Le Mariage de Proudhon (Paris: Stock, Delamain et Boutelleau, 1955), 231.
115. Le Peuple, November 8–15, 1848.
116. Ibid., November 8–15, 1848. The paper appeared as a weekly until November 28, when it became a daily.
117. Ibid.
118. Ibid., December 18, 1848.
119. Guillemin, 91.
120. Dautry, 234.
121. Dautry, 211. Reports that "les soirs pour se déclasser, les réactionnaires parisiens vont au Vaudeville applaudir la Propriété, c'est le vol, folie socialiste en 3

actes et 7 tableaux, où la proclamation de la République est acceuillie au premier acte par une choeur qui chante des airs d'enterement, où au second acte, censé passé en 1852, la fidelité au droit au travail détermine les vitriers à casser toutes les vitrines d'un appartement pour les remplacer, et les dentistes d'arrocher les dents de ceux qui ne leur demandent rien. Passons sur les actes suivantes qui sont de la même force. Tout le long de la pièce, Proudhon apparait avec ses lunettes et ses favories, copieusement ridiculisé, tellement ridiculisé que le gouvernement et le président de l'Assemblée, Arrmand Marrast, crurent devoir intervenir offieusement pour 'l'atteinte à l'inviolabilité de la représentation nationale.'" Bourgin, 102. Describes *Le Propriété, c'est le vol* as a very popular play.

122. *Le Peuple*, January 26, 1849.
123. *Ibid.*, January 27, 1849.
124. The charges can be found in *Le Moniteur Universel*, January–March 1848, no. 134, p. 293.
125. *Le Peuple*, January 29, 1849.
126. *Ibid.*, January 30, 1849.
127. Letter to M. Abram, May 31, 1848. *Correspondance*, ii:333.
128. Letter to Maguet, February 2, 1849. *Ibid.*, 357–58.
129. The Assembly's resolution appears in *Le Moniteur Universel*, 495–496.
130. Letter to Maurice, February 16, 1849. *Correspondance*, ii:359. The official circulation rose to 40,000 by the end of April. See the letter to Maurice, 370.
131. *Le Peuple*, February 26, 1849.
132. Letter to M. P***, March 2, 1849. *Correspondance*, ii:363–64.
133. Letter to Maurice, June 7, 1849. *Ibid.*, 383.
134. *Carnets*, iii:212.
135. For a description and analysis of Herzen's collaboration with Proudhon on *La Voix du Peuple*, see Raoul Labry, *Herzen et Proudhon* (Paris: Editions Bossard, 1928), ch. vi.
136. *La Voix du Peuple*, October 1, 1849.
137. *Ibid.*, October 17, 22, and 30, 1849.
138. P.-J. Proudhon, *Les confessions d'un révolutionnaire pour servir à l'histoire de la révolution de fevrier* (Paris: Rivière, 1929).
139. *Ibid.*, p. 113.
140. *Ibid.*, p. 111. The emphases are his.
141. For a different example of this sort of analysis, see Stanley Moore, "Marx and Lenin as Historical Materialists," *Philosophy and Public Affairs*, 4 (1975):171–94.
142. *Idée générale de la révolution au XIXe siècle*, 199.
143. *Confession d'un révolutionnaire*, 58.
144. *Idée générale de la révolution au XIX siècle*, 178, 182–84; see also John Ehrenberg, *The Dictatorship of the Proletariat: Marxism's Theory of Socialist Democracy* (New York: Routledge, 1992).
145. *Idée générale de la révolution au XIX siècle*, 240.
146. *Ibid.*, 203.
147. *Ibid.*, 344.
148. See *La Voix du Peuple*, December 26–27, 1849 and January 7, 8, 10, and 12, 1850.
149. *Ibid.*, December 28, 1849.
150. In a letter to Guillemin of December 3, 1849, Proudhon commented on his plans for approaching Louis-Napoleon as follows: "Si cette affaire venait à se conclure, la Montagne, les communistes, les icariens, les phalansteriens, tout

serait écrasés; Louis Bonaparte aurait, de façon ou d'autre, une place dans la République, ce qui me trouble au fond assez peu; autant lui que Louis Blanc. *Correspondance*, iii:62.

151. Proudhon stated the Banque's three aims as follows:

"1. Appliquer les principes de constitution sociale ... et préluder à la réforme politique par une exemple de centralisation spontanée, indépendente et sociale;

"2. Attaquer le gouvernementalisme, qui n'est autre chose que l'exageration du communisme, en donnant l'essor à l'initiative populaire, en procurant de plus en plus la liberté individuelle par la mutualité;

"3. Assurer le travail et le bien-être à tous les producteurs, en les organisant les uns à l'égard des autres comme principe et fin de production, en autres termes, comme capitalistes et comme consommateurs." *Confessions d'un révolutionnaire*, 247.

152. *Carnets*, iii:222.
153. *Ibid.*, 253.
154. *Ibid.*, 277.
155. *Ibid.*, 284–85.
156. *Ibid.*, 169–70.
157. *Ibid.*, 190.
158. *Ibid.*, p. 354. This quote appears in a postscript, having been written in October 1851 for the second edition of the book.
159. *La Voix du Peuple*, November 15, 1849.
160. Dautry, 270.
161. Bourgin, 132.
162. Guillemin, 278.
163. Karl Marx, *The Eighteenth Brumaire of Louis Bonaparte* (New York: International Publishers, 1963), 110. The emphases are his.
164. Dautry, 277.
165. Guillemin, 437.
166. Guérard, 127.
167. See his articles in *La Voix du Peuple* of January 28 with his letters to Darimon of January 15, 16, and 22, 1850. *Correspondance*, iii:83–89.
168. *Correspondance*, iii:121–26.
169. *La Voix du Peuple*, March 25, 1850.
170. *Ibid.*
171. *Ibid.*, March 28, 1850.
172. *Ibid.*, April 16 and 19, 1850.
173. Letter to Mathey, May 6, 1850. *Correspondance*, iii:244.
174. *Carnets*, iii:365–68.
175. See, for example, *Le Peuple de 1850*, July 10, 1850, which featured an attack on Louis Blanc and Ledru-Rollin.
176. Letter to Darimon, August 15, 1850. *Correspondance*, iii:320.
177. *Idée générale de la révolution au XIXème siècle*, 128.
178. *Ibid.*, 239.
179. *Ibid.*, 245.
180. *Ibid.*, 266.
181. *Ibid.*, 332.
182. Marx, *Class Struggles in France 1848–1850*, 125–26.

5

Squaring the Circle

PROUDHON AND BONAPARTE

Proudhon was released from prison on June 4, 1852, six months after Louis-Napoleon's *coup*, and found himself at the beginning of a decisive stage in French history. The third period of his intellectual and political career was shaped by the extensive economic changes which began to transform France and Europe in the early years of the Second Empire, changes which were precipitated by the rapid growth of heavy industry organized around coal and iron. Industrial expansion had been relatively slow during the July Monarchy, but the political stabilization which put an end to the events of 1848 and culminated in the Second Empire accompanied a tremendous expansion of characteristically modern economic activity.[1]

The most important social consequences of this dramatic spurt of industrialization were the accelerated proletarianization of broad strata of the petty bourgeoisie and the greatly-intensified exploitation and misery of all the working poor. This stimulated the political reawakening of workers and small proprietors alike, and for the first time the modern proletariat was in a position to lead the opposition to the regime. Its first tendency was to organize itself.

As the French workers slowly revived after their catastrophic June defeat and the artificial boom of the early 1850s began to wear off, the labor movement began to set up associations, mutual-aid societies, and political clubs. As it did so it gradually moved away from the political influence of the democratic petty bourgeoisie and began to develop a variety of socialist and mutualist tendencies. The openly partisan character of the regime drove the workers to political activity before long, and they were soon running their own candidates for political office. Louis-Napoleon never succeeded in gaining the support of the French working class, and from 1857 on the proletariat formed the core of all significant opposition to the Empire.[2] This pushed its own consciousness forward.[3]

As the labor movement turned to sustained political activity, it began to develop a distinctly modern form of socialism which was increasingly prepared to call private property in the means of production into question and to contemplate the use of political power to interfere with market processes in the name of social democracy. The workers were assisted by many intellectuals like Proudhon who were themselves stimulated by the renewal of activity. As the revived workers' movement began to develop an independent political, organizational, and ideological orientation it came into contact with the rapidly-developing democratic radicalism of France's enormous mass of small proprietors. The political relationship between the socialist proletariat and the democratic petty bourgeoisie dominated the French left throughout the Second Empire, until the Paris Commune put an end to all the illusions of peaceful change which had so impressed the post-1848 generation of social critics and political activists.

The systematically reactionary Empire of the 1850s was economically liberal, and the long boom which marked its early years made left-wing labor politics exceedingly difficult. The regime had considerable room in which to maneuver for some time, and it did so through management and manipulation rather than relying on repression and terror alone. With three recent revolutions and a highly politicized population behind it, the French bourgeoisie had to take account of "the people" even if it seemed to have finally discovered the political formula to ensure its unchallenged supremacy. Louis-Napoleon relied on universal manhood suffrage and the fraudulent glories of the Second Empire, but it was his use of democratic forms for frankly antidemocratic purposes which was so problematic—and so modern. The Emperor's claim that he ruled on behalf of oppressed nationalities, his use of the bureaucracy to reward the regime's friends and punish its enemies, his appeals to the working class, and his attempt to represent himself as the agent of change and social progress made a mockery of the democratic potential of the franchise, but universal suffrage also provided the nascent proletariat with a chance to appeal directly to the petty bourgeoisie. This is why people like Proudhon were so important.

Whatever his longer-term importance would prove to be, Proudhon had been disappointed by the lack of mass opposition to Bonaparte's *coup*. His immediate conclusion was that the people had been passive because they were ignorant, and his disillusionment carried over several months later:

> in everything they have accomplished, the masses have always been openly or secretly pushed and solicited by elite spirits which form among them . . . each time the people has been left to itself, it has only known, like students imitating their teachers, how to copy what it has before its eyes into the margins and thus move society backwards.[4]

The people were badly in need of education and Proudhon was convinced that the Church had become the most serious threat to freedom.[5] He would have liked to gain the neutrality of the Elysee so he could continue his war against the "parti prètre," and this desire may help explain the curious conclusions to which he soon came about Louis-Napoleon. The 1852 publication of *La Révolution sociale démontrée par le coup d'état du 2 décembre* represented his attempt to explain recent political events in what he thought was their proper context.[6]

It was important for all the leading leftists of the period to understand and explain what had happened in France since February. The revolution had been lost and the counter-revolution was supreme—that was clear to all. But from that point socialists and communists, radicals and republicans, could and did come to very different conclusions. Marx and Engels, for example, were forced to revise their earlier optimistic expectation that 1848 was the beginning of the continent-wide proletarian revolution by recognizing that the events of the period had marked the consolidation, rather than the disintegration, of bourgeois hegemony.[7] But where their reevaluation of the period's events encouraged them to refine their historical analysis, Proudhon thought it necessary to explain that the *coup* would come to serve the revolution regardless of the wishes of its protagonists. He had already come to believe that "the revolution" was a permanent idea in history which operated independently of individual wishes or desires and always moved in the direction of equality and social progress.[8] If "a man, in all the circumstances of his life, is only the expression of an idea," then he felt it necessary to demonstrate how a counter-revolutionary man might serve the revolutionary idea.[9] If the new period belonged to the bourgeoisie, Proudhon hoped he could make it serve the Revolution *quand même*. To do so he called upon the rudimentary theory of history he had outlined earlier and recently adapted to his new purpose.

The first epoch in human history—the "religious"—took shape when Jesus gave voice to mankind's collective conscience and provided humanity with its first chance to take its moral life into its own hands. Man's independent ethical development was predicated on Jesus's support for the poor and oppressed, his genuinely democratic and plebeian orientation to the political and theological issues of the day, and his demands for a sweeping transformation of society. But once a cult, a theology, and a bureaucracy developed out of the network of scattered and persecuted Christian sects, the liberatory content of Jesus's life was transformed into its opposite. By the end of the second century Christianity had lost its subversive and critical edge and had become reconciled to power, inequality, and property. It preached obedience and submission, postponing the possibility of collectively transforming this world for the promise of individual salvation in the next. This attitude carried over to the present day. Basing its teaching on the antihuman doctrine of Original Sin and the ineradicable depravity of humanity, the Church now preaches acceptance of misery, evil, and inequality in the here and now, makes right and morality into empty duties mechanically imposed from above, places the source of moral authority outside the conscience of the individual, represses independent virtue, and pronounces labor a punishment for sin. Claiming that justice is unattainable without it, the Church has ritualized and trivialized Jesus's words, deprived them of their fundamental moral content, and tried to create a world after its own image.[10]

The Enlightenment's "philosophic" attack on the Church's rigidity, arrogance, and absolutism ushered in the second liberatory period in human history. Its affirmation of individual reason and conscience, freedom, equality, and science led to the appearance of social contract, popular sovereignty, mutual respect, and reciprocity as durable principles for social organization. Man now has an openness and flexibility of spirit which could no longer be stifled by religion. Individual conscience and free criticism became the indispensable vehicles of moral and social progress. God was now irrelevant to a science which began looking for truth in the relation between things instead of by examining fixed entities "in themselves."[11]

The separation of theology from science and the resulting commitment to analyze facts made it possible to develop a science of society based on the "real" social structure of the present. Despite the tremendous accomplishments of Adam Smith, whose discoveries opened the path to a systematic organization of social cooperation based on exchange, the "philosophic" period came to a close with the French Revolution. Like Christianity, the Great Revolution had taken initial shape as a spontaneous expression of man's collective conscience. It had proclaimed the permanence of justice, equality, and science; created a new public and private morality; and promoted equality, democracy, and emancipation as the fundamental goals of any social order worthy of man. Equality was now on humanity's historical agenda, and nothing could remove it.

Even if the Jacobins' hyperpolitics and the bourgeoisie's backwardness had temporarily stalled "the revolution's" advance, history is inexorably tending toward equality of all men before reason—the second great revolution. But the reason it proclaimed became private and personal, a commodity of market society to be used in the pursuit of individual goals. To establish it as the guiding principle of the social order requires a third "revolution," this time in the social sphere where labor waited to become the equal of capital.[12]

Proudhon hoped that Louis-Napoleon's *coup* would be the most recent manifestation of "the revolution." Although illegitimate because it broke the law, it would serve the people's interests in the long run because the president's motion conformed in every important respect to the revolution's goals: the solution of the social problem, the absorption of politics into the economy, and the substitution of ordered anarchy for the despotism of parties.[13]

Louis-Napoleon did not represent a party, a class, or even himself: "even a hereditary chief of state does not represent a party, he inherits a necessity."[14] The Napoleonic state might serve progress despite itself and rescue politics from the abyss into which it had fallen by coordinating Proudhon's reforms:

> If there is a government, it can only result from a delegation, convention, federation, in a word from the free and spontaneous consent of all the individuals which make up the People, each one of them insisting on and canvassing for the guarantee of his own interests. Thus the government, if there is one, instead of being Authority as hitherto, will represent the relationship between all the interests created by free property, free labor, free trade, free credit and will itself have a value only through what it represents.[15]

If the president's objective effect was to advance the revolution, this did not mean that Louis-Napoleon's intentions were noble. Indeed, Proudhon felt that Bonaparte's ability to serve the revolution might be continually frustrated by his vain attempts to make it serve him and subordinate the general interests of the country to his ill-conceived and reckless dynastic ambitions. Proudhon wanted the Prince-President to become the conscious agent of history, and he appealed to him to recognize necessity and act accordingly:

> The Revolution has foreseen everything, understood everything; it has outlined everything beforehand. Search and when with a straight and a calm heart you have found, don't concern yourself, with the rest of the country, with anything but execution.[16]

"I accept the fait accompli," Proudhon declared in the beginning of the book,[17] and if his apparent defense of the president and the *coup* enraged much of the left, his hope was not to apologize for Louis-Napoleon but to salvage some good out of what initially seemed a hopeless situation. His overwhelming desire to reconcile the increasingly antagonistic interests of different classes stood behind his retreat from the opposition to despotism which had characterized his attitude during the previous four years. Proudhon did not really support the *coup* but it appeared that he was at least compromising with it. His flirtation with Louis-Napoleon reflected his political isolation. He had repudiated most of the classical left and was looking for some alternative source of progress, convinced as he was that "no progress at all is possible as long as it remains the affair of the former democratic party and the old republican bands."[18]

In the long run, however, Proudhon's apparent willingness to compromise with the government stemmed much more from his fundamental political project than from some sort of fearful indecisiveness or his rupture with the left. His constant desire to protect independent economic activity and the small property on which it was based had driven his intellectual and practical activity from the beginning. The two greatest threats to the *petite bourgeoisie* whose interests rested at the heart of his work were the concentrated wealth of the *haute bourgeoisie* and the propertylessness of the rapidly-growing proletariat. Proudhon's efforts to establish a niche between the two great classes of modern society would be shaped by how he understood France's social structure and how he proposed addressing her social problems. After years of reflection, his studies led him to an important sketch of the country's principal actors:

> The *bourgeoisie*—I include in this class all those who live from the return on capital, from the rental of property, from the privileges of office, from the dignity of employment and sinecures, rather than from the real products of labor. Thus defined, the modern bourgeoisie is a sort of landed and capitalist aristocracy, analogous by its numbers and the character of its employment to the ancient nobility; having near-total control of the banks, railroads, mines, insurance, transportation, of great industry and big commerce, and having as a base of operations a public debt, mortgages, indentures and stocks amounting to 20–25 billion.
>
> The *middle class*—This is composed of entrepreneurs, owners, shopkeepers, manufacturers, farmers, scientists, artists, etc., living, like the proletarians and differently from the bourgeoisie, much more from their personal products than from their capital, privileges and property, but differing from the proletariat in that they work, as we commonly say, for themselves, that they are responsible for their own losses and can enjoy the full benefit of their labor, while the proletariat works for a wage.
>
> Finally, the *Working Class* or *Proletariat*—Like the preceding, it lives much more from its work than from its capital, possesses no industrial initiative, and merits in every respect the name of *mercenary* or *salaried*, ... like the middle class, composed in general of the most capable and energetic producers, living far below the bourgeoisie in terms of security; at the same time the proletariat is composed of a poor, if not miserable, multitude, having only a dream of well-being all its life, hardly knowing the use of wheat, meat and wine in many places, shod in wooden shoes, clothed in cotton or cloth, and the great majority of whom cannot read. The economists have described the proletariat's misery in moving terms; they have proven that this misery is the cause of weakening public morality and of the degradation of the race.[19]

At first sight Proudhon seemed to be dividing society into a bourgeoisie, a proletariat, and a *petite bourgeoisie* standing between the two. The "bourgeoisie" seemed to be the same as the "upper bourgeoisie" and was characterized by its ownership or control of the means of production. Since it did not have to work but lived off the labor of others, Proudhon thought of it as the modern equivalent of the feudal aristocracy, different from its ancestor only because the source of its wealth was different. His continuing emphasis on "la féodalité capitaliste" was based on older analyses of the July Monarchy, analyses which were rapidly becoming obsolete. Because industry had not yet come to dominate the economy in the 1830s and early

1840s, the bourgeoisie as a whole was not yet led by its fraction which derived its wealth from industry. Since they had been in opposition to the "haute bourgeoisie financière" during the July Monarchy, Proudhon did not consider the industrialists to be a part of the ruling class. His analysis of the financial, commercial, and industrial bourgeoisie relied on the political economy of an earlier period and was too narrow for the 1850s, although it should be remembered that *La révolution sociale* was published before the great industrial explosion of the Second Empire had begun.

Proudhon included the industrialists in the "classe moyenne" because he thought they worked for themselves and did not depend on appropriating the labor of others. The "middle class" represented the combination of work and ownership which he had always favored. This analysis was carried over from an earlier period and reflected some of the preindustrial tendencies which were inherent in Proudhon's socialism. Focusing on their nonexploitative qualities, Proudhon thought that the "middle class" and the workers shared more with each other than did different fractions of the bourgeoisie. The "middle class" stood between the workers and the "new aristocracy" and could serve as a social and political bridge between the classes whose growing antagonism so worried him.[20] His desire to place the petty bourgeoisie's interests at the center of his work was now plainly stated:

> Resolve the bourgeoisie and the proletariat into the middle class; the class which lives from its investments and the one which lives from its wages into the class which, properly speaking, has neither investments nor wages but which invents, which tries things, which improves, which produces, which exchanges, which alone constitutes the society's economy and truly represents the country: this is, as we have said, the real question of February.[21]

Since the revolution's purpose was "to ensure that everyone without exception would have capital, work, markets, freedom, and leisure in equal proportion," Proudhon was really holding that the universalization of the petty bourgeoisie was France's only salvation. Failure to generalize small production and reform society along the lines he had been suggesting for years would have disastrous consequences:

> There exists in France, and so long as the revolution is not made in the economy there will exist: (1) a *bourgeoisie* which pretends to maintain forever the ancient relations between capital and labor even though work is no longer being rejected as servitude but is being demanded as a right and since the circulation of products can proceed almost without interruption, capitalist privilege has no more reason to exist; (2) a middle class at the heart of which lives and moves the spirit of freedom, which has knowledge of the future and which, repelled from above and below by capitalist insolence and proletarian envy, still forms the heart and mind of the nation; (3) a proletariat, full of its power, which socialist soothsayers have intoxicated and which, with good reason, is showing itself to be unmanageable.[22]

"I have preached class conciliation, symbol of the synthesis of doctrines," Proudhon wrote his friend Langlois.[23] But his desire to compromise now had a solid theoretical base. From 1850 until the end of his life, his chief political and ideological goal was to detach the independent "middle class" from the political influence of the "haute bourgeoisie" and move it toward the workers. Desperate to organize a political alliance of the workers and small proprietors against the parasitical "nouvelle féodalité," he appealed to the *petite bourgeoisie* to support the workers and simultaneously called for the proletariat to protect small property. As he put it, he wanted to "separate first the manufacturing and financial aristocracy, that is to say the bank, stock exchange, mines, big manufacturing works like Creusot, in a word all the industrial and mercantile feudalism of the bourgeoisie properly so called, from the middle class."[24]

Proudhon's hope that Louis-Napoleon would come to his senses and embrace the revolution was quickly shattered. The economic expansion that provided the basis for the Empire's consolidation continued uninterruptedly until 1857. When combined with the Anglo-French victory over Russia in the Crimean War and the birth of a son to the Empress, prosperity made the years 1855–56 the high points of the Empire.[25] Unbroken reaction ruled France from the summer of 1848 until the end of the Empire as the regime continued the work of repression begun immediately after June.[26] Administrative centralism and political reaction stifled public life and made a mockery of universal suffrage. The press was rigidly controlled, candidates for elective office were nominated and supported by the central government, election meetings were prohibited, and all political clubs and parties were banned. Police spies were everywhere, the universities were purged and the press controlled, and what debate and discussion there were took place in a void. Opposition to Louis-Napoleon did not surface until economic difficulties at home and setbacks abroad undermined the Emperor's claim that despotism and adventurism were necessary for order and prosperity.

The "good years" of the Empire were unhappy ones for Proudhon and for much of the left. He was bitterly disappointed at Louis-Napoleon's failure to move in the direction he had recommended. He found the country's wealth hard to accept, knowing that it would consolidate the counter-revolution.[27] The Emperor's popularity led him to the reluctant conclusion that Bonaparte had become the incarnation of military despotism and he became a "defeatist" during the Crimean War, hoping that the fall of the regime would be worthwhile even if it led to nothing more than a bourgeois monarchy or a bourgeois republic.[28]

To his distress at political events was added financial hardship and the beginning of the physical deterioration that plagued him for the rest of his life. The whole family came down with cholera in the spring of 1854.

Proudhon's youngest daughter Marcelle died and he himself never fully recovered from the effects of the disease; the cerebral anemia which caused his premature death was a direct outgrowth of the cholera. By the end of 1855 his accumulated hardships had driven him to the brink of despair:

> By my thought and my conscience, I have always been elevated well above this proletarian filth, but the realities of my life always plunge me into it. Am I destined to see myself poorer, more miserable, fallen further below my birth than I haven't been in eighteen years? I don't know. But so long as I curse wealth, it takes revenge on my curse. Poverty isn't good for anything.[29]

His difficulties notwithstanding, Proudhon had maintained his lifelong interest in moral matters since his egalitarianism had driven his early criticism of property. The 1855 publication of a Church-supported slanderous attack on him prompted a development and summation of his moral, economic, and political views. *De la Justice dans la révolution et dans l'église* was published in April 1855, and is the most ambitious project Proudhon ever undertook. Primarily a work of moral philosophy, it was his first substantial move beyond his earlier analyses of 1848 and represented a major step in Proudhon's attempt to articulate an integrated and comprehensive social theory.

MUTUALIST JUSTICE

A moral commitment to equality of conditions had always rested at the core of Proudhon's social theory. All the criticisms he had advanced and the reforms he had suggested were designed to overcome the chaos and the inequality which mocked France's pretensions to have realized the principles of the Great Revolution and organized a just society. Now, scandalized by the corruption of the Second Empire and the helplessness of the population to set things right, Proudhon began to develop the outline of a moral theory which would serve as the foundation of his subsequent activity.[30] Her outward energy and glitter notwithstanding, France had

> a middle class which is killing itself from cowardice and stupidity; commoners who are sinking into indulgence and bad advice; women feverish with luxury and lewdness, brazen youth who are grown-up children, a priesthood dishonored by scandal and revenge, having no faith in itself any longer and hardly challenging the silence of public opinion with its still-born dogmas; that's the profile of our century.[31]

Proudhon was still convinced that economic disorganization was at the heart of all France's difficulties, and he was now trying to elaborate a moral principle which could aid in social reconstruction. For him "the creation of an economic science based on the analysis of industrial phenomena and on justice is the final word of revolutionary theory."[32] Like the rest of the French left, he had moved a long way from the barricades of June.

If a principle of justice could help organize an egalitarian economy, Proudhon's discussion of it began with a distinction between the "principle of transcendence" and the "principle of immanence," the major representatives of which in human affairs he took to be the Church and the "Revolution." The Church understands justice not as the voluntary adhesion of a free conscience to a moral law but as the revealed commandment of an external and alien God. It had become a mortal enemy of freedom because its expression of the "principle of transcendence" placed it in direct opposition to mankind's moral self-determination.[33] The "principle of transcendence" was *droit divin*, external authority, politics, force, arbitrariness, and the police—anything that located justice outside of human consciousness and thus arbitrarily limited man's capacity for self-definition. "Authority," the enemy of justice, was expressed in religious affairs by the Church, in economics by capital, and in politics by the state. These institutions constituted the "fatal trinity," the basis of all absolutism.

If authority was inherently alien and enslaving, Proudhon's "principle of immanence," *droit humain*, was manifested in and reinforced by the free individual conscience, the source of liberty, preserver of morality, guarantor of reciprocity, and foundation of mutual service.[34] It is the opposite of the "principle of authority" and finds its social expression in justice, mutualism, and federated anarchy. Proudhon's justice rests on "a social order established on a reciprocal system of free and guaranteed transactions interpreted by the city's intervention."[35] It would serve as the core of Proudhon's attempt to reconcile substantive equality of conditions with the requirements of market society, one of the defining theoretical struggles of his life. This orientation would lead him to understand justice as the preservation of the integrity of every existing social unit. His desire to guarantee the safety of different classes had underlain his earlier suggestion that economic equality would follow from the free exchange of equivalencies, and it formed the root of his conception of justice as well:

> Man, by virtue of the reason with which he is endowed, has the faculty of feeling his dignity in the person of a fellow man as in his own person, of affirming himself as an individual and as species simultaneously.
> JUSTICE is the product of this faculty; it is *respect, spontaneously felt and reciprocally guaranteed, for human dignity, in whatever person and whatever circumstance it finds itself jeopardized, and at whatever risk its defense exposes us to.*
> From the definition of Justice are deduced those of right and of *duty*.[36]

If justice is the principle of mutual respect, it cannot be realized in a social vacuum. Proudhon was as critical of the amoral individualism of commercial culture as he was of the stifling communalism of much of the traditional left and tried to establish the framework of a rationally-determined individual moral life which would be developed and lived in association with one's fellows. Rights-based individualism repelled him as much as Rousseau's attempt to locate morality exclusively in a community which claims to represent the general interest.[37] Both extremes struck him as equally arbitrary because equally absolute, and his earlier notion of an "être collectif" had expressed his sense that man is always encountered in a network of social relations outside of which he cannot function as a civilized moral being. If "the personality of collective man is as certain as the reality and the personality of the individual,"[38] it follows that this "collective being" is "as real, as personal, as endowed with will and intelligence as the individuals of which it is composed."[39] If the potential for justice was immanent in man and if society was his natural environment, it follows that justice must be founded on the recognition and defense of difference.[40] Such respect must involve the willingness to take any action necessary to defend someone else's integrity. Justice implies duties to others and requires much more than the formal recognition of rights in a social environment which makes their practical realization impossible:

> To feel and affirm human dignity, at first in everything which concerns us and then in the person of our neighbor—and this without returning to egoism or considering divinity or community: that it *right*.
> To be ready in any situation to energetically undertake the defense of this dignity, even against one's own interests: that is *justice*.[41]

This understanding of justice was based on the egalitarianism which had always rested at the heart of Proudhon's work; "justice, law of the material, intellectual, and moral world, has *equality* as its formula," he declared.[42] Now understood as mutual respect, justice could be realized only if organized on a basis of widespread economic equality.[43] Such equality was the law of nature, the inequality which characterized social life the result of an "anomaly":

> All individuals of whom society is composed are, in principle, of the same essence, the same calibre, the same type, the same model; any difference between them comes not from the form but from the external circumstances in which individuals are born and develop. It is not by virtue of this inequality, grossly exaggerated in any event, that society maintains itself, it is in spite of it.[44]

If human history had a direction, it was passing from the regime of authority to the regime of liberty, from the Church to the Revolution, from inequality to independence. Proudhon never equated progress with technology and economic growth alone. It had a moral content as well; only justice can order societies so personal freedom can coexist with social welfare.[45] The problem "consists in discovering how to make the best of the physical, intellectual, and economic powers which nature is incessantly discovering, with the goal of reestablishing a social equilibrium which is momentarily troubled by accidents of climate, generation, education, illness, and necessity."[46]

If justice was expressed as equilibration and balance, Proudhon's treatment of it was shaped by an understanding of dialectics which was far less critical in the *Justice* than it had been in his earlier works. His method before 1848 had required combining or balancing two terms of a contradiction to get a third which, while not resolving the contradiction, would at least hold it in temporary equilibrium by suppressing each term's "negative" side and developing its "positive" side. Thus possession had stood between property and communism, expressing the positive aspects of both and keeping the contradiction between them manageable. The "middle class" had likewise stood between the bourgeoisie and the proletariat. Its mechanical quality notwithstanding, this early method had been based on a dynamic view of social relations and had pointed to the possibility of changes in the terms of the contradictions.

Proudhon's use of the dialectical method in the *Justice*, however, was decidedly more conservative and dropped the dynamic element, seeking to conciliate both terms of a contradiction, to hold them in balance pretty much as they were. Equilibrium played the same role for Proudhon that process played for Hegel. "In order for the social power to be able to act with all its strength," he said, "all the functional forces of which it is composed must be in equilibrium. Now this equilibrium cannot result from an arbitrary discrimination; it must come from a balance of forces acting upon one another in complete liberty and leading to a mutual equation."[47] Equilibrium and stability were now his ultimate goals.[48] This meant that he would continue his movement away from an attempt to suppress the "bad" sides of the bourgeoisie and the proletariat by merging both into the petty bourgeoisie to an effort to establish rules for a just social order which would permit all existing classes to exist largely unchanged.

Proudhon wondered "by what virtue, by what law, man can retain personal activity and free will while multiplying his power through association?"[49] Economic forces could equilibrate one another only through their "mutual opposition," property balancing community, competition balancing privilege, and so on: "like the natural world, the moral world exists by itself, resting on certain laws and equilibrated in all its parts."[50] As presently constituted, politics cannot help but be as arbitrary and unstable as the economy which is its base; but with an egalitarian economy equilibrated through a mutual balancing of economic forces which would guarantee the integrity of existing groupings, society can now organize itself along its "natural" lines:

> In what concerns the substance and organization of social life, I was the first to show what belongs to the group from the excess of social power which sur-

passes the sum of individual powers which composes it; I gave the second law when I showed that it resolves itself into a sort of equilibration of forces, services and products which makes the social system a general equation, a balance. For an organism, society, the moral being *par excellence*, differs fundamentally from living creatures, in whom the subordination of organs is the law of existence. This is why society rejects every suggestion of hierarchy while it expresses the principle that all men are equal in dignity by nature and must become equivalent in conditions through work and justice.[51]

"Justice" in government must be expressed as substantive equality of conditions, but now it is an equality whose function is to hold all parts of society in mutual balance.[52] Proudhon was always disposed to search for a "law of equilibrium" which would enable society to "naturally" regulate itself with spontaneous social forces set in motion by an equilibrated economy and unhampered by alien political structures. The juridical expression of his notion of justice was "equal and reciprocal respect for possessions and interests in conditions posed by law and whatever it costs envy, greed, laziness and inability."[53] A theory of justice which had been deeply subversive when married to an egalitarian criticism of property had evolved into a sort of pluralism which derived its strength from the market relations to which it declared itself opposed. Proudhon's earlier critiques of bourgeois social relations were now phrased as the attempt to defend all the classes connected with capitalism from the inevitable consequences of capitalism. He wanted to generalize private property while safeguarding the independence of every class. He repeated his earlier demand that the workers receive as much value as they create through their labor; justice now demanded that, while the bourgeoisie would retain its ownership of the means of production, the workers themselves would appropriate all the surplus value they created. This did not require that the workers be substantively equal between themselves, since Proudhon's notion of justice was perfectly compatible with any market-based system of ethics:

> In order for service to be reciprocal, the master or the representative of the enterprise must return to the worker as much as the worker gives him: this implies, not the equality of all salaries among themselves including the directors, since salaries cannot be equal and the social equality of people does not demand the substantial equality of services, but equality between the *wages* of each worker and the value of his *product*.
>
> Equality of product and wage, this is the exact translation of the law of reciprocity and the principle which has supposedly been governing society since the Revolution.[54]

As might be expected, his powerful desire for equilibrium and social peace led Proudhon in some profoundly reactionary directions. His notorious views about women and the family were motivated by his desire to protect stable social institutions in a period of rapid social change. During the Revolution of 1848 he had linked an analysis of the family to the character of the wider social order and exposed the hypocrisy of bourgeois platitudes about the joys of family life by accusing the capitalists of corrupting morality, creating misery among the proletariat, and spreading disorder through laziness and greed. The specimen copy of *Le Peuple* which had appeared on September 2, 1848, contained the following declaration addressed to its readers:

> You, whose ambition is to earn whatever it takes to nourish a woman and make her happy, do you want to know who are the enemies of the family? Go to your neighbor the capitalist, the stock-holder, the speculator, the adventurer, the idle; look into his private life; question his wife, his maid, his little boy, and you will know who, by his greedy egoism and his disorderly romances, corrupts public morality and undermines the family. It's misery which makes the worker a libertine and a fornicator; he has a natural horror of vice and an impulse toward virtue. It's luxury which makes the rich incestuous and adulterous; with them, overindulgence and laziness are the invincible agents of disorder.

Despite this apparently progressive inclination to blame bourgeois hypocrisy and self-indulgence for social decline, Proudhon was an extreme male supremist and his views about the family were so traditional as to be considered reactionary even by his contemporaries. Virtually the only socialist of his generation who was not a feminist, he compromised his egalitarianism by seeking to strengthen an institution he thought indispensable for social life. Prudish in his sexual and social views, his suspicion of women doubtless originated in his rationalist claim that morality requires man to hold his animal side in check and be guided in all things by his reason. His opinions were deeply held, and they long preceded the outbreak of the revolution in 1848.[55]

The publication of the *Justice* offered him a chance to prove that women are inferior to men in three important areas of life. Since reproduction is their *raison d'être*, their resulting physical passivity and weakness is derived from nature. Intellectually inferior because they cannot reflect, women are incapable of understanding, receiving an idea or following a deduction. At home in the world of the irrational, they cannot think like men and were "a sort of middle term between them and the rest of the animal kingdom."[56] Their moral inferiority derived from an undeveloped conscience which rendered them unable to deal with freedom or justice: "relative to us, the woman can be described as an *immoral being*."[57] Since women were inferior to men, it followed for Proudhon that they should not be treated equally in the home or in society. If they are superior to men in "the grace of their figure and spirit, the pleasantness of character and the tenderness of heart," this in no way made up for their inferiority in physical, intellectual, and moral matters:[58]

since every question of preponderance in the government of human life results either from the economic order or from the philosophic or juridical area, it is obvious that the superiority of beauty, even intellectual and moral, cannot help women, whose condition remains subordinate. Men and women can be equivalent before the Absolute; they are not equal, and cannot be, either in the family or in the city.[59]

Proudhon thought it important to demonstrate the inferiority of women because he badly wanted to strengthen the traditional patriarchal family as a bulwark of social peace. Afraid that any change in relations between men and women would weaken the family, he insisted that it could prepare its members to be good citizens and good people because it would protect its members against political despotism. Proudhon's was an old-fashioned and badly outdated view, and the tenacity with which he clung to it demonstrated that he had run out of hope that people could find safety from the autocratic parasitical state unless the most deeply-rooted and traditional social structures were protected. Having provided a theoretical defense of this position in his definition of justice, Proudhon seemed to hope that the family would be the seat of justice, the guarantor of individual autonomy, and the source of revolution as well:

> love, marriage, paternity, family, natural institutions, prior to religion herself, are suspect to the Church; this is because they are the home of liberty, independence, free will, genuine charity, inviolable Justice: a fortress built by the human heart against theocracy and absolutism from which the Revolution will come sooner or later if the priesthood doesn't make off with it first.[60]

Proudhon wanted to make the family the moral and productive cell of society.[61] His defense of inheritance, with the sole limitation that no one be able to transmit more property than could be immediately used in production, dovetailed with his defense of the family, both being based on his desire to defend and generalize small production. He defended his views until the end of his life, never losing sight of a social order "founded on indissoluble marriage, on marital and paternal authority, on moral rigidity, individual and familial property, sacrosanct and inalienable property."[62]

Even Proudhon's good friend Alexander Herzen was disappointed and repelled by his discussion of women and the family in the *Justice*. He thought Proudhon had denied the most positive aspects of his antiauthoritarianism in relying upon Roman conceptions of authority and defending an autocratic family. Calling this part of the book "the testament of an old man," Herzen broke with Proudhon in June 1859 by publishing a long attack on him in the *Northern Star*, then an important Russian socialist publication.[63]

Proudhon's views about slaves and Jews were hardly more advanced than his contempt for women. He suggested that slaves in the American South could not be liberated by Union troops or Lincoln's government but would have to wait for a complete social transformation before they could be free. In the absence of such an unlikely development, emancipation would do no more than exchange one set of masters for another and it might be better for the slaves to remain with their present owners and seek progress through self-improvement.[64] His anti-semitism was deeply rooted in petty-bourgeois anxieties and drew from the popular identification of Jews with banking and finance. For Proudhon, their legal emancipation by the French Revolution removed their excuse that restrictive laws left them no choice of occupation, and Jews had become that with which they had formerly been charged. "The Jew remained a Jew, a parasite race, hostile to work, addicted to all practices of an anarchical and lying trade, gambling, speculation and usurious banking." More than kings and emperors, "they are the sovereigns of the epoch" and Proudhon intended to "expose" them:[65]

> JEWS—Do an article against this race, which poisons everything, thrusting itself everywhere, without ever blending with any people.
> Call for its expulsion from France, except for individuals married to Frenchmen; abolish the synagogues; admit them to no employment; in fact, abolition of this creed.
> It is not for nothing that Christians have called them god-killers. The Jew is the enemy of the human race. It is necessary to send this race back to Asia, or exterminate it.
> H. Heine, A. Weil, and others are nothing but secret spies; Rothschild, Cremieux, Marx, Fould—evil, bad-tempered, envious, sour, etc., etc. beings who hate us.
> By means of iron or fusion or expulsion, it is necessary that the Jews disappear. Tolerate the old ones who can no longer beget children.
> Work to be done.—What the people of the Middle Ages hated by instinct, I hate on reflection, and irrevocably.
> The hatred of the Jew as of the English must be an article of religious faith.[66]

Proudhon had written his *Justice* because he wanted to prove that a moral category like justice could generate principles which could organize the economy.[67] The categories he had examined in 1846 would continue to exist as such; balanced and equilibrated by justice, they would now be the source of harmony and peace. With mutualism serving as the expression of equality, the market's chaotic destructiveness would be replaced by equal exchange and social peace. Everything would be changed into its opposite and the result would be "good" capitalism, capitalism without profit, chaos, or suffering:

> property balanced by property, even though always absolute for its owner, resolves itself into a pure delegation according to public reason; credit, always self-serving for the lender, into an interest-free mutuality; commerce, speculative by nature, into equal exchange; the government, imperative in its essence, into a balance of forces; work, repugnant to intellect, into an exercise of intellect; charity into right, competition into solidarity, unity into series, etc.[68]

Proudhon's desire to defend the petty bourgeoisie drove the moral theory he developed in the *Justice*; his purpose was not substantially different during the 1850s from what it had been during the previous decade. He still believed that the destruction of the *petite bourgeoisie* and the small property on which it rested fatally undermined the redemptive power of the market that the political economists were describing. The progress of which they spoke was nothing more than a redistribution of wealth from the poor to the rich, and Proudhon condemned it precisely because of the threat it carried for the petty bourgeoisie:

> They say that there has been an increase of commerce, increase in profits, thus increase in well-being. False calculation and false conclusion. There has been a displacement of commerce, displacement of profits, displacement of well-being, all to the detriment of the many small industries which comprise productive democracy and to the benefit of the great industry which presently comprises the new feudalism. In admitting that his displacement has been accompanied by a certain increase in commerce because of lower costs, this increase is balanced by a subordination of producers who were formerly independent and are salaried today, falling from the petty bourgeoisie into the proletariat ... the number of exploited being greater today than earlier, there has been a retrogression.[69]

De la Justice dans la révolution et dans l'église was seized as soon as it was published. The government's alliance with the Church was shaky because Louis-Napoleon's backing of Italian unification appeared to threaten the Pope's autocratic and unpopular regime in the Papal States, but in internal matters the state was very clearly the Church's guardian. The frequent attacks on the Church in the *Justice* were too much for the government, and despite Proudhon's appeal to the Senate he was convicted in June of "attack on the family, attack on respect for the laws, exciting hatred among the citizens." Sentenced to three years in prison and a fine of 4,000 francs, he left for Belgium and exile a month later. His family joined him in December. That the *Justice* was intolerable to the Second Empire was more an indication of the regime's despotism than of Proudhon's subversiveness, for the moral and political positions elaborated in the book were little more than a warmed-over pluralism and did not come close to calling into question the fundamental principles of market society. Seeking to combine the greatest possible area of individual development with a measure of social solidarity, Proudhon's mutualism had emerged at the center of his thinking. Its demand for respect and tolerance was the practical expression of his understanding of justice and was put forward as a framework within which the individual could be reconciled with the community, his misogyny and antisemitism notwithstanding. "Authority" emerged as the chief antagonist to liberty and freedom, and if Proudhon was not an extreme individualist who denied the existence of an objective world or the moral worth of learning to come to terms with it, it is no less true that the *Justice* sketched out a picture of an equilibrated stateless market society which did not deviate in any important way from some varieties of classical liberalism. When all is said and done, what Proudhon wanted was to organize a just version of capitalism. When he said that free contracts must replace the state's authority—which he says repeatedly throughout the book—he described contracts which were expressions of mutuality, transactions of equal exchange in which one gets back exactly as much as one puts in. These contracts are the concrete expressions of equality, justice, and mutuality in the conditions of daily life. The concrete form of moral self-direction, they will express the diversity which Proudhon so badly wished to protect. He wanted to make it possible for each individual or group to confront and negotiate directly with each other unhampered by hierarchy, law, power, or any other distorting influence.[70] The fusion of liberty and order which Proudhon thought he had organized in the notion of justice would be the dissolution of the state, and his hostility to politics—one of his most important and problematic legacies—seemed to have found a moral expression. It remained for him to amplify it.

PROUDHON IN BRUSSELS

Political exile is often difficult, and Proudhon's four years in Belgium were no exception. He followed French internal and external affairs closely and kept up an active correspondence with several friends in Paris, but his theoretical work was not noticeably affected by the changed perspective that came with his first extended stay outside France. Proudhon had always been preoccupied by French matters and shared little of the internationalism which was becoming a permanent feature of the European left, but the years of exile in Brussels when coupled with Louis-Napoleon's Italian adventure encouraged him to consider international affairs a little more closely than he had previously. The path which would culminate in his theory of federalism was shaped by the entire body of his earlier France-based work, however, even if it was affected in the short run by international developments.

Personal hardships had much to do with shaping the general character of the exile. His nervous disorder got progressively worse, each attack leaving him weaker and more frightened than before. His morale suffered a great deal at times, aggravated by occasional family illness and permanent poverty. The period was not a happy one for Proudhon: isolated, vulnerable, sick, poor, and under continuous attack from all quarters, he alternated between blaming the French people for the Empire and wondering why no one took him seriously.

He remained convinced that the apparent strength of the Empire was illusory, an artificial glitter which could mask inner weakness and decay for only so long. He was sure that the regime's vulnerability had led it to ban the *Justice*, for a system founded upon a lie cannot tolerate the search for truth.[71] The regime was supported by only "its guards, its jesuits, its speculators, its whores and a few functionaries," and he predicted a war between the government and the country that would end in France's renewal.[72] He would be happy with any change. "If my predictions aren't wrong," he said, "we are moving toward a restoration of revolutionary ideas, a restoration whose external, political sign will be the replacement of despotism by a representative regime (monarchical or republican)."[73]

To his hope that the regime would fall of its own corruption was added the conviction that Louis-Napoleon's irresponsible restlessness would hasten the day of liberation—even if such liberation might assume a political form in the short run. He was sure that the Empire would have to go to war to divert France's attention from internal difficulties and dismissed the regime's professed concern for the independence and unification of Italy, which led to a short war with Austria in 1859, as a "chauvinistic joke which is masking other designs."[74] He was sure that irresponsible leadership, lack of domestic support, and international isolation were leading the regime to a serious crisis. "In other countries," he said, "it is clear that our country appears unhappier than it has ever been; the imperial government is universally hated, the nation scorned, all of Napoleon's projects frustrated, the country isolated, deprived of her freedom internally, of respect abroad, and her liberty in overall decline."[75]

To his disgust with Louis-Napoleon and the "cretins" who supported him was added renewed illness and war in the spring of 1859.[76] Proudhon was still preoccupied with the moral consequences of France's political and economic crisis.[77] He was angry and bitter at popular support for Bonaparte's Italian adventure and turned his attention to war and the "national question" as national movements developed in central, eastern, and southern Europe.[78] He was deeply ashamed that France had become the most reactionary Papalist nation on the continent, and even in exile he imagined that he might be the "very powerful engineer" who could reestablish French society.[79]

La Guerre et la paix was published in May 1861, and is the only full-length work Proudhon produced while in exile. He had begun to think about war as a "category" in reaction to the events of 1859, but the book appears as a sidelight; his serious attempt to deal with the issues raised by Italian unification was his theory of federalism, the elaboration of which was the major project of his last years. Proudhon tried to do the same thing for the "principle of war" that he had done earlier for the economic categories; he tried to isolate war, to analyze its inner contradictions and identify its "good" and "bad" aspects in the hope that he could develop the "positive" side and reduce the impact of the "negative" side.[80] Such a "scientific" approach had seemed to suffer from only technical problems in 1846, but now Proudhon's attempt to apply the same method led to great difficulties. Besides the fact that Tolstoy named his great novel after Proudhon's book, the important thing about *Guerre et Paix* was not so much what it put forward about war but why Proudhon's intentions were so misunderstood.

If he wanted to describe a "metaphysic of war and a physics of peace" in the book,[81] his real effort was to demonstrate that—like everything else— war was a manifestation of the principle of justice. "I've reestablished war to her ancient prestige," he claimed; "I've made it clear, contrary to the opinion of legal people, that it is essentially just."[82] As destructive as it can be, war can also be the expression of mankind's highest and most nearly divine characteristics. It is a pure manifestation of man's inner life, a law of his soul, a necessary condition for human purification.[83] The foundation of our social life and the reflection of mankind's highest achievements, war has served as a way for man to develop his moral life, organize equality, and express his higher faculties:

> War is divine, that is to say, primordial, essential to life, to the production of man and society. Its health is rooted in the depths of the conscience, and it encompasses in its idea all human relationships. Through war our most elevated faculties have revealed and exposed themselves from the beginning of history: religion, justice, poetry, fine arts, social economy, politics, government, nobility, bourgeois, royalty, property. Through war in subsequent epochs morality strengthens itself, nations renew themselves, states balance themselves, progress unfolds, justice establishes its dominion, liberty finds its guarantees . . . Without war, peace cannot comprehend itself; it has nothing positive, it is deprived of value and significance; it is nothing. Even so, humanity flees war and strains toward peace with all its might. Contradiction between the fundamental givens of a society and its operations.[84]

As silly as all this may sound, Proudhon did not want to leave the discussion at this point. If "war is a form of our reason, a law of our soul and a condition of our existence like the beautiful, the just and the useful,"[85] it is also true that it can disorganize societies and contribute to their further disarray if economic reforms do not "constitute" society. Until then, war will be "extradialectical," fatal, contradictory, and destructive. Like everything else, war will have a radically different impact on a society which has been reorganized than it has on one which is as fundamentally disturbed as contemporary France. For Proudhon, the failure of the revolution degraded war and made it an enemy of man's moral liberation. Its positive and ennobling aspects would come out only if society were "organized" along the lines he had been suggesting for years.[86]

Proudhon's intentions notwithstanding, the publication of *La Guerre et la paix* provoked violent reactions from his friends and enemies alike. His apologies for war were blown far out of proportion, separated from their connections to his wider social theory, and made to seem much more central to the book's purpose than they were. Proudhon's reaction to the recent publication of Darwin's *Origin of Species* doubtless contributed to the confusion, but whatever the cause he was forced to spend a great deal of time trying to explain that his only desire had been to scientifically isolate and analyze the phenomenon:

> I begin by observing that war contains a moral and juridical element in it; that it is the combination of this moral element with the spilling of blood and massacre, which are not moral at all, which gives war its *divine*, mysterious character; I say that to decipher this myth, we must study war, no longer on the field of battle, but in humanity's conscience with the understanding that without this we will understand nothing and that, understanding nothing about it, we will always be its victims.[87]

If injustice was the cause of war, it followed that conflict could not be eliminated until society was reorganized along egalitarian lines. Proudhon had wanted to prove that the reign of political economy would be the reign of peace, finding it difficult to believe that people really thought he was defending militarism.[88] He wanted to "be done with" with war, but he stated his thoughts in such a way as to confuse his friends and make them wonder what his intentions really were:

> to be done with war, it is not enough to declaim against it like the *pacifists*; we must begin by recognizing that it has something great, moral, juridical, sublime and by revealing its principle, its role, its mission, its goal; having done that, one can then—and only then—see that with war having accomplished all or almost all of its mission, it is finished, not by the good will of nations or governments, but by the accomplishment of its mandate.[89]

Sometimes Proudhon seemed to think that he was in trouble because he had found it difficult to express his ideas clearly. At other times he blamed his critics, proclaiming that they were attacking him because he was the last representative of the principles of 1848.[90] Yet he felt that he had to express what he honestly felt to be the truth even at the expense of his popularity,[91] and the continuous attacks to which he was subject undermined his confidence at times. "More than ever," he said, "I wonder if I am of this world, if I matter in it, or if I should regard myself as a troubled soul who returns to frighten the living and is refused their prayers. My success is enough for my family's subsistence and for my pride as an author; but I would like to have some influence in the world, and this is the area from which I find myself excluded."[92] An important cause of the difficulties in which he found himself, however, was that his aim remained "the complete reconciliation of the medium bourgeoisie with socialism as I have always understood it."[93] As the continuing decay of the Second Empire compelled him to make some difficult choices, his continuing desire to find safety for the petty bourgeoisie began to impart a decidedly conservative tone to his thoughts and words during this period. "You know," he told his friend Charles Beslay, "that my ambition is, after having been the most revolutionary spirit of my age, to become, without changing my ideas one iota and even by the success of these very ideas, *the most conservative*."[94]

Proudhon received a full pardon from Louis-Napoleon on December 12, 1860, as the Empire began to swing to the "left."[95] He stayed in Belgium for almost two more years because of his fear that he would not be able to get his works published in France.[96] He was ultimately forced to flee because his opposition to the national movements in Italy and Germany made him a target of Belgian nationalists. When he suggested that support of Italian and German nationalism was equivalent to supporting the annexation of Belgium by France, a mob—which he always suspected was organized by the Belgian police—forced him to hastily return to France. His return guaranteed that his future development would be dramatically affected by his proximity to the reawakening French working class, the major influence on him during his last years and the source of the spurt of creativity which characterized his final works.

THE THEORY OF FEDERALISM

Proudhon returned to find France in a far more general crisis than he had imagined.[97] He immediately set out to provide the remedy, and he decided to state his preliminary conclusions regarding the "principle of nationalities" as soon as possible.[98] He was working on *Du principe fédératif* partly to defend himself against the suspicions coming out of Belgium, and he described his hopes for the book to a friend:

> It's a demonstration, after a style of mine, of this proposition: that all governments known to this day are discordant fragments of the true social constitution which is unique, true for all people, and can be called *federative republic*, that there is no liberty, law, morality or good will outside of that . . . In brief, this is what I call the *solution of the political problem*, the definition of the Republic.[99]

Proudhon had concluded that federalism was the political form of justice and the most dependable way to organize the victory of liberty over authority. Worried above all by the development of large unitary states, he dissented from the universal support which national movements enjoyed from the left, a position which he knew would be unpopular and whose publication could only deepen his already bothersome isolation.[100] He was also becoming troubled by the deeply-rooted collectivism of the reviving workers' movement and wanted to organize federalism as the political form of mutualism because each existing unit would be able to preserve its autonomy and avoid the potential dangers of relying too much on centralization or association. The maintenance of diversity had become a central goal of Proudhon's political and social theory and stood behind his increasing emphasis on finding local solutions to local problems. His drive to disintegrate the increasingly centralized nation-state system was paralleled by his desire to avoid the tendency to search for answers to social problems in politics. Despite his reservations, he was so sure that federalism was the answer to Europe's problems that he went ahead and published the *Du Principe fédératif* in February 1863. To his surprise, the book was an instant success and had some subsequent influence among the Communards, the right-wing thinkers of Third Republic France, and the English pluralists.

He started by posing the contradiction between authority and liberty as the root contradiction of the political order, a technique reminiscent of earlier works. Each of these "principles" had its own history and identity, but was simultaneously dependent on the other for its self-definition. The never-ending struggle between them determined the course of political development.

Where Proudhon would have tried earlier to find a third term between the two which would be the "synthesis" or "solution" of the equation, his new understanding of dialectics led him to suggest that "all political constitutions, all systems of government . . . can be summarized by this formula, the *balance of authority by liberty* and *vice versa*."[101] Politics would be unstable "until universal reason has discovered how to master these two principles and equilibrate society by the regularization of these antagonisms."[102] Proudhon was beginning to move away from his radical antistatism as he called for subordinating politics to social structure and converting it into a tool of emancipation. The state is still an "alienation de la force collective" which renders political power incapable of accurately representing the general interest, but if free contracts among substantive equals are made the center of gravity of social structure and political organization, then a reformed state could serve justice.[103]

Proudhon intended to solve the contradiction between authority and liberty by using the "law of contract," convinced as he was that freedom can be found only in the social relations of civil society. Following the arguments of the *Justice*, a just contract returns to all the parties at least as much value as they contribute while simultaneously helping them defend their freedom, initiative, and independence.[104] The unitary centralized state inexorably destroyed the autonomy of its parts, but Proudhon was sure that a federative system would preserve the balance between authority and liberty by making it possible to organize a nonpolitical, nonauthoritarian, and nonhierarchical variety of freedom. It would erect an insurmountable barrier to the grasping, despotic centralization of contemporary politics while safeguarding the autonomy of each individual.

Proudhon's theory of federalism provided the political expression of the moralism espoused in the pages of the *Justice*. It incorporated a theory of mutualism generalized across the entire society and supported by a far more developed theory of contract than he had elaborated up to now. "If I began with *anarchy* in 1840 as the conclusion of my criticism of the governmental idea, now I finish with *federation*, necessary legal base for Europeans and, later, of organization for all states."[105] Centralization could not organize equality or reconcile authority with liberty. The false unity which the centralized nation-state offers could not establish social solidarity; the autonomy of local communities can express freedom only on the basis of spontaneous self-organization. Free voluntary contract can serve as a social cement only if it is actively encouraged and protected by a federated political apparatus.

Having outlined his suggestions for the reorganization of the state, Proudhon turned his attention to its economic foundation. His real objective was to pose the political form of federalism as the basic framework for the economic reforms he envisaged; all his later writings have the organization of a mutualist economy at their center.[106] A "fédération agricole-industrielle" was the highest application of the "principle" of mutuality, the answer to the "féodalité financière."[107] The state would guarantee and if necessary execute what now emerged as the summation of all Proudhon's teachings to date:

> All my economic ideas, developed over twenty-five years, can be summarized in three words: *agricultural-industrial federation.*
>
> All my political ideas are reduced to a similar formula: *political federation* or decentralization.
>
> And since I do not use my ideas as either a party instrument or a tool of personal ambition, all my hopes for the present and the future are expressed by this third corollary term: *progressive federation.*[108]

Proudhon had begun to move away from his radical anarchism in the *Justice*, where he had tried to suggest some reforms which he hoped would enable the state to support equality and freedom. He continued this motion in *Du principe fédératif*, his basic goal having changed to finding a balance between authority and liberty, state, and individual.[109] He was now interested in impregnating the state with justice.[110] His anarchism had blended into federalism, yet it is important that the political federalism was designed to support a mutualist economy.[111] Federalism meant political decentralization, long one of Proudhon's cherished goals:

> I am curious to know how it happens that liberty and equality can result from the unity of power, from administrative centralization, from the concentration of economic forces, from the accumulation and supremacy of capital, how economic mutuality could be anything but a federation.[112]

Proudhon had sketched out the outline of his theory of mutuality in the *Justice*. The expression of justice founded on universal respect for others' autonomy, mutuality would protect small producers by replacing authority, centralization, and hierarchy with a network of free exchange. This theme had run throughout all his writings; he was merely giving it a political form at this time, convinced as he was that

> in theory and practice, federation completely resolves the problem of the rela-
> tion between freedom and authority, giving to each its just measure, its sphere
> of competence and all initiative. Consequently, only it guarantees order, justice,
> stability and peace with inviolable respect for the citizen and the state.[113]

Free and just contracts would regulate the balance between producers, eliminate egoism, and organize social intercourse.[114] They would replace abstract formal law as the political organization of mutualism and justice. They would replace the arbitrariness of the state and equilibrium, now guar-anteed by a network of contracts between equals, would replace political force.[115] Proudhon's understanding of socialism, decisively influenced by his petty-bourgeois orientation, was now expressed as "freedom of trade and of industry, mutuality of security, reciprocity of credit, equal distribution of taxes, equilibrium and security of fortune, participation of the worker in the risks of the enterprise, inviolability of the family in hereditary trans-mission."[116] The authentic revolution, he said,

> is the realization of the sovereignty of the people everywhere and always; sover-
> eignty of man in everything the individual is and can be; sovereignty of the
> commune in everything common; sovereignty of fathers and mothers in every-
> thing about the family, sovereignty of the producer in everything about work,
> commerce and industry; sovereignty of the locality in everything local; sover-
> eignty of national representation in only those matters which touch the most
> general interests.[117]

Proudhon's target at this time was the political and administrative cen-tralization that was so characteristic of French politics in general and of the Second Empire in particular. Like many others, he saw the Napoleonic state growing like a parasite, choking spontaneity, and deadening political life. Yet he was no longer interested in destroying the state or even in dissolving it back into society. His primary wish was to maintain the equal-ity of exchange between autonomous centers of production.[118] His federal-ism was perfectly designed to accomplish this goal. If different poles of production could be preserved within the framework of a mutualist and egalitarian social order, that would be the equivalent of the disappearance of the state. Federalism provided the political framework for unity and di-versity, authority and freedom, coordination and justice:

> In a free society, the role of the state or the government is above all a role of
> legislation, institution, creation, inauguration, installation; it's least of all a role

of execution. In this regard, the name of *executive power*, by which one designates one aspect of sovereign power, has powerfully contributed to falsifying ideas . . . the state, whatever it dictates, whatever it does or oversees, is the generator and the supreme director of the movement.[119]

Proudhon's views concerning the "national question" had appeared in *Guerre et Paix* and were stimulated by the appearance of national movements in Italy, Germany, Poland, and Hungary. Where most of the European left supported such movements, however, he characteristically declared that the real duty of the French left was to attack the "principle of nationalities" itself. This position was largely shaped by Louis-Napoleon's intervention in Italy,[120] and he was able to maintain his critical distance from the Empire, "me, proof that the supposed question of nationalities, as far as they understand it, is a false principle, a false idea, an anachronism which I deny and break into pieces."[121] His task was to oppose all national movements regardless of their leadership.[122] The Italian revolution, he asserted, must be directed as much against Cavour, Garibaldi, Mazzini, and Victor-Emmanuel as against the Pope, Napoleon, and Franz-Joseph:

> I declare that such a world, a world of speculators, thugs, intriguers, whores, adventurers, greedy and unprincipled bourgeois, seems a thousand times worse to me than the good Catholic-imperial people of the Peninsula; that the peasant from the Papal States who carried a candle to the Madonna in good faith seems infinitely more respectable to me than the liberal from the school of Cavour and Garibaldi . . .[123]

Proudhon's federalism had become central to his thought.[124] He was confident that justice could be realized only in a federal republic resting on a mutualist economy.[125] Such an arrangement would reconcile rights and duties and make it possible for self-sufficient and morally sovereign individuals to enter into equal and voluntary social relations as a matter of free choice. A network of free contracts would replace states and mitigate the harmful effects of the Church and capital. Neither man's moral life nor his public affairs would stand in the stark opposition to the vital processes of his social life as they did at present. If "the first and most fatal error which has burdened humanity is to have put the government above society,"[126] then his solution was tailored to rectify it, for "what we put in place of government is industrial organization . . . what we put place of political power are economic forces."[127] His fundamental desire was still to erect a theoretical model for protecting the material interests of all social classes, a project which boiled down to sheltering France's small proprietors from the ravages of industrialization. This project had engaged his attention for twenty-five years, but now the important work he undertook toward the end of his life turned to a different set of problems and was clearly stimulated by the rapid development of the labor movement. It is ironic indeed that one of Proudhon's most enduring legacies was the advice he offered to the nascent trade union movement.

PROUDHON AND THE WORKERS' MOVEMENT

In characteristic Bonapartist fashion, the Empire swung "left" during the early 1860s as economic crisis and foreign adventure forced Louis-Napoleon to appeal to the liberal bourgeoisie, the bulk of the petty bourgeoisie, and the proletariat. Yet the workers and the small proprietors had never given up their attachment to socialism, democracy, and republicanism, and the slight relaxation of the atmosphere only encouraged the development of a robust opposition centered in the labor movement. The elections of 1863 resulted in a victory for the opposition in Paris, and the government's monopoly of the countryside was seriously challenged for the first time since the *coup*.[128] Nothing could conceal the fact that great blocs of the population were beginning to move away from the regime. The Empire was soon faced with the same alternatives that had confronted the July Monarchy: in the light of increasing resistance to its rule, any attempt to maintain despotism might lead to revolution, but relaxation and concessions would allow the opposition to develop in great depth.

The elections of 1863 were a serious blow to the regime, and the steady rise in popular resistance to the "settlement" of 1851 dominated French political life for the next seven years. For the proletariat, the elections signalled the beginning of its overt struggle against the Empire, a process that was intimately linked to its accelerating ideological independence and political organization. It increasingly came to dominate the opposition.[129]

The determining factor in French politics was that the proletariat was beginning to find its own leaders, articulate its own needs, and move away from the democratic petty bourgeoisie. The socialism of the 1860s was more mature, experienced and militant than that of the 1840s. Dominated as it was by concentrated factory workers,[130] it placed primary emphasis on solidarity and organization—particularly *political* organization, which alone would make it possible to win allies and seriously contest for state power. Workers' candidates ran for office in 1863 and although one of their leaders was badly beaten in a partial election the following year, the class struggle could not be diluted by an electoral defeat:

> Tolain got 424 votes. The bourgeoisie attained its goal. But it attained another which it had not sought. It got the workers used to relying on no one but themselves; it confirmed their developing understanding of the class struggle; it pushed them bit by bit on to the path of revolution.[131]

A big step forward in the development of the French workers' movement was taken on February 17, 1864, when a letter signed by sixty workers appeared in *L'Opinion Nationale*. The publication of the "Manifeste des Soixante" is one of the defining events in the history of the French working class. It was a class document, the result of a distinctly proletarian consciousness, written by, addressed to, and expressing the interests of an important part of the proletariat. It stated its support for the fullest measure of political democracy, committed itself to the struggle for social emancipation and substantial equality of conditions, demanded the right to form trade unions, advised the workers to elect their own parliamentary representatives from their own ranks, pointed out to the petty-bourgeois democrats and the bourgeois liberals that they could do nothing without the active support of the workers, demanded free credit, and insisted on mandatory public education. Its publication announced the appearance of an ideologically class-conscious and politically independent proletariat in French political life. The reactionary papers invoked the "spectre rouge" once again, and liberal papers kept repeating that there were no class antagonisms in France and accused the "sixty" of seeking to arbitrarily divide a unified country along imaginary lines. The formation of the International Working-Men's Association on September 28, 1864, was another milestone in the development of the French proletariat.

Proudhon had been consulted by the "sixty" before their letter was published and was delighted to see the working class begin to organize itself, even if he remained suspicious of political activity. He was a strict abstentionist at this time and urged the workers to abstain from voting in the elections of 1863, arguing for nonparticipation on both principle and tactical grounds.[132] He thought of it as the highest form of civil disobedience because the "right" of abstention was prior to that of insurrection. Abstention appealed to him because it was legal, although he did acknowledge that anything would be legitimate if Louis-Napoleon continued to hold on to power after half the French people had refused to participate in elections.[133] He was also hopeful that abstention would enable the workers' movement to maintain its ideological independence of the bourgeoisie, since he considered the proletariat's attachment to collective political activity little more than a ratification of the worst aspects of the *status quo*. He was still interested in reconciling the goals of the "classe moyenne" and the workers, and he remained convinced that the workers should stay away from bourgeois politics because abstention would make the desired reconciliation easier. "Little by little a rapprochement will take place between the proletariat and the class of artisans, small manufacturers, small owners, petty bourgeois—the grouping which is most mistreated by the existing regime and is the healthiest part of the social body."[134] When all was said and done, Proudhon wanted to give the bourgeoisie every conceivable chance to meet the citizens' demands:

according to principles, and considering that all the *forms, conditions* and *guarantees* of *universal suffrage* are violated by the present regime, the citizens' duty is to abstain until the government has done justice to their demands and recognized the sovereignty of the nation with a number of changes.[115]

Proudhon expected that Louis-Napoleon would continue to use universal suffrage to confuse and divide the people.[136] "But be aware, my friend," he wrote a correspondent, "that the most backward and retrograde thing in all countries is the mass—what you call the democracy."[137] His fear that the regime would be able to continue its maneuvering through deception and manipulation merged with his more general distrust of political activity to produce the abstentionist position.

Proudhon was pleased with the results of the elections of 1863 because almost a third of the Parisian voters abstained or mutilated their ballots and the rest began to move away from the Empire.[138] He approved of the general thrust of the "Manifeste des Soixante," taking issue only with its support of workers' candidates and continuing to hold that abstention from all political activity was the only way the workers would be able to independently organize.[139] He continued to believe that elections simply legitimized the enslavement of the proletariat, confirmed its political impotence, aided the regime, and sowed confusion in the minds of the population. He wanted to limit all political activity to protest and had come to feel that boycotting elections was always the correct strategy.

His nervous disease got progressively worse during 1864, and by the fall it was clear that he was dying. Life had become a continual crisis for him,[140] yet he was still trying to convince the proletariat that its only course lay in separating itself from any and all connections with the bourgeoisie. He died on January 19, 1865, while dictating the last pages of *De la Capacité politique des classes ouvrières* to his daughter.[141] Proudhon's recommendations to the French proletariat complemented his writings on federalism and may be said to be his "testament."

Given that "the people" were clearly coming to a new level of social consciousness and political organization, he considered it more essential than ever that the workers separate themselves completely from bourgeois politics.[142] Society was becoming more divided into two classes, those who must labor and those who can live without working from their rents, pensions, or capital.[143] The interests of the two classes were becoming more and more antagonistic, the bourgeoisie having gotten progressively more corrupt and retrograde since its great victory in 1789.[144] Such a position was quite different in its implications than much of his earlier work. Even so, Proudhon was not ready to embrace a theory of class war or countenance a political struggle for state power. If the proletariat and the bourgeoisie were drawing away from each other that might advance the workers' level of understanding for the moment, but only on condition that they meet again sometime in the future. Even as he advocated abstention from all political activity on his deathbed, he looked forward to the same fusion of work and property which had animated his work from the beginning:

> Whether the bourgeoisie knows it or not, its role is over; it cannot go any further, and it cannot be reborn. But it should give up the ghost peacefully! The victory of the common people will not lead to its elimination, in the sense that the commoners will replace the bourgeoisie in its political domination after having replaced it in its privileges, property, or enjoyment, any more than the bourgeoisie would replace the commoners in their wage-labor. The present well-established distinction between the classes, proletariat and bourgeoisie, is a simple revolutionary accident. Both must be reciprocally absorbed in a higher consciousness; the day when the common people, organized as a majority, will have seized power and proclaimed social and economic reform according to the new law's hopes and science's formulas will be the day of final fusion.[145]

The *Capacité* had an immediate impact on the French working class, although its full importance was not felt until several years after Proudhon's death.[146] His considerable posthumous influence in the First International, the Paris Commune, and the later development of the French working class resulted largely from the role that he and his followers played in the great debates about the role of politics in the proletariat's struggle against capitalism.[147] Proudhon's hostility to politics had been modified to some extend as he developed his theory of federalism, but a general orientation toward the economic and social roots of inequality was a logical outgrowth of his ideas and experience as they had developed throughout his life.[148] It derived from his fundamental attachment to small production and reflected his fierce desire to safeguard the sanctity of the individual. His mutualism had been developed to reconcile liberty with equality, but he remained suspicious of both the bourgeoisie's politics and the proletariat's collectivism. His opposition to strikes reflected his desire to organize an equilibrium of classes. When the revived workers' movement forced a repeal of the notorious Le Chapelier Law which had banned workers' associations since the Revolution, Proudhon denounced it in no uncertain terms. "The law permitting unions is fundamentally anti-legal, anti-economic, contrary to all society and all peace," he said. "There is no more right to organize than there is a right to blackmail or theft, any more than there is a right to incest or adultery."[149] His hostility to unions and strikes was so deeply felt and so provocatively stated that he sometimes sounded like the most reactionary industrialist. His apology for a state massacre of strikers became infamous:

> The authority which had the miners of Rive-de-Gier shot was disastrous. But it was acting like Brutus, who was placed between his love for his father and his

duty to his consul: he had to sacrifice his children to save the republic. Brutus didn't hesitate and posterity doesn't dare condemn him.[150]

This curious position, like most others to which Proudhon came, derived from his desire to restrict and circumscribe the class struggle. He wanted to keep it legal and manageable, nonpolitical and, in the final analysis, nonthreatening. His socialism had always been a socialism of exchange rather than of production, and he had always wanted to mitigate the effects of the bourgeoisie's appropriation of society's "collective force" without calling the organization of production into question. His overwhelming desire was to treat workers' cooperatives, mutual-aid societies, and the like as the germs of an alternative to capitalism and to resist any tendency to treat the class struggle as a political phenomenon with consequences for the society as a whole.[151] His many disciples in France, Spain, Italy, and Switzerland followed in his footsteps and always sought to make the First International into a cooperative society which would organize work, make credit available, and stay out of all workers' political struggles.

Proudhon continued to believe that history had passed from the age of politics to that of economics, but his attempt to separate the political from the economic aspects of the working class movement was theoretically mistaken and tactically dangerous. He preferred to leave political activity to the bourgeoisie and had given up the orientation toward general and comprehensive activity that a commitment to politics implied. Like the other socialists of the period, he was trying to understand how the proletariat ought to relate to a bourgeoisie which had betrayed it time and time again. The Paris Commune proved to be the graveyard of almost all varieties of "anti-political" socialism, but Proudhon's stubborn abstentionism continued to have some residual influence until the rapid growth of the proletariat swept it away in the 1890s.

Proudhon's final formulations about property were expressed in the *Théorie de la propriété*, also published several months after his death and representing his last attempt to "balance" property and possession with each other and with other antinomies.[152] Since he now believed that antinomies were eternal and absolute and that justice requires that they be against other antinomies,[153] his intention was to find the conditions which would make property an organ of equality.[154] He had come some distance since his early writings, but the method of analysis and the underlying goals remained the same. He still tried to analyze the institution "as such" and discuss its purposes and its "internal" functioning. His idea of the positive role of property followed from what had become his primary concern in his later years:

> If the citizen is to become something in the state, it is not enough . . . that he be free in his person; like the state, his personality must support itself on a piece

of matter which he possesses exclusively, just as the state which has sovereignty over the public domain. This condition is fulfilled by property.[155]

Property had become the term of another equation and was to serve as a counterweight to the state. With the patriarchal family, it was now to be a main line of defense against autocracy. His intentions notwithstanding, Proudhon's commitment to small property was driving him toward classical liberalism. Focusing almost exclusively on the public, political nature of power and authority, he was increasingly disposed to ignore their private, economic roots. He had become convinced that the indivisibility and inalienability of property must be preserved so the individual could defend himself against the state. He wanted to limit the ability of landowners to divide and sell their holdings, concerned that this would destroy the material foundations of small rural property.[156] Faced with the capitalist transformation of agriculture and the dangers to which it subjected the rural petty bourgeoisie and peasantry, he was still trying to universalize small property and defend the petty bourgeoisie against both the propertyless proletariat and the modern capitalist.

His political orientation took an ideological form, for Proudhon was able to criticize property against the bourgeois political economists but felt that he had to defend it against the socialists. The issue for him was no longer the radical transformation of the existing social order—if it had ever been—but rather its gradual improvement. This required suppressing the conflicts between equality, liberty, the division of labor, competition and the like. When the political economists said that substantive equality of conditions must yield to liberty and freedom, he replied that the laws of the jungle were insufficient to create a just social order. When the socialists sought to substitute association for competition or community of goods for private property, he replied that he was unwilling to sacrifice liberty or property. The goal was still to universalize "possession," for if uncontrolled property was the domination of the weak by the strong, then communism was the domination of the strong by the weak and both were equally unjust. The protector of liberty and privacy, property can reinforce justice in a mutualist system. "To serve as a counterweight to public power, balance the state and by this means to assure individual freedom—this will be property's principal political function."[157] If property were distributed equally, the state would become a liberating institution because it would now be "owned" by all its citizens and the equal division of property would enable citizens to both protect and develop themselves:[158]

> Property is the natural and necessary counterweight to public power; the civil right of property is the controller and determinant of state policy. Where there is no property or where it is replaced by slave or feudal possession, there is despotism in the government and instability throughout the system.[159]

Proudhon had found "possession" inadequate and, faced with the political and economic developments of the 1850s and 1860s, ended by justifying the same sort of property against which he had waged such a prolonged struggle at the beginning of his career. His goal having remained constant throughout, he had moved from an initial suspicion of bourgeois society and a willingness to regulate property to an embrace of a modified form of market society and a reluctance to interfere with liberty. The constancy of his project shone through the variations in the means by which he intended to protect the independence and approximate equality of small centers of production.[160]

Proudhon's late writings were riven by the same kind of problems that were present at the beginning of his career. He seemed to be trying to deal with new subjects, yet his purposes remained fairly constant throughout his life. He seemed to be heading in new directions much of the time, yet he often paid only lip service to vexing problems and glibly concluded that everything would be fine when society was organized. He seemed to recognize the need for wide social change, yet he consistently denied that state power could serve social progress. He wanted to provide political and ideological leadership yet his thinking often lagged behind the events of the day. When he tried to escape from this predicament he sometimes unconsciously lent his support to reaction; very seldom did he really defend the proletariat. Deeply aware of the contradictions of modern capitalism and standing at the edge of modern socialism, he had one foot in the past and one foot in the present. The resulting tensions and dilemmas were intrinsic to his purpose and vividly reflected the character of the small proprietors whose combination of work and ownership he had respected for so long and wanted to guarantee forever.

NOTES

1. Albert Leon Guérard, *French Civilization in the Nineteenth Century* (New York: Century, 1914), 138–40. See also Albert Thomas, *Le Second Empire* (Paris: Jules Rouff, 1907).
2. Guérard, 203.
3. Charles Morazé, *La France Bourgeoise* (Paris: Armand Colin, 1946), 98.
4. Letter to Boutteville, October 8, 1852. *Correspondance* (Paris: Lacroix, 1875), v:57–58.
5. Letter to Darimon, September 5, 1852. *Ibid.*, 7–9.
6. P.-J. Proudhon, *La Révolution sociale démontrée par le coup d'état du 2 décembre* (Brussels: Lacroix, Verboeckhoven et Cie., 1868).
7. See Engels's Introduction to Marx's *Class Struggles in France 1848–1852* (New York: International Publishers, 1964).

8. *La Revolution sociale démontrée par le coup d'état du 2 décembre*, 37.
9. *Ibid.*, 60.
10. *Qu'est-ce que la propriété?* (Paris: Rivière, 1926). 146; *De la création de l'ordre dans l'humanité* (Paris: Rivière, 1927), 54–56; *Les confessions d'un révolutionnaire pour servir à l'histoire de la révolution de février* (Paris: Rivière, 1929), 60, 72, 73; *Système des contradictions économiques* (Paris: Rivière, 1923), i:354.
11. *De la création de l'ordre dans l'humanité* 89; *Idée générale de la révolution au XIXème siècle* (Paris: Rivière, 1924). 344–45; *Les confessions d'un révolutionnaire*, 137; *La révolution sociale démontrée par le coup d'état du 2 décembre* 144, 145.
12. *Système des contradictions économiques*, i:65–66, 134; ii: 395; *Idée Générale de la révolution au XIXème siècle*, 126, 151, 334; *Confessions d'un révolutionnaire* 345; Letter to Bergmann Sept. 28, 1859, *Correspondance* ix:181–2; Letter to Langlois Oct. 16, 1859, *ibid.*, ix:206.
13. *Ibid.*, 8.
14. *Ibid.*, 42.
15. *La révolution démontrée par le coup d'état du 2 décembre*, 288.
16. *Ibid.*, 162.
17. *Ibid.*, 2.
18. *Carnets* (Paris: Rivière, 1960–68), iv:214.
19. *Ibid.*, 15–16. The emphases are Proudhon's.
20. Roger Garaudy, *Les Sources françaises du socialisme scientifique* (Paris: Editions d'Hier et Aujourd'hui, 1948), 121.
21. *La Révolution sociale démontrée par le coup d'état du 2 décembre*, 93.
22. *Ibid.*, 158.
23. Letter to Langlois, 18 May 1850. *Correspondance*, iii:263.
24. Letter to Darimon, August 15, 1850. *Ibid.*, iii:322.
25. J. M. Thompson, *Louis Napoleon and the Second Empire* (Oxford: Blackwell, 1954), 144.
26. Guérard, 143.
27. "Je regarde les avantages matériels comme neant, s'ils ne sont pas commandés par les principes de l'honneur et de la justice; . . . je proteste contre toute scission que l'on voudrait faire dans la société, et conséquemment contre toute pensée de compensation entre le *bien-être* et le *vertu*." Letter to Trouessart, September 16, 1853. *Correspondance*, iii:244. The emphases are Proudhon's.
28. Letters to Charles Beslay, April 3, 1855. *Ibid.*, 155 and to Alexander Herzen, July 23, 1855, vi:220.
29. Letter to Maurice, December 5, 1855. *Ibid.*, 279.
30. P.-J. Proudhon, *De la Justice dans la révolution et dans l'église* (Paris: Rivière, 1930), i:423.
31. *Ibid.*, 252.
32. *Ibid.*, 260.
33. *De la Justice dans la révolution et dans l'église*, (Brussels: Lacroix, Verboeckhove et Cie., 1868), ii:67–72.
34. *Ibid.*, 147ff.
35. *De la Justice dans la révolution et dans l'église*, i:306.
36. *Ibid.*, 422.
37. Aaron Noland, "Proudhon and Rousseau," *Journal of the History of Ideas*, 28:1 (January–March 1967), 33–54.
38. *Système des contradictions économiques*, i:123.
39. Letter to Michelet, April 11, 1851. *Correspondance*, iv:361.

40. *Ibid.*, 301.
41. *De la Justice dans la révolution et dans l'église*, i:414. The emphasis is his.
42. *Ibid.*, 220.
43. *De la Justice dans la révolution et dans l'église* (Paris: Rivière, 1931), ii:61.
44. *Ibid.*, 69.
45. Letter to Villiaume, January 24, 1856. *Correspondance*, vii:16.
46. *De la Justice dans la révolution et dans l'église*, ii:69.
47. *Ibid.*, 281.
48. "Modesty and equilibrium, this was in fact the programme which, in *Justice*, he offered to preach to the people, if Cardinal Mathieu, on his side, would undertake to recall the rich to their duties." Henri de Lubac, *The Un-Marxian Socialist: A Study of Proudhon* (New York: Sheed and Ward, 1948), 33.
49. *De la Justice dans la révolution et dans l'église*, i:309.
50. *De la Justice* dans la révolution et dans l'église (Lacroix), ii:125.
51. *Ibid.*, iii:114.
52. *Ibid.*, 340.
53. *De la Justice dans la révolution et dans l'église*, i:302.
54. *De la Justice dans la révolution et dans l'église* (Rivière), ii:76.
55. *Carnets* (Paris: Rivière, 1961), ii:11.
56. *De la justice dans la révolution et dans l'église*, iv:135.
57. *Ibid.*, 155. The emphasis is Proudhon's.
58. *Ibid.*, 219.
59. *Ibid.*, 219–20.
60. *De la Justice dans la révolution et dans l'église* (Lacroix), ii:78.
61. Eugene Fournière, *Les théories socialistes au XIXeme siècle* (Paris: Alcan, 1904), 221. See also Jacques Chabrier, *L'Idée de la révolution d'après Proudhon* (Paris: Editions SomatMontchrestien), 1935), 75–76.
62. Boris Souvarine, "P.-J. Proudhon: cent ans après," *Le Contrat Social*, ix:2 (March–April 1965), 93–94.
63. See Raoul Labry, *Herzen et Proudhon* (Paris: Editions Bossard, 1928), 138.
64. *Carnets*, ii:81.
65. *De la Justice dans la révolution et dans l'église*, iv:458.
66. *Carnets*, ii:337.
67. Letter to Marc Dufraisse, October 28, 1857. *Correspondance*, vii:291.
68. *Justice*, iii:101.
69. *Ibid.*, 251.
70. Alan Ritter, "Proudhon and the Problem of Community," *Review of Politics*, October 1967, 470.
71. He expressed his conviction that the regime could not tolerate an expose of its weakness in a letter to his friend Charles Beslay on October 12, 1858. *Correspondance* viii:221–22: J'ai toujours pensé, vous ne l'ignorez pas, que l'Empereur n'était pas le système; je le pense plus que jamais aujourdhui. Les vrais motifs de l'interdiction de mon Mémoire sont l'abîme profond qu'il découvre entre la société moderne et l'Eglise, et la situation juridique fait à celle-ci; la critique que j'ai fait du mauvais esprit qui règne dans la magistrature et le parquet, je dirai meme la démonstration de leur ignorance; enfin, les considérations politiques placées au commencement et à la fin de mon travail. On en est venu à ne pouvoir souffrir un mot de vérité, une pensée originelle ou spirituelle. Tout fait peur à ce monde dérouté; car on ne peut pas me reprocher la moindre véhémence à l'addresse de personne. J'ai poussé si loin

la modération, tant à l'égard de l'Eglise qu'a l'égard du gouvernement, que mes bons amis les rouges ont découvert que je négociais ma réconciliation. Mais ce monde ne compte plus, si c'est peut-etre parmi les bêtes."

72. Letter to Maguet, November 28, 1858, *ibid.*, 306. He expressed the same hope in a letter to Beslay, December 10, 1858, *ibid.*, 326.
73. Letter to Gustave Chaudey, March 14, 1859. *Ibid.*, ix:33.
74. Letter to Boutteville, January 16, 1859. *Ibid.*, viii:368.
75. Letter to Mathey, October 7, 1860. *Ibid.*, x:171.
76. Letters to Beslay, April 27, 1859, *ibid.*, ix:73 and to Gouvernet, July 20, 1859, *ibid.*, 111.
77. See, for example, his letter to Mathey, October 29, 1860. *Ibid.*, 204–10.
78. His letters to friends at the beginning of the Franco-Austrian war of 1859 express his feelings. See the letters to Gouvernet of May 26, 1859, *ibid.*, 90 and to Gustave Chaudey, June 18, 1859, *ibid.*, 100–101.
79. *Ibid.*, 209.
80. Georges Guy-Grand, *Pour connaître la pensée de Proudhon* (Paris: Bordas, 1947).
81. *La Guerre et la paix* (Paris: Lacroix, Verboeckhoven et Cie., 1868), i:1.
82. *Ibid.*, i:xvi.
83. J.-L. Puech, "Proudhon et la guerre" in Michel Auge-Laribé et al, *Proudhon et notre temps* (Paris: Chiron, 1920), 208.
84. *La Guerre et la paix*, i:30.
85. *Ibid.*, i:35.
86. *Ibid.*, 213.
87. Letter to M. X, June 5, 1861. *Correspondance*, xi:112. The emphasis is Proudhon's.
88. Celestin Bouglé, *La Sociologie de Proudhon* (Paris: Armand Colin, 1911), ch. viii.
89. Letter to Beslay, June 17, 1861. *Correspondance*, xi:118–19.
90. Letter to Gouvernet, January 2, 1862. *Ibid.*, 315–16.
91. He expressed his problem in a letter to Doctor Clavel on October 26, 1861: "il faut choisir: ou faire de la politique dans le mauvais sens du mot, en manoeuvrant à travers les caprices et les rouages de l'opinion, ou bien affirmer envers et contre tous la vérité pure, ou du moins ce que je crois en mon âme et conscience être la vérité. J'ai préféré ce dernier parti . . ." *Ibid.*, 260.
92. Letter to Gouvernet, December 19, 1861. *Ibid.*, 297.
93. Letter to Chaudey, March 7, 1862. *Ibid.*, xii:14.
94. Letter to Charles Beslay, May 21, 1861. *Ibid.*, xi:82. The emphasis is Proudhon's.
95. He had hoped to be included in the general amnesty for political offenders in August 1859, and was overjoyed at the thought of returning to France. Several days later he discovered that because he had been convicted for an "outrage to public morals," his was not a political crime and hence did not fall under the terms of the amnesty. The news evoked a bitter reaction which he expressed in a letter to Maurice of September 8, 1859: "L'amnistie ne me regarde pas; le ministère Delangle s'en est expliqué formellement. M. Proudhon n'est pas un *condamné politique*. Sans doute, si l'Empereur fait une anmnistie pour les auteurs des romans obscènes, j'y serait compris, selon M. Delangle. Que ce gens sont bêtes avec leur hypocrisie!" *Ibid.*, ix:151.
96. See Woodcock, *Pierre-Joseph Proudhon* (London: Routledge and Kegan Paul, 1956), 240–44 for some interesting details concerning Proudhon's departure from Belgium. Proudhon himself referred to the incidents which finally forced him to leave in letters to M. Lebegue, September 18, 1862, *Correspondance*,

xii:193–94 and to Felix Delhasse, September 21, 1862. *Ibid.*, 195–98.

97. See his letter to Madier-Montjau, September 26, 1862. *Ibid.*, 201–2.
98. *Ibid.* See also a letter to Felix Delhasse, November 19, 1862. *Ibid.*, 235.
99. Letter to Buzon, January 31, 1863. *Ibid.*, 269. His emphasis.
100. See the letter to Lebegue, February 25, 1863, *ibid.*, 306, and the "avant-propos" to his *Du principe fédératif et de la nécessité de reconstituer le parti de la révolution* (Paris: Lacroix, Verboeckhoven, et Cie., 1868).
101. *Du principe fédératif*, 11. The emphasis is his.
102. *Ibid.*, 37.
103. *De la justice dans la révolution et dans l'église*, ii:267.
104. *Ibid.*, 47.
105. Letter to Millet, Nov. 2, 1862. *Correspondance*, xii:219–20.
106. *Ibid.*, 79.
107. *Ibid.*, 80–81.
108. *Ibid.*, 83–84.
109. Alan Ritter, *The Political Thought of Pierre-Joseph Proudhon* (Princeton: Princeton University Press, 1969), 155.
110. Georges Gurvitch, *Les fondateurs française de la sociologie contemporain: Saint-Simon et Proudhon*, vol. ii: *P.-J. Proudhon sociologue* (Paris: Centre de Documentation Universitaire, 1955), 65.
111. Ritter, 156–57.
112. *Du Principe fédératif*, 199.
113. *Ibid.*, 238.
114. Chabrier, 78–79.
115. Edouard Dolléans, *Proudhon* (Paris: Gallimard, 1948), 217.
116. *Du Principe fédératif*, 99.
117. *Carnets*, iii:365.
118. Pierre Ansart, *Naissance de l'anarchisme* (Paris: Presses Universitaires Francaises, 1970), 205 and Soltau, 287.
119. *Du Principe fédératif*, 326–27. His emphasis.
120. See, for example, his letter to Governet, February 8, 1859. *Correspondance*, ix:20–23.
121. Letter to Beslay, February 6, 1859. *Ibid.*, 12.
122. Letter to Ferrari, November 7, 1859. *Ibid.*, 224–25.
123. *Ibid.*
124. Bernard Voyenne, "Le Federalisme de Proudhon" in *Actualité de Proudhon* (Brussels: Editions de l'Institut de Sociologie de l'Universite Libre de Bruxelles, 1967), 141–50.
125. *Ibid.*, 149.
126. *Carnets*, ii:257.
127. *Idée générale de la révolution au XIXéme siècle*, 302.
128. Thomas, 159. The results for the whole country were as follows:

eligible	9,938,685
voting	7,262,623
government	5,308,254
opposition	1,954,369

129. *Ibid.*, 160.
130. Paul Louis, *Histoire du socialisme en France* (Paris: Rivière, 1946), 130.
131. Thomas, 231.

132. Letter to Gustave Chaudet, January 28, 1863. *Correspondance*, xii:259–61.
133. *Ibid.*, 260.
134. *De la Justice dans la révolution et dans l'église*, iii:475.
135. Letter to Darimon, April 18, 1863. *Correspondance*, xiii:15. The emphasis is Proudhon's.
136. *Ibid.* and Thomas, 154.
137. Letter to X, October 12, 1861. *Ibid.*, xi:222.
138. Letter to Beslay, June 6, 1863. *Ibid.*, xiii:99.
139. Letter "Aux Ouvriers," March 8, 1864. *Ibid.*, 247–66.
140. See, for example, his letter to Maurice of July 20, 1864. *Ibid.*, xiv:12–13.
141. *De la Capacité politique des classes ouvrières* (Paris: Lacroix, Verboeckhoven, et Cie., 1868).
142. *Ibid.*, 30.
143. *Ibid.*, 45–46.
144. *Ibid.*, 50–51.
145. *Ibid.*, 51–52.
146. Thomas, 163–64.
147. Almost any of the classic histories of the working-class movement during the Second Empire describe the influence of "Proudhonisme." See, for example, Edouard Dolléans, *Histoire du mouvement ouvrier* (Paris: Armand Colin, 1946); Daniel Guérin, "Proudhon et l'autogestion ouvrière" in *Actualité de Proudhon*, 67–88; Annie Kriegel, "Le Syndicalisme révolutionnaire de Proudhon," *ibid.*, 47–66; H. Lagardelle, *Syndicalisme et socialisme* (Paris: Rivière, 1908); J. Maitron, *Le Syndicalisme révolutionnaire* (Paris: Editions Ouvrières, 1952); and Gaëtan Pirou, *Proudhonisme et le syndicalisme révolutionnaire* (Paris: Arthur Roussseau, 1910).
148. Maxinme Leroy is one of many commentators who sees Proudhon as a syndicalist first and foremost. See his "Le Retour à Proudhon," *Pages Libres*, 2:61 (April 10, 1912), 613.
149. *De la Capacité politique des classes ouvrières*, 387–88.
150. *Ibid.*, 380.
151. M. Harmel, "Proudhon et le mouvement ouvrier," Auge-Laribé et al, 47.
152. P.-J. Proudhon, *Théorie de la propriété* (Paris: Lacroix, Verboeckhoven, et Cie., 1868), 53.
153. *Ibid.*, 206.
154. *Ibid.*, 65.
155. *Ibid.*, 138.
156. *Ibid.*, 94–98.
157. *Ibid.*, 138.
158. *Ibid.*, 189–90.
159. *Ibid.*, 196.
160. Aime Berthod, *P.-J. Proudhon et la propriété, un socialisme pour les paysans* (Paris: V. Giard et E. Brière, 1910), 159.

6

Accomplishments and Limits

The turbulent and unsettled character of France's industrialization subjected her large and vulnerable *petite bourgeoisie* to continuous economic and political pressure through most of the nineteenth century. Because its interests were so important to him and because the period in which he was living framed public matters with particular clarity, Proudhon's work is an uncommonly reliable gauge of the social and ideological forces which shaped French public life during a period of rapid change. He was not alone in his efforts to diagnose and cure the country's social *malaise*, but he was more overtly partisan than many of his contemporaries and his work can serve as a way of grasping some of the forces that were shaping modern history. And since he was primarily interested in the welfare of a grouping whose inherent instability is rooted in its objective social position, his career may tell us something about ideology and class which is of general applicability to contemporary political affairs.

By the time he died in 1865, France was well on her way toward building a modern industrial civilization based on coal and iron. Even with the twists and turns occasioned by her singular political history and social structure, it had been clear for some time that French developments would follow the general pattern first established by England and Holland. As uneven as it was, the country's industrialization was giving rise to a distinctly modern social structure and to a series of correspondingly dramatic ideological developments. The rise of a modern working class, which had made its first appearance in national affairs during the Revolution of 1848 and continued to constitute itself with increasing independence of the petty bourgeoisie throughout the century, posed a new set of ideological and political problems for the French left which older spokesmen were only partly able to understand. The gradual development of a distinctly proletarian current in national life raised the issue of the use of political power as a tool of social transformation in a direct and unambiguous fashion, for the propertyless workers had little stake in, and even less interest in defending, the prevailing institutions of market society. As they became more active and self-reliant, they tended to look to politics to help settle some of the social issues which earlier upheavals had been able to pose but not resolve.

One of the most intractable contradictions of the French Revolution was that a profoundly democratic political transformation had given rise to an individualistic and unequal social order which undermined both the promise of formal equality before the law and the possibility of substantive equality of conditions. Economic liberalism had been in conflict with social democracy for some time, and it soon became clear that the central pivot of a rejuvenated workers' movement would be a call for some sort of regulation of the market in the name of a broader goal than the traditional bourgeois demand for "liberty."[1] As the century proceeded, working-class socialism and the left wing of petty-bourgeois democracy increasingly shared a willingness to subject market society to public supervision in the service of social welfare, and this common orientation provided important opportunities for political cooperation. At the same time, the workers tended to go much further than the small proprietors, and this provided equally-important opportunities for conflict and betrayal.

The intrinsic collectivism and militancy of the workers' movement was a new phenomenon for left-wing activists, and more modern socialists often clashed with people like Proudhon who were trying to analyze contemporary society with modes of thought which were partly derived from a preindustrial culture. The utopians had tended to confuse a criticism of the specifically capitalist form of modern society with a criticism of industrialization as such and were tempted to turn the clock back to a mythical era of harmony and stability in reaction to the market's chaotic destructiveness. Proudhon's tentative reactions to the labor movement's collectivism and militancy revealed far more about France's social structure and the insecurities of her small proprietors than was immediately apparent. Even if he did not go so far as to fall into Fourier's errors, his desire to preserve the petty bourgeoisie's working ownership led him to echo the liberal claim that social harmony could arise spontaneously through the liberation of private initiative. The rise of a distinctly proletarian trend which was increasingly oriented toward abolishing the institutions of market society proved sufficiently problematic for Proudhon that he tried to forge a "third path" which would go beyond bourgeois liberalism to establish substantial equality of conditions but would stop short of modern socialism's drive to strike at private ownership of the means of production. These two goals could not be accomplished separately, but there is no way Proudhon could have known this.

Much of this had been prefigured during the Revolution of 1848, and the June catastrophe had only delayed the appearance of a politically and ideologically independent proletariat. Proudhon's contradictory motion during the revolution can be understood as an example of the petty bourgeoisie's desire to stand between the two great antagonists of the day by remaining independent of both, for its preservation depended on its ability to maneuver between them and buy time so it would not have to confront either alone. If the Revolution of 1848 marked the beginning of the end for the older socialist sects and currents, then Proudhon's death—coming as it did between the Founding Congress of the First International and the outbreak of the Paris Commune—came toward the end of the end. His life and work straddled the passage from one kind of social order to another and from one set of ideological presuppositions to another. He can serve as a mirror through which the contradictions of a period of deeply wrenching transition become visible. The development of a national market, a national state, a national culture, and a national polity were driven by powerful forces which had been building up for some time, and Proudhon's reactions were particularly revealing of what was shaping nineteenth-century France and what would mark the history of other societies as well.

In a very real way, the triumph of coal and iron seemed to have completed the historical task of the French Revolution. Many hoped that the broad political and ideological promises which had accompanied the bourgeoisie's struggle against feudal particularism and privilege could now be redeemed by an industrial civilization which could finally realize universal human aspirations in a national framework. The conscious satisfaction of basic human needs now seemed to be within associated humanity's grasp. If the Revolution had created the near-perfect legal, institutional, and ideological conditions for modern civilization, perhaps industry could overcome the few social and economic barriers which seemed to be remnants of the past.

But the industrial present was also a capitalist present, and as the century wore on the deep contradictions of an exploitative social order became more apparent and more destructive. As a classic bourgeois class structure began to emerge, the universal promises of 1789 and 1793 seemed to fade into the background. But the nineteenth-century history of France illustrates that the Great Revolution simply refused to go away, particularly for those who regarded themselves as the guardians of its democratic content. It became clear to many socialist intellectuals and labor militants that the Revolution's promises could be realized only if the country's social structure was transformed, and this meant that democracy had to be extended from the polity to the market, from the state to the society. The social revolutionaries of the nineteenth century imagined themselves to be the heirs of the political revolutionaries of the eighteenth, and Proudhon was not alone in his contention that solving "the social question" would bring "the Revolution" to a close. France's political history came together with his own work to pose a set of questions which could have been asked only at the beginning of contemporary history. Resolving them remains humanity's fundamental project, and this is one reason why Proudhon remains inter-esting more than a hundred years after his death.

Nineteenth-century French history continuously displayed both the bourgeois revolutions of the past and the proletarian revolutions of the future, and even if he was unable to find a "formula" which could reconcile them to each other, no one knew better than Proudhon that things were changing. If the Republic, the July Monarchy, and the second Bonaparte defined the triumphant bourgeoisie's politics and expressed its ideology, then the June Days and the Paris Commune embodied the workers' hopes and served as harbingers of the future. A constitutional monarchy yielded to a revolu-tionary and then a conservative republic, and a new imperial despotism was succeeded by the first victorious proletarian insurrection in history. But the different wings of the French bourgeoisie had an unexpectedly hard time elaborating a political form within which they could exercise their joint rule, and it is also true that the July Revolution, the June Days, and the *coup d'état* of December 2 were considerably more than vulgar imitations of the past. They changed the form of the state with which the French bour-geoisie responded to and organized a developing national society. A central problem revealed by nineteenth-century France's tortuous history is how such a developed capitalist society was so manifestly unable to master its own political history. One of Europe's most thoroughly bourgeois social orders was also one of its most unstable and undependable.

Generally speaking, the social roots of capitalism lie in the economic processes of civil society. It is the market, after all, which generates and reinforces bourgeois relations of production, and this is why the market has proven so difficult for socialists to manage. Both the circumstances of its rebellions against the feudal state and its roots in commodity production and exchange seem to require that bourgeois revolutions strike at a grasp-ing and interfering political order. The French bourgeoisie, having come to power during *the* classic bourgeois revolution, was ideologically liberal through-out much of the nineteenth century, but its social instability, ideological vulnerability, and political shallowness compelled it to rely on the state to a much greater extent than one would expect. The long history of French bureaucracy and centralism contributed to this, but Proudhon was confronting a classic bourgeois state apparatus when he began laying the foundations for the political theory of anarchism.

French petty-bourgeois resistance to the country's relentlessly centraliz-ing state goes back at least 300 years, and the devastating evolution of bourgeois social relations only accelerated an ideological trend which had been simmering just below the surface of her public life for some time.[2] The long history of French bureaucratic centralization had nurtured a broad tradition of criticism of the state which had deeper roots than the petty bourgeoisie's reactions to its immediate difficulties.[3] At the same time, the development of capitalist social relations and the increasing demands of the state went hand in hand throughout much of the nineteenth century, and the petty bourgeoisie found itself having to resist both. Proudhon faithfully articulated its demands for protection from the market's discipline and its preference for local solutions to local problems, both of which had considerable anticapitalist potential. Resistance to centralization and to the capitalist market seemed to be two sides of the same coin. The defense of local interests against the claims of the national market and the state would gradually yield to more modern and conscious political movements which would accept the fundamental accomplishments of the capitalist transformation of France, but this was only beginning when Proudhon died. He was able to combine elements of a decidedly precapitalist localism with extremely insightful criticisms of bourgeois society because both past and future lived in him and animated his work.

It was during the nineteenth century that one of the most pronounced tendencies of modern history became apparent. The development of a national market and the attendant consolidation of a national state were accompanied by a popular effort to resist, or at least to attenuate, their effects. As the modern articulated bureaucratic state began to cover the entire society and penetrate into every locality, workers, peasants, and small producers tended to band together in opposition to the effects of the free market and the authoritarian state. As the century developed and the concentration of capital was matched by the intrusiveness of national authorities, the bourgeois character of both became more obvious. The evident partiality of the political apparatus drew broader and broader strata of the population into sustained public activity, and the twin development of the modern bourgeois market and the modern bourgeois state created the conditions for modern political life.

The bourgeoisie had been the first ruling class whose material interests were sufficiently comprehensive to demand a modern political structure for their protection. Its roots may lie in the property relations of civil society, but when the bourgeoisie spoke as a class it did so in the political arena. Its development from a welter of medieval estates had necessitated a modern state because it had to protect its home market against foreign rivals and its property against domestic enemies. It had taken huge strides forward during the Great Revolution, but it was the nineteenth century's economic developments which fully created the material conditions for its rule. The bourgeoisie's general and comprehensive activity imparted a unique breadth to its politics which dramatically affected every other stratum of French society. Its political hegemony notwithstanding, the need to develop a stable national framework for its rule was sufficiently new and complex that it took the better part of the century to accomplish.

Since it sprang up in and was sustained by local trade and relatively restricted conditions of production and exchange, the petty bourgeoisie tended to be somewhat narrower in its ambitions and perspectives than the bourgeoisie *proprement dite*. This is why theorists like Proudhon tended to demand local self-government, political and economic decentralization, and protection from predatory concentrations of wealth. For the most part France's small proprietors were content to live alongside other groupings, and their spokesmen tended to develop conciliatory conceptions of shared power and local autonomy. But the same considerations did not shape the workers' perspectives, for they were formed by the same powerful forces of industrial production which were conditioning the political activities of their antagonists. Even though they were initially drawn to political activity by their need to defend themselves, they soon acquired a breadth of view and a comprehensiveness of activity which set them apart from their erstwhile petty-bourgeois allies. As the labor movement began to turn toward the socialist intellectuals, its tactics shifted from sabotage and mutual aid to strikes and trade unions, demonstrations and political parties. The petty-bourgeois opposition tended to trail behind these developments because the conditions of its existence and its immediate aspirations did not call forth the same breadth of view or seem to require the same sort of militancy, but before long it was clear that the socialist proletariat and the democratic petty bourgeoisie had a great deal in common even as their different relationship with property simultaneously tended to drive them apart.

Proudhon stands as one of the best representatives of the variety of nonpolitical radicalisms which arose during the consolidation of the modern national state system, flourished for a time before World War I, and eventually withered as the Russian Revolution encouraged modern socialists to develop a comprehensive political orientation toward the bourgeoisie and its state. His work reflected the economics, politics, and ideology of a transitional period during which the perspectives of France's beleaguered *petite bourgeoisie* dominated those of its nascent proletariat. The industrial workers and the socialist intellectuals did not begin to turn toward each other until after his death, but when they did they imparted to French socialism a distinctly political orientation which persisted for decades and accounted for the partial eclipse of Proudhon's influence.

In the meantime, the major social formation for which he spoke and which proved most receptive to his ideas were small proprietors and independent artisans who were under intense pressure in a rapidly-industrializing environment. The Great Revolution had granted formal equality before the law to all citizens, but as the century wore on it became clear that the deep social roots of oppression had not been touched. Bourgeois notions of liberty and equality were perfectly compatible with social exploitation and economic inequality, and many social theorists concluded that a formal statement of abstract liberties and rights did not conflict with, but were necessary conditions of, the free commerce which was built on and reinforced intractable social misery. It was clear that the market transformed formal equality into substantive inequality and that class interest rather than theoretical immaturity accounted for the bourgeoisie's failure to address "the social question." For all its accomplishments, the French Revolution had clearly failed to extend democracy into the marketplace and bridge the gap between the formal claims of the state and the real operations of the society.

Under these circumstances, it was easy to conclude that socialist intellectuals and labor activists should stay away from political activity. If the Revolution's hyper-political Jacobinism had fed popular hopes that all social dilemmas were susceptible to political solution, the persistence of these problems encouraged the retreat from politics which was so characteristic of the century.[4] Proudhon was a very important representative of this tendency, and his hostility to politics emerged as the core of his thinking and constituted his most important legacy to a generation of followers. His attempt to carve out an area of private initiative where the individual would be free to pursue his interests without interference reflected a widely-held liberal prejudice that our most important associations are private and that our basic needs can be met in small intimate associations which must be nurtured and protected from public officials. His claim that a willingness to use public power to change the organization of civil society would lead to an arbitrary power-hungry statism which would trample individuals' private rights prefigured a good deal of contemporary liberal anticommunism.[5] Marxism did not come to dominate working-class socialism until some time after Proudhon's death, and only when it did was it possible to move away from the assortment of nonpolitical socialisms which had arisen in reaction to the failed Revolutions of 1848.[6] Even within the ranks of those who explicitly based their activity on the theoretical legacy from Marx and Engels, the transition to a *political* socialism which would focus on the conquest of state power as the first step in the social revolution was a long and difficult one.

Proudhon's sort of antistatism was particularly characteristics of agrarian people who made their living from the soil and lived as independent and self-supporting a life as conditions permitted. The state had been seen as the parasitical enemy for hundreds of years—the instrument of the cities, the national market, the army, and the bureaucracy. "When the French peasant paints the devil," remarked Marx, "he paints him in the guise of a tax collector."[7] The anarchists' desire for the immediate "abolition of the state" always resonated well in such an environment, and rural anarchism has traditionally scoffed at socialists' suggestions that it might take some time for a reconstructed state to help construct the material conditions for the transition to a classless society.[8]

Early socialism was tied by a thousand threads to the many small producers who were being transformed into proletarians, and Proudhon served as an important link between it and older agrarian patterns of resistance which fed on a visceral hostility to the state and everything it stood for. He expressed the deeply-held belief that politics was an enemy of freedom and could never be anything more than a parasitical excrescence pure and simple. But the state could not be "abolished" until "society" was able to take over its functions, and Proudhon did not recognize that modern political institutions still had a considerable role to play. This was the stumbling-block on which anarchism broke its neck theoretically—the indisputable fact that an entire historical period would be necessary before the necessary functions performed by the state could be freely discharged by social institutions. For all its rhetoric, the socialism of Proudhon's generation was unable to develop a theoretically credible theory of the state or to explain how it might be "abolished" for one eminently simple reason: *the state had become a social necessity.* There was no way around it, and wishes could not substitute for facts. Proudhon's criticism of the state might have been driven by his own quintessentially petty-bourgeois egalitarianism and hostility to authority, but he was no more able to demonstrate that society could dispense with the state than were any of his contemporaries.

Proudhon was many things at once because he was an honest and principled social critic who rejected the organizing core that only a political orientation could have provided. He started his career as a radical egalitarian critic of property but was variously known—and described himself—as a socialist, an anarchist, a mutualist, a pluralist, a moralist, a reformer, a federalist, an anti-theist, a revolutionary, a sociologist, and a political economist. He was all of these things because of the way the market worked and because he was sincerely trying to understand how its destructive effects could be ameliorated. He began life as an egalitarian because he was appalled by the persistence of social inequality despite the accomplishments of the French Revolution. He was a socialist because he recognized the economic root of France's difficulties; he was an anarchist because he developed a systematic criticism of the bourgeois state; he became a mutualist in reaction against the market's foundation in a competitive individualism. Similar explanations could be advanced for all the categories into which Proudhon fit because they were all developed in response to the very palpable effects of industrial society. He was a pluralist because of the market's reckless destructiveness, he was a moralist because its rationality demanded that people treat each others as means to privately-determined ends, and he was a reformer because the revolutionaries of his day had so clearly run out of plausible answers. His federalism tried to counter the inexorable economic and political centralization of his time, his hostility to the political and ideological role of the Church drove his antitheism, and his partial insights into the nature of bourgeois property occasionally led him to sound very much like a revolutionary. Along the way, he also helped develop some of the methodological and conceptual foundations of modern social science. He was a remarkably talented individual for one who had so little formal education, and his career reveals a variety of interests and a breadth of view which were remarkable even in the nineteenth century.

But in the long run he lacked a theoretical center of gravity which could have helped him provide some coherence to what remains an eclectic and somewhat incoherent body of work. He was unable to grasp the key link that would have helped him develop an integrated understanding of his own era because he was most interested in the welfare of those who populated a vanishing world of independent small producers, worked hard for a living, and did not exploit their employees. His own fragmented and splintered view was a perfect ideological reflection of the real conditions in which the petty bourgeoisie lived and worked, for small producers were always responding to others' initiatives and could not develop a stable economic niche or an ideological perspective of their own. Industry made their lives increasingly difficult during Proudhon's lifetime, and the scattered character of their politics reflected the dispersed character of their economic activities. It was very difficult for small proprietors to transcend the narrow and restricted conditions which their isolated and vulnerable economic activity continually created and recreated.

Unable to see the forest for the trees, Proudhon focused on selected manifestations of oppression and was unable to understand how they were connected. He could not penetrate to their common root because he did not understand the general and comprehensive character of politics. There were many compelling reasons why he developed such a clear criticism of the state and of politics but the ambiguous legacy of the French Revolution, the failure of the classical French left, and the contradictory logic of the marketplace failed to provide a viewpoint which was broad enough so Proudhon could generalize, integrate, and summarize. Only politics could have provided such a perspective, but he was unable to see that classes speak as classes when they speak politically and that raising the question of state power could have helped him understand how the scattered manifestations of a single phenomenon were related. In the absence of such a comprehensive view, Proudhon could go no further than to contest this or that aspect of the existing order.

In the long run, the absence of a powerful and independent working-class movement had a powerful influence in shaping the character of Proudhon's worldview. He lived during a transitional period during which the petty bourgeoisie had lost, but the proletariat had not yet gained, the strength and coherence that could enable it to lead France's democratic movement. When he died in 1865 the industrial future was apparent to some but the character of left-wing and labor politics remained hidden. If 1848 had proven anything, it was that the absence of a powerful and independent working-class movement guaranteed that the social relations of bourgeois society would work their will and exert a powerful pull on the *petite bourgeoisie*. The situation was only marginally different seventeen years later, and this is why Proudhon's fundamental theoretical project was to save France's small proprietors from the vestiges of feudalism, the reality of capitalism, and the possibility of socialism. His basic desire was to protect the union of work with ownership, a union which he considered fundamental for a just and harmonious social order. If he failed to arrive at a broadly-based political theory, this in no way detracts from his very real accomplishments. At the same time, his intellectual and political biography contains many lessons for the present—the most important of which is that the lack of both a central political core and durable connections with a healthy labor movement produces a socialism which surrenders in advance to the marketplace and can go no further than endlessly exploring the politics of difference.

The strata and groupings which were located between the bourgeoisie and the proletariat were tied to the former through their ownership of some land, instruments, and capital. They were tied to the proletariat because they partly had to work for a living. Insignificant numbers of them joined the bourgeoisie during the nineteenth century, but great numbers were impoverished and sank down into the proletariat. The great majority of the petty bourgeoisie were subject to considerable pressure, were constantly driven to bankruptcy and unemployment, and urgently demanded economic and political democracy. That Proudhon was unable to articulate a comprehensive understanding of their situation does not detract from his very real accomplishments. His critiques of political economy, bourgeois defenses of property, clericalism and the Church, malthusianism, and the doctrinaire left were incisive and influential. His emphasis on the "social question" during the 1840s and his insistence that capital be "subordinated" to work accompanied his clear understanding that the state was an agent of class domination. He had genuine sympathy for the most impoverished and oppressed elements of French society and understood something of the creation and appropriation of surplus value. He was committed to the Revolution and the Republic as he understood them, defended democracy when it was dangerous to do so, and often manifested a great deal of courage. He was a talented, original, and imaginative theoretician who tried his best to acquire the knowledge of his age and bring it to the people to whose welfare he was sincerely dedicated. Like him, we are living in a period during which the old is in plain crisis but the new cannot yet be born. Considering how little progress has been made in resolving many of the deep problems to which he drew attention over a century ago, we may have more to learn from people like him than we think.

NOTES

1. See Andrew Levine, *Liberal Democracy: A Critique of Its Theory* (New York: Columbia University Press, 1981).
2. Charles Tilly, *The Contentious French: Four Centuries of Popular Struggle* (Cambridge: Harvard University Press, 1986).
3. Preston King, *Fear of Power: An Analysis of Anti-Statism in Three French Writers* (London: Frank Cass, 1967).
4. For a related but different analysis, see Sheldon Wolin, *Politics and Vision: Continuity and Innovation in Western Thought* (Boston: Little, Brown, 1960), ch. 10.
5. For a different view, see Georges Gurvitch, *L'idée du droit social* (Paris: Sirey, 1932) and Pierre Ansart, *Sociologie de Proudhon* (Paris: Presses Universitaires de France, 1967).
6. See George E. McCarthy ed., *Marx and Aristotle: Nineteenth-Century German Social Theory and Classical Antiquity* (Savage, MD: Rowman and Littlefield, 1992).
7. Karl Marx, "The Class Struggles in France 1848 to 1850," *Marx and Engels Collected Works* (New York: International Publishers, 1975–), x:118.
8. See E. J. Hobsbawm, *Primitive Rebels: Studies in Archaic Forms of Social Movements in the 19th and 20th Centuries* (New York: Norton, 1965). For further discussion of these issues, see my *The Dictatorship of the Proletariat: Marxism's Theory of Socialist Democracy* (New York: Routledge, 1992).

Bibliography

ARTICLES, NEWSPAPERS, AND PERIODICALS

Avron, Henri. "Proudhon et le radicalisme allemand." *Annales: économies, sociétiés, civilisations* 6: 2 (1951): 194–201.

Berthod, Aimé. "L'attitude social de P.-J. Proudhon." *Bulletin de la société d'histoire de la Révolution de 1848* 5: 30 (January–February 1909).

———. "La théorie de l'état et du gouvernement dans l'oeuvre de Proudhon." *Revue d'histoire économique et sociale* xi (1923): 270–304.

Bouglé, Celestin. "La Première Philosophie de Proudhon." *Revue du mois* x (October 1910): 424–34.

———. "Le progrès intellectuel de Proudhon avant 1848." *Revue du mois* xii (September 10, 1911): 273–87.

———. "Proudhon fédéraliste." *Revue du mois* xx (1919): 502–13.

Bourgin, Maurice, "Des rapports entre Proudhon et Karl Marx." *Le Contrat social* ix: 2 (March–April 1965).

Chiaromonte, Nicola. "P.-J. Proudhon: An Uncomfortable Thinker." *Politics* iii (January 1946): 27–29.

Cobban, Alfred. "The 'Middle Class' in France, 1815–1848." *French Historical Studies* 5: 1 (Spring 1967): 41–56.

Dayan-Herzbrun, S. "Proudhon critique de Platon." *Revue philosophique de France et de l'étranger* 97 (January–March 1972): 15–25.

Douglas, Dorothy. "P.-J. Proudhon: A Prophet of 1848." *American Journal of Sociology* xxxiv (1929): 781–803; xxxv (1930): 35–59.

Draper, Hal. "A Note on the Father of Anarchism." *New Politics* 8: 1 (Winter 1969): 79–93.

Elwit, Sanford. "Politics and Ideology in the French Labour Movement." *Journal of Modern History* 49: 3 (1977): 468–80.

Gaillard, Jeanne. "Les associations de production et la pensée politique en France (1852–1870)." *Le Mouvement social* 52 (1965): 59–84.

Gillouin, René. "Le Mysticisme social. Fourier. Proudhon." *Grande revue* cv (March 1921): 63–70.

Guiral, P. "Proudhon et la Révolution Française." *Annales de la Révolution Française* 184 (April–June 1966).

Gurvitch, Georges. "Proudhon et Marx." *Cahiers internationaux de sociologie* 40–41 (1966): 7–16.

Hanagan, Michael. "The Politics of Proletarianization." *Comparative Studies in Society and History* 21 (April 1979): 227–30.

Harbold, William H. "Progressive Humanity: In the Philosophy of P.-J. Proudhon." *Review of Politics* 31: 1 (January 1969): 28–47.

Hoffman, Robert. "Marx and Proudhon: A Reappraisal of their Relationship." *The Historian* xxix: 3 (May 1967): 409–30.

Jackson, John Hampden. "Proudhon: A Prophet for our Time." *Contemporary Review* clxv (March 1944): 156–59.

La Voix du Peuple. September 25, 1849–May 14, 1850.

Lacroix, Jean. "Proudhon et la souveraineté du droit." *Politique* 7: 12 (December 1973).

Lair, Maurice. "Proudhon, père de l'anarchie." *Annales des sciences politiques* 24: 5 (September 15, 1909): 588–618.

Le Moniteur Universel. August 1, 1848–January–March 1849.

Le Peuple. September 4, 1848–June 13, 1849.

Le Peuple de 1850. June 15, 1850–October 13, 1850.

Le Représentant du Peuple. February 27, 1848–August 9, 1848.

Leroy, Maxime. "Le Retour à Proudhon." *Pages Libres* 2: 61 (April 10, 1912).

_____. "Citoyen ou producteur?" *Revue de métaphysique et de morale* xxvi (1919): 669–84.

L'Europe en Formation 62. (May 1965).

Marx, Karl. "The Class Struggles in France 1848 to 1850." *Karl Marx and Frederick Engels Collected Works.* New York: International Publishers, 1975–. x: 45–145.

McDougall, Mary Lynn. "Consciousness and Community: The Workers of Lyon, 1830–1850." *Journal of Social History* 12: 1 (Fall 1978): 129–45.

Moss, Bernard. "Producers' Associations and the Origins of French Socialism: Ideology from Below." *Journal of Modern History* 48 (March 1976): 69–89.

Noland, Aaron. "Pierre-Joseph Proudhon: Socialist as Social Scientist." *American Journal of Economics and Sociology* xxvi (July 1967): 313–28.

_____. "Proudhon and Rousseau." *Journal of the History of Ideas* 28: 1 (January–March 1967): 33–54.

_____. "History and Humanity: The Proudhonian Vision." In Hayden V. White ed., *The Uses of History.* Detroit: Wayne State University Press, no date: 59–105.

Noyelle, H. "La Notion de justice dans l'oeuvre économique de Proudhon." *Revue d'histoire des doctrines économiques et sociales* 11: 2 (1923).

Puech, J.-L. "Le Centenaire de Proudhon." *Revue de la paix* 14: 1 (January 1909).

Reichart, William O. "Pierre-Joseph Proudhon: One of the Fathers of Philosophical Anarchism." *Journal of Human Relations,* xiii (1965): 81–92.

_____. "Natural Right in the Political Philosophy of Pierre-Joseph Proudhon." *Journal of Libertarian Studies* 4 (Winter 1980): 77–91.

Rist, Charles. "La pensée économique de Proudhon." *Revue d'histoire économique et sociale* 33: 2 (1955): 129–65.

Ritter, Alan. "Proudhon and the Problem of Community." *Review of Politics* October 1967: 457–77.

Schapiro, J. Salwyn. "Pierre-Joseph Proudhon, Harbinger of Fascism." *American Historical Review* 1: 4 (July 1945).

Schnerb, Robert. "Marx et Proudhon devant le coup d'état du 2 décembre." *Revue socialiste* 1947: 526–36.

Sewell, William H. Jr. "Property, Labor, and the Emergence of Socialism in France, 1769–1848." In John M. Merriman ed., *Consciousness and Class Experience in Nineteenth-Century Europe.* New York: Holmes and Meier, 1979: 45–63.

Silbener, Edmund. "Proudhon's Judeophobia." *Historica Judaica* xi: 1 (April 1948): 61–80.

Sorel, Georges. "Essai sur la philosophie de Proudhon." *Revue philosophique de la France et de l'étranger* 17: 6 (June 1892).

Souvarine, Boris. "P.-J. Proudhon: cent ans après." *Le contrat social* ix: 2 (March–April 1965): 86–94.

Spear, Lois. "Pierre-Joseph Proudhon and the Myth of Universal Suffrage." *Canadian Journal of History* 10 (December 1975): 295–306.
Vialatoux, J. "La Justice selon Proudhon." *Economie et humanisme* vi: 106 (1957): 400–404.
Viard, Jacques. "Pierre Leroux, Proudhon, Marx et Jaurès." *Revue d'histoire moderne et contemporaine* 29 (April–June 1982): 305–23.
Watkins, Frederick. "Proudhon and the Theory of Modern Liberalism." *Canadian Journal of Economics and Political Science* xiii: 3 (August 1947): 429–35.
Woodcock, George. "Proudhon, An Appreciation." *Dissent* ii: 4 (Fall 1955): 394–405.
_____. "The Solitary Revolution: Proudhon's Notebooks." *Encounter* xxxii: 3 (September 1969): 46–55.

BOOKS

Actualité de Proudhon. Brussels: Editions de l'Institut de Sociologie de l'Universite Libre de Bruxelles, 1967.
Ansart, Pierre. *Naissance de l'anarchisme*. Paris: Presses Universitaires de France, 1970.
_____. *Socialisme et anarchisme*. Paris: Presses Universitaires de France, 1969.
_____. *Sociologie de Proudhon*. Paris: Presses Universitaires de France, 1967.
Artz, Frederick B. *Reaction and Revolution 1814–1832*. New York: Harper and Brothers, 1934.
Auge-Laribé, Michel et al. *Proudhon et notre temps*. Paris: Chiron, 1920.
Bancal, Jean. *Proudhon: pluralisme et autogestion*. Paris: Aubier Montaigne, 1970.
Beloff, Max et al eds. *L'Europe du xixe et du xxe siècle*. Milan: Marzorati, 1959.
Berth, Edouard. *Du 'Capital' aux 'Réflexions sur la Violence'*. Paris: Rivière, 1932.
Berthod, Aimé. *P.-J. Proudhon et la propriété, un socialism pour les paysans*. Paris: V. Giard et E. Brière, 1910.
Bouglé, Celestin. *La Sociologie de Proudhon*. Paris: Armand Colin, 1911.
_____. *Chez les prophètes socialistes*. Paris: Alcan, 1918.
_____. *Socialismes Français*. Paris: Armand Colin, 1951.
Bougeat, Jacques. *P.-J. Proudhon, père du socialisme français*. Paris: Denouïl, 1943.
Bourgin, Gorges. *1848: naissance et mort d'une république*. Paris: Les Deux Sirènes, 1948.
Bravo, Gian Mario. *Les socialistes avant Marx*. Paris: Maspero, 1970.
Brogan, Denis William. *Proudhon*. London: Hamish Hamilton, 1934.
Buber, Martin. *Paths in Utopia*. Boston: Beacon, 1949.
Buchanan, Allen. *Marx and Justice: the Radical Critique of Liberalism*. Totowa, NJ: Rowman and Littlefield, 1982.
Carr, Edward Hallett. *Studies in Revolution*. London: Macmillan, 1950.
Chabrier, Jacques. *L'idée de la révolution d'après Proudhon*. Paris: Les Editions Somat-Montchrestien, 1935.
Coginot, Jacques. *Proudhon et la démagogie Bonapartiste*. Paris: Editions Sociales, 1958.
Cole, G. D. H. *A History of Socialist Thought*. vol. i: *The Forerunners*. New York: St. Martin's, 1965.
Condit, Stephen. *Proudhonist Materialism and Revolutionary Doctrine*. Sanday, Orkney: Cienfuegos Press, 1982.
Cornu, Auguste, et al. *A la lumière du Marxisme*. vol. ii: *Karl Marx et la pensée moderne*. Paris: Editions Sociales Internationales, 1937.
Crowder, George. *Classical Anarchism: The Political Thought of Godwin, Proudhon, Bakunin, and Kropotkin*. New York: Oxford University Press, 1991.

Cuvillier, Armand. *Proudhon*. Paris: Editions Sociales Internationales, 1937.
_____. *Hommes et ideologies de 1848*. Paris: Rivière, 1956.
Dana, Charles. *Proudhon and His 'Bank of the People'*. Chicago: Charles Kerr, 1984.
Dautry, Jean. *1848 et la Deuxième République*. Paris: Editions Sociales, 1957.
_____. *Histoire de la Révolution de 1848*. Paris: Editions d'Hier et Aujourd'hui, 1948.
Dickinson, G. Lowes. *Revolution and Reaction in Modern France*. London: Allen and Unwin, 1952.
Doleans, Edouard. *Histoire du mouvement ouvrier*. Paris: Armand Colin, 1946.
_____. *Proudhon*. Paris: Gallimard, 1948.
and Puech, J.-L. *Proudhon et la Révolution de 1848*. Paris: Presses Universitaires de France, 1948.
Dommanget, Maurice. *Les grands socialistes et l'éducation*. Paris: Armand Colin, 1970.
Dunham, Louis. *The Industrial Revolution in France 1815–1848*. New York: Exposition Press, 1955.
Duprat, Jeanne. *Proudhon: sociologue et moraliste*. Paris: Alcan, 1929.
Droz, Edouard, P.-J. *Proudhon*. Paris: Librarie des "Pages Libres," 1909.
Ehrenberg, John. *The Dictatorship of the Proletariat: Marxism's Theory of Socialist Democracy*. New York: Routledge, 1992.
Elbow, M. H. *French Cooperative Theory 1789–1948*. New York: Columbia University Press, 1953.
Etudes sur la philosophie morale au xixe siècle. Paris: Alcan, 1904.
Fourier, Charles. *Oeuvres complètes*. 12 vols. Paris: Editions Anthropos, 1966–68.
Fournière, Eugene. *Les Théories socialistes au XIXe siècle de Barbeuf à Proudhon*. Paris: Alcan, 1904.
Furet, Francois. *Marx and the French Revolution*. Chicago: University of Chicago Press, 1988.
Garaudy, Roger. *Les Sources françaises du socialisme scientifique*. Paris: Editions d'Hier et Aujourd'hui, 1948.
Gide, Charles and Rist, Charles. *A History of Economic Doctrines from the Time of the Physiocrats to the Present Day*. Trans. R. Richards. Boston: Heath, nd.
Gooch, G. P. *The Second Empire*. London: Longmans, Green, 1960.
Gray, Alexander. *The Socialist Tradition: Moses to Lenin*. London: Longmans Green, 1946.
Guérard, Albert. *French Prophets of Yesterday: A Study of Religious Thought Under the Second Empire*. London: T. Fisher Unwin, 1913.
_____. *French Civilization in the Nineteenth Century*, New York: Century, 1914.
_____. *Napoleon III*. Cambridge: Harvard University Press, 1943.
Guerin, Daniel. *Anarchism*. New York: Monthly Review Press, 1970.
Guillemin, Henri. *Le Coup du 2 décembre*. Paris: Gallimard, 1951.
Gurvitch, Georges. *L'idée du droit social*. Paris: Sirey, 1932.
_____. *Les Fondateurs français de la sociologie contemporaine: Saint-Simon et Proudhon*. Vol. i: P.-J Proudhon. Paris: Centre de Documentation Universitaire, 1955.
_____. *Proudhon et Marx: une confrontation*. Paris: Centre de Documentation Universitaire, 1964.
_____. *Proudhon: Sa vie, son oeuvre avec un exposé de sa philosophie*. Paris: Presses Universitaires de France, 1965.
Guy-Grand, Georges. *Pour connaître la pensée de Proudhon*. Paris: Bordas, 1947.
Halévy, Daniel. *Proudhon d'après ses carnets inédits*. Paris: Sequana, 1944.
_____. *Le mariage de Proudhon*. Paris: Stock, Delamain et Boutelleau, 1955.

Hall, Constance Margaret. *The Sociology of Pierre-Joseph Proudhon.* New York: Philosophical Library, 1971.

Haubtmann, Pierre. *Marx et Proudhon: leurs rapports personnels 1844–1847.* Paris: Editions Economie et Humanisme, 1947.

Hobsbawm, E. J. *The Age of Revolution 1789–1848.* New York: New American Library, 1962.

_____. *Primitive Rebels: Studies in Archaic Forms of Social Movements in the 19th and 20th Centuries.* New York: Norton, 1965.

_____. *The Age of Capital 1848–1875.* New York: New American Library, 1975.

Hoffman, Robert. *Revolutionary Justice: The Social and Political Theory of P.-J. Proudhon.* Urbana: University of Illinois Press, 1972.

Hyams, Edward. *Pierre-Joseph Proudhon: His Revolutionary Life, Mind, and Works.* New York: Taplinger, 1979.

Jackson, John Hampden. *Marx, Proudhon, and European Socialism.* London: English Universities Press, 1957.

Jaurès, Jean ed. *Histoire socialiste.* Vols. vii–ix. Paris: Jules Rouff, 1907.

Joll. James. *The Anarchists.* Cambridge: Harvard University Press, 1980.

Kemp, Tom. *Industrialization in Nineteenth-Century Europe.* London: Longmans, 1969.

King, Preston. *Fear of Power: An Analysis of Anti-Statism in Three French Writers.* London: Frank Cass, 1967.

Kolakowski, Leszek. *Main Currents of Marxism,* vol. 1: *The Founders.* Oxford: Oxford University Press, 1978.

Kracauer, Siegfried. *Orpheus in Paris: Offenbach and the Paris of His Time.* Trans. Fwenda Davis and Eric Mosbacher. New York: Knopf, 1938.

Labrousse, E. *Le Mouvement ouvrier et les théories sociales en France de 1815 à 1848.* Paris: Centre de Documentation Universitaire, 1948.

Labrusse, Laurent. *Les Conceptions proudhoniennes du crédit gratuit.* Paris: Jouve et Cie, 1919.

Labry, Raoul. *Herzen et Proudhon.* Paris: Editions Bossard, 1928.

Lagardelle, H. *Syndicalisme et socialisme.* Paris: Rivière, 1908.

Landauer, Carl. *European Socialism: A History of Ideas from the Industrial Revolution to Hitler's Seizure of Power.* Westport, CT: Greenwood, 1976.

Langlois, Jacques. *Défense et actualité de Proudhon.* Paris: Payot, 1976.

Lefebvre, Georges. *La Monarchie de Juillet,* Paris: Centre de Documentation Universitaire, 1936.

Leroy, Maxime. *Histoire des idées sociales en France.* 3 vols. Paris: Gallimard, 1946–54.

Levasseur, Emile. *Histoire des classes ouvrières en France de 1789 à 1870.* Paris: A. Rousseau, 1904.

Levine, Andrew. *Liberal Democracy: A Critique of its Theory.* New York: Columbia University Press, 1981.

Leys, M. D. R. *Between Two Empires: A Study of French Politicians and People Between 1814 and 1848.* Lordon: Longmans, Green, 1955.

Lhomme, Jean. *La Grande bourgeoisie au pouvoir 1830–1880.* Paris: Presses Universitaires Francaises, 1960.

Lichtheim, George. *The Origins of Socialism.* New York: Praeger, 1969.

Louis, Paul. *Histoire du socialisme en France.* Paris: Rivière, 1946.

Lu, Shi Yung. *The Political Theories of P.-J. Proudhon.* New York: Gray, 1922.

Lubac, Henri de. *The Un-Marxian Socialist: A Study of Proudhon.* New York: Sheed and Ward, 1948.

McCarthy, George ed. *Marx and Aristotle: Nineteenth-Century German Social Theory and Classical Antiquity*. Savage, MD: Rowman and Littlefield, 1992.

Maitron, J. *Le Syndicalisme révolutionnaire*. Paris: Editions Ouvrières, 1952.

Manuel, Frank. *The Prophets of Paris*. Cambridge: Harvard University Press, 1962.

_____. *French Utopias*. New York: Free Press, 1966.

Marcuse, Herbert. *Reason and Revolution: Hegel and the Rise of Social Theory*. Boston: Beacon Press, 1960.

Marx, Karl and Frederick Engels. *Collected Works*. 50 vols. New York: International Publishers, 1975–.

Michel, Henry. *L'Idée de l'état*. Paris: Hachette, 1896.

Moore, Barrington Jr. *Social Origins of Dictatorship and Democracy*. Boston: Beacon, 1966.

Moraze, Charles. *La France bourgeoise*. Paris: Armand Colin, 1946.

Moss, Bernard. *The Origins of the French Labor Movement 1830–1914: The Socialism of Skilled Workers*. Berkeley: University of Caliornia Press, 1976.

Pirou, Gaetan. *Proudhonisme et syndicalisme révolutionnaire*. Paris: Arthur Rousseau, 1910.

Plamenatz, John. *The Revolutionary Movement in France 1815–1871*. London: Longmans, 1952.

Plekhanov, George. *Anarchism and Socialism*. Trans. Eleanor Marx Aveling. London: Twentieth Century Press, 1906.

Poster, Mark ed. *Harmonian Man: Selected Writings of Charles Fourier*. Trans. Susan Hanson. Garden City: Doubleday, 1971.

Proudhon, Pierre-Joseph. *Candidature à la Pension Suard*. Paris: Rivière, 1926.

_____. *Carnets*. 3 vols. Paris: Rivière, 1960–68.

_____. *Correspondance*. 14 vols. Paris: Lacroix, 1875.

_____. *De la Capacité politique des classes ouvrières*. Paris: Lacroix, Verboeckhoven et Cie, 1868.

_____. *De la Célébration du dimanche considérée sous les rapports de l'hygiène publique, de la morale, des relations de famille et de cité*. Paris: Rivière, 1926.

_____. *De la Création de l'ordre dans l'humanité, ou principes d'organisation politique*. Paris: Rivière, 1927.

_____. *De la Justice dans la révolution et dans l'église*. 3 vols. Brussels: Lacroix, Verboeckhoven, 1868–69.

_____. *De le Justice dans la révolution et dans l'église*. 2 vols. Paris: Rivière, 1931.

_____. *Du Principe fédératif et de la nécessité de reconstituer le parti de la révolution*. Paris: Lacroix, Verboeckhoven, 1868.

_____. *Idée générale de la révolution au XIX siècle*. Paris: Rivière, 1924.

_____. *La Guerre et la paix*. Paris: Lacroix, Verboeckhoven, 1868)

_____. *La Révolution sociale démontrée par le coup d'état du 2 décembre*. Paris: Lacroix, Verboeckhoven, 1868.

_____. *Les Confessions d'un révolutionnaire pour servir à l'histoire de la révolution de février*. Paris: Rivière, 1929.

_____. *Qu'est-ce que la propriété? ou recherches sur le principe du droit et du gouvernement*. Paris: Rivière, 1926.

_____. *Qu'est-ce que la propriété? 2e Mémoire*. Paris: Lacroix, Verboeckhoven, 1867.

_____. *Système des contradictions économiques, ou philosophie de la misère*. 2 vols. Paris: Rivière, 1923.

_____. *Théorie de la propriété*. Paris: Lacroix, Verboeckhoven, 1868.

Ridley, F. F. *Revolutionary Syndicalism in France*. Cambridge: Cambridge University Press, 1970.

Ritter, Alan. *The Political Thought of Pierre-Joseph Proudhon*. Princeton: Princeton University Press, 1969.

_____. *Anarchism: A Theoretical Analysis*. Cambridge: Cambridge University Press, 1980.

Robertson, Priscilla. *Revolutions of 1848: A Social History*. New York: Harper and Row, 1952.

Roll, Eric, *A History of Economic Thought*. Englewood Cliffs: Prentice-Hall, 1956.

Rostu, Georges du. *Proudhon et les socialistes de son temps*. Paris: Giard et Brière, 1913.

Rousseau, Jean-Jacques. *The First and Second Discourses*. Ed. and trans. Roger Masters. New York: St. Martin's Press, 1964.

Ruggiero, Guido de. *The History of European Liberalism*. Boston: Beacon Press, 1959.

Saint-Simon, Henri de. *Catéchisme politique des industriels*. Paris: Ad. Naquet, 1832.

_____. *La Physiologie sociale: oeuvres choisies*. Ed. Georges Gurvitch. Paris: Presses Universitaires de France, 1965.

_____. *Selected Writings*. Ed. and trans. F. M. H. Markham. New York: Macmillan, 1952.

_____. *Social Organization, The Science of Man and Other Writings*. Ed. and trans. Felix Markham. New York: Harper and Row, 1964.

Sainte-Beuve, Charles. *P.-J. Proudhon: sa vie et sa correspondance*. Paris: Costes, 1947.

Schatz, Albert. *L'Individualisme économique et social*. Paris: Armand Colin, 1907.

Schlatter, Richard. *Private Property: The History of an Idea*. New Brunswick: Rutgers University Press, 1951.

Schochet, Gordon J. *Patriarchialism in Political Thought*. Oxford: Oxford University Press, 1975.

Soboul, *The Sans-Culottes*. Trans. Remy Inglis Hall. Princeton: Princeton University Press, 1980.

Soltau, Roger Henry. *French Political Thought in the 19th Century*. New York: Russell and Russell, 1959.

Sudan, Elisa. *L'Activité d'un socialiste de 1848*. Friburg: Imprimerie Galley et Cie., 1921.

Thompson, J. M. *Louis Napoleon and the Second Empire*. Oxford: Basil Blackwell, 1954.

Tilly, Charles. *The Contentious French: Four Centuries of Popular Struggle*. Cambridge: Harvard University Press, 1986.

Tilly, Charles, Louise, and Richard. *The Rebellious Century 1830–1930*. Cambridge: Harvard University Press, 1975.

Tocqueville, Alexis de. *Correspondance and Conversations with Nassau William Senior 1834–1809*. Ed. and trans. M. C. Simpson. New York: Augustus M. Kelley, 1968.

_____. *Recollections*. Ed. J. P. Mayer., Trans. Alexander Teixeira de Mattos. New York: Columbia University Press, 1949.

Vernon, Richard ed. *The Principle of Federation by P.-J. Proudhon*. Toronto: University of Toronto Press, 1979.

Vincent, K. Steven. *Pierre-Joseph Proudhon and the Rise of French Republican Socialism*. New York: Oxford University Press, 1984.

Voyenne, Bernard. *Le Fédéralisme de P.-J. Proudhon*. Paris: Presses d'Europe, 1973.

Wolin, Sheldon. *Politics and Vision: Continuity and Innovation in Western Thought*. Boston: Little, Brown, 1960.

Woodcock, George. *Pierre-Joseph Proudhon*. London: Routledge and Kegan Paul, 1956.

Index